Great Battles
of the Classical
Greek World

Great Battles of the Classical Greek World

Owen Rees

Pen & Sword
MILITARY

First published in Great Britain in 2016 by
Pen & Sword Military
an imprint of
Pen & Sword Books Ltd
47 Church Street
Barnsley
South Yorkshire
S70 2AS

ISBN 978 1 47382 729 5

Typeset in Ehrhardt by
Mac Style Ltd, Bridlington, East Yorkshire
Printed and bound in the UK by CPI Group (UK) Ltd,
Croydon, CRO 4YY

Pen & Sword Books Ltd incorporates the imprints of Pen & Sword
Archaeology, Atlas, Aviation, Battleground, Discovery, Family
History, History, Maritime, Military, Naval, Politics, Railways, Select,
Transport, True Crime, and Fiction, Frontline Books, Leo Cooper,
Praetorian Press, Seaforth Publishing and Wharncliffe.

For a complete list of Pen & Sword titles please contact
PEN & SWORD BOOKS LIMITED
47 Church Street, Barnsley, South Yorkshire, S70 2AS, England
E-mail: enquiries@pen-and-sword.co.uk
Website: www.pen-and-sword.co.uk

Contents

Acknowledgements

An independent historian is an isolated creature who relies heavily upon the kindness of his or her wider network. For this reason I am eternally grateful to any and all who have helped me along the way, patiently answering my enquiries and my annoying, niggling, follow-up questions. My aim was to fill this book with the most up-to-date information possible, and that would not have been possible if not for the kindness of strangers, and the patience of friends: I hope that I have not missed anyone out.

First and foremost, my thanks go to all of the teachers and lecturers who have suffered me as a student. My thanks go especially to Prof. Helen King and Prof. Peter Kruschwitz; this book could not be any further from your interests, but the passion you both hold for your topics was infectious and has continued to influence me to this day.

Within the wider historical community my inquiries and requests have always been met with good grace and humour. Specific thanks go to Dr. Andreas Konecny for sending me his works, and for all of his advice, on the layout of Plataea and the logistical issues surrounding the siege; and to Dr. John W. Lee for his patience with my constant questioning about the Persian military. Further thanks go to Dr. Matthew Sears, Prof. Christopher Tuplin and Prof. Paul Cartledge for their timely assistance to a complete stranger.

My thanks go to my editor Philip Sidnell at Pen & Sword Books, who took a gamble on a new author and gave me the freedom to change the aims and format of this book on more than one occasion. I hope I have not disappointed.

I am indebted to my friends and peers who have helped keep alive a boyish passion for ancient Greek Warfare. From a tiny seminar group in London, to PhDs and book deals, I can always rely on Cezary Kucewicz for his support and misguided optimism. In Dr. Roel Konijnendijk I have been lucky enough to have moral support and erstwhile academic critique throughout the drafting of this book. While we did not always agree, his disapproving gaze forced me to re-evaluate my work time and time again. I have no doubt that this book is in better shape because of his dutiful eye. Finally my thanks go to Dr. Josho Brouwers for always being willing to engage in random discussions on Greek warfare by email; it has been procrastination at its most useful.

A very special thank you to Joseph Hall who has been subjected to this book for a long time, and has been kind enough to proofread drafts for me. I have appreciated his friendship along the way, and I am amazed that, to this day, we have still not met in person!

To my family and in-laws, I thank you for your patience for a project that has consumed the last two years of my life. You have not always understood, or agreed with the decisions I made in writing this book, but you have always supported me wholeheartedly and I am forever grateful.

But my biggest thanks must go to my poor wife, Carly, and my children Matilda and Henry. You have suffered the most and have never complained. I could not have done this without you and, maybe now, we can have our evenings back… It is to you that I dedicate this book.

Any mistakes that remain in this book are unequivocally mine and mine alone.

Preface

This project was conceived with one simple goal in mind: to create a desire in the reader to want to learn more about Greek warfare. For that reason I have drawn inspiration, not from the scholastic tradition but from the student tradition. This does not mean that I have written this book while intoxicated, but that I have tried to recreate the passion and enthusiasm that I experienced among my peers in seminar groups and conversations in the bar, rather than recreate the traditional narratives to be found in a plethora of books that exist already. There are times when an anecdote from Herodotus or Thucydides is just so ridiculous that it should be discounted, but these anecdotes offer flavour and colour to Greek history. Where an academic would analyse and, most likely, discount them from their narratives, I have chosen to leave them in and allow you to question their validity – or in turn just enjoy them for the quirky eccentricities that they so often are.

Each chapter follows a similar formula of narrating the background to a battle, followed by a description of the battlefield, then the opposing armies, the battle narrative, and finally the aftermath – all except those in the section on sieges have a minor variance.

I decided to try and use a main source for each battle - either Herodotus, Thucydides or Xenophon - which were then supplemented by a multitude of other authors when the main source is lacking in information or, to be honest, colour and interest. This means that the source information has been made available at the beginning of each chapter, and then again at the subheading of 'The Battle' for the reader's convenience. This allows the narrative to flow without interruption, and also prevents the page becoming consumed by a million endnote citations. It also means that the notes become free to highlight disparities and extra information that do not fit within the narrative-based format of the book – it is here you will find the wider academic debate surrounding these battles and warfare in general. Finally this format allows you, the reader, to either ignore my notes completely and simply read the narrative while knowing what the main sources are, or follow my notes without rolling your eyes at yet another short citation to a passage in Herodotus.

This project had the aim of being as up-to-date as possible with regard to academic research surrounding Greek battles, with the added ambition of bringing new information into the public sphere, which can otherwise become lost behind the paywalls of internet depositories, such as JSTOR. While I do not claim to have achieved that in its entirety, I hope that each reader can take something new from these fascinating battles.

What should hopefully become clear from reading this book is how much we still do not yet understand about Greek warfare, and just how much there is yet to study. Whether you are a history enthusiast who wants to know more about the Greeks, or an erstwhile scholar forging forwards into new realms of understanding, I hope this book (re)ignites an interest, a passion, that I desire to share with you.

One important element of Greek warfare missing from this book is naval battles. These were originally considered for this project, but due to the sheer volume of potential candidates it was decided that they merit their own publication.

Finally, it should be noted that Greek names are rendered into their Latinized form, as these are what most people will be familiar with. However, technical terms have been rendered as transliteration from the original Greek (see Glossary).

Introduction

The history of classical Greece can come across as a series of tales of war and bloodshed. Modern Western civilization is thought to owe a debt, culturally and philosophically, to ancient Greece. It is perhaps curious, then, that ancient Greek culture and democracy did not rest on the shoulders of giants but on the strength in limb of its heavy infantry hoplites. The strength of those hoplites in turn rested on the unity of their formation, the justly famous phalanx. If the phalanx ever failed, so in turn would the hoplites, leaving the cultural capitals exposed and vulnerable to the whims of the victor.

The hoplite and his phalanx were considered so important to the Greeks that almost every contemporary battle narrative focused solely on them, ignoring the peripheral forces of cavalrymen, archers and lightly armed troops. Our sources were only interested in the beating heart of their army, the heavily armoured hoplite. But the aim of this book is to show that the hoplite did not act alone, and that Greek tactics as a whole were full of ingenuity and adaptability. It is also the aim to present battles, not as isolated incidents within a short campaign, but as part of a much wider background which influenced the decisions that were made by the commanders.

The Hoplite and the Phalanx

A hoplite was a heavily-armed infantryman with a characteristically large round shield (*aspis*) that he held in one hand and a spear in the other. He was a citizen-soldier, most commonly enlisted by his city-state (*polis*) to serve in exchange for very humble financial reparations. Citizens of age who could afford the equipment had the duty to serve as hoplites – the state did not supply them with weapons or armour, so hoplites were often drawn from among the wealthy, property-owning citizens. This does leave some confusion in visualizing Greek armies because the fluctuation in financial wealth between citizens made it inevitable that some hoplites were better equipped than others. You may have seen depictions of men with large helmets, chiselled body armour (cuirass) and leg greaves, but these only depict the possible forms of armour available; they do not represent what every hoplite would have looked like throughout the Classical Greek period. As the period progressed, so too did the choice of armour; leg guards became thinner, whereas the cuirass became obsolete and was replaced with a linen corselet (*linothorax*).

There were exceptions to this general picture, due to the fact that Greece was not a singular state but was made up of hundreds of little city-states. The biggest exception to this image would be the citizen-army of Sparta, which consisted of a meritocratic, professional leisure class who had the time and social drive to prepare themselves for war on a daily basis. Yet, towards the end of our period other city-states began to introduce their own elite forces who were given similar freedoms. It is also pertinent to observe that smaller city-states would have been forced to call up all able-bodied men, irrespective of wealth or equipment, in defence of their walls, and to expect these troops to have been as fully kitted as the Spartans or the wealth-laden Athenians, is unrealistic. So, as long as a man had his shield, a weapon such as a spear or sword, and could stand in formation he would have been considered a hoplite.

This formation is known as the phalanx. The phalanx was, in theory, a regimented line-up where the shields of the hoplites could overlap, and protect the hoplite as well as the man directly to his left, and the second rank's spears would protrude over the linked shields of the front rank. This image is based upon a static formation, and epitomizes it in its strongest, defensive position; but, truth be told, the formation was rarely static, and almost every battle commenced with a 'charge' to the enemy, and so the lines of hoplites were seldom as steadfast as this.

There was no general rule to the length and depth of the phalanx because it could change according to terrain as well as tactical considerations. We have evidence of phalanxes ranging from them being hypothetically one man deep, to those that were fifty men deep. As long as the formation was wider than it was deep it can comfortably be described as a phalanx.

How phalanxes actually fought in battle is the subject of huge scholarly debate, with the 'orthodox' view being reminiscent of a rugby scrum culminating in a big push (*othismos*); body mass against body mass, shield against shield until one line finally gave way. The 'revisionist' view presents a more fluid formation with greater space between the ranks, and between the opposing lines. Revisionists describe the concept of *othismos* as being a metaphorical big-push rather than a literal one. Rather than wade into the argument, all reconstructions presented here will be as literal an interpretation of the original sources as possible, and the reader can choose which model, if any, fits best.

The phalanx's great strength lay in its unity. With a complete shield wall it was virtually impenetrable from the front, making it a very effective defensive formation. Unfortunately, as mentioned above, most phalanxes were not in a rigid formation due to the Greeks' habitual charge into combat. Furthermore, the phalanx had some weaknesses. One such weakness lay in the lack of speed available to both the unit as a whole and the heavy laden hoplite individual. Another issue was the poor protection available to the flanks and rear of the formation. Finally, Greek hoplites had a nasty habit of crowding behind their protective shields, making the formation edge to the right-hand side as they marched.

Cavalry and Light Infantry

Cavalry and light infantry (including archers, slingers and *peltasts*) were underrepresented by the classical Greek historians and so we have very little information about them. This is made all the more strange by the fact that one of these historians, Xenophon, actually wrote a book about horsemanship and cavalry tactics. But this was his attempt to right the glaring tactical errors being made by Greek commanders rather than an accurate reflection of contemporary tactics. The geography of mainland Greece did not lend itself kindly to the development of cavalry tactics, but there were Greek areas that were famous for their horsemanship, most notably Thessaly and Boeotia; yet, due to the southern geographical bias in our sources this element of the wider Greek world does not receive a great representation.

Cavalry and light infantry represent two ends of a military, as well as social, spectrum. As with hoplites, both would have been expected to supply much of their own equipment. Horses were obviously expensive, thus only in the remit of the very wealthy, and only those who could not afford the hoplite panoply would choose to forgo the social position of honour in favour of the light infantry.

For all of the silence within the sources, the Greek historians could not hide the important roles these two elements played within Greek warfare. Light infantry in particular, in the form of *peltasts*, were instrumental in shaping Greek tactics and shattering military ideals towards the end of our period. Archers have a very poor reputation in Greek texts, often depicted as unmanly, and yet Athens had a standing force of 1,600 archers at the start of the Peloponnesian War (431 BC). As for the cavalry, when they are described in battle it is most often with devastating results. From the massacre of Greeks at Plataea by Boeotian cavalry fighting for the Persians, to the cavalry's tactical importance at the Battle of Delium, Greek cavalry are integral to our understanding of Greek warfare.

The Nature of Greek Combat

For all of the depictions and all of the battles that have captured the western world's imagination for centuries, classical Greece actually saw very little in the way of large-scale pitched battles. The histories are full of raids, skirmishes and a surprising number of situations where two large armies come close to blows before leaving and not a drop of blood was spilt, but large land battles were few and far between. It may also surprise some that for all of the rhetoric and hyperbole from historians (including my own) it was very unusual for a Greek-on-Greek battle to have a large body count. The reason is self-explanatory from the description of the phalanx above; if a formation broke its ranks to chase the routing enemy, they were just as susceptible to a massacre as the enemy were, so the pursuit was almost always left to the cavalry and the light infantry. If a fleeing army ever regrouped, or joined with a new infantry force, the pursuing cavalry and light infantry would have no choice but to abandon the chase.

But this should not take away from the experience of combat for the individuals, who still ran the risk of serious injury if not death. Battle was long, it was loud, it would have been exhausting, and it would have been disorientating; in the words of Thucydides, 'those who take part in an action have a clearer idea of it, though even then they cannot see everything, and in fact *no one knows much more than what is going on around himself*', (the emphasis is mine).

Great Battles

The biggest issue with any list of Great Battles is which battles to choose and which ones to leave out. While battles such as Spartolus (429 BC) and Solygeia (425 BC) are important to our understanding of battle tactics, the sources do not allow for a thorough reconstruction like they can for Delium (424 BC) or Leuctra (371 BC).

Most controversially, I have chosen to leave out the battle of Thermopylae (480 BC), arguably one of the most famous battles of the classical Greek period. Thermopylae has been overlooked for one simple reason: it is an amazing story of human endurance and military efficiency, but tactically it is very boring. The Spartans hemmed their joint forces into a small pass and repelled the waves of Persian men as they tried to force a way through. On the third day of battle the Persians found a route to approach the pass from behind the Greek lines and killed all the Greeks who had remained to fight. It is a popular story, and makes a riveting read, but it shows us very little about Greek warfare. If anything, it creates myths of Greek battle which need to be meticulously unpicked.

The battles here have been chosen to follow a simple chronology of classical Greek warfare, starting with the Peloponnesian War, which was the first fully reported conflict that pitched hoplite against hoplite. This is followed by the Spartan period of hegemony which shows the period in which Sparta gained and lost its position of authority in Greece.

The last two sections are thematic, dealing with variances of Greek warfare. Sieges were chosen to highlight an underappreciated aspect of Greek warfare. Greek sieges were varied, and at times experimental, but they were always gruesome and bloody affairs. There was no illusion of honour or integrity within a siege environment, it was a ferocious battle for survival that included women and children amongst its participants.

The final thematic section, on the Greco–Persian conflicts, needs a little more explaining. It is the standard practice to start a book on classical Greek warfare with the Greco–Persian Wars, because this starts the chronology that is generally accepted as the classical Greek period. However, the placement of the battles of Marathon and Plataea at the beginning of a book about hoplite based warfare begins with an anomaly of Greek military action. What is clear is that the Greeks did not fight the Persians in the same manner in which they fought each other, but placing this conflict at the beginning allows a false image to arise concerning Greek battle, and Greek tactics in turn. I have chosen to create an image of Greek warfare through their internal conflicts, before the Persian conflicts are shown as a separate tactical issue.

Three Persian battles have been chosen to highlight the variance of tactics utilised by the Greeks, based upon the unique situations as they arose. But, due to the inevitable crossover with information regarding the Greeks that can be found in earlier narratives within this book, I have chosen to emphasise the Persian perspective, which serves a secondary purpose of attempting to rebalance the pro–Hellenic stance of the traditional narratives.

Glossary

agora - marketplace

boeotarch – a Boeotian commander in command of a division of 1,000 hoplites and 100 cavalrymen.

decarchies – oligarchies implemented by Lysander the Spartan, consisting of 10 men each.

Eparitoi – an elite hoplite force picked by the Arcadian Federation, following the Spartan defeat at Leuctra.

ephors – a group of 5 *spartiates* who were elected on an annual basis to 'oversee' Sparta and her two kings.

epilectoi – an elite force of citizen soldiers who received military training on an almost professional basis. For example, the Eparitoi (see above) were the *epilectoi* of the Arcadians.

hamippoi – light infantry force that ran inside, and alongside, a cavalry force.

helot – unfree peasants living in Messenia. Served as a slave populace to the Spartans.

Hippeis – elite force of 300 Spartiates who served as a bodyguard to one of the Spartan kings in battle. The name literally meant 'horsemen' but they fought on foot in the phalanx.

lochos (plural *lochoi*) – generally used as a term for a military 'unit'. It is used more specifically as a military sub-unit, comprising half a Spartan *mora*.

machanai – siege machines.

metic – alien resident of a *polis*.

metropolis – the mother city to a colony.

mora (plural *morai*) – a Spartan regiment.

navarch – naval commander.

othismos – the debated term that influences how we recreate Greek warfare. It refers to a big push, which is either literally taken to describe a mass shoving contest between opposing phalanxes, or refers to a metaphorical push which describes an increased effort or exertion at particular points in the battle.

paean – A type of chant that varied between Greek communities. In this context it is best thought of as somewhere between a hymn or prayer and a war song.

peltast – Originating in Thrace, the *peltast* was a light infantryman who carried a originally crescent-shaped shield and threw javelins.

perioeci – free residents of Laconia, but they did not have the citizen rights of *Spartiates*.

peripoloi – frontier guards, or territorial police, of Athens.

plethron (plural *plethra*) – unit of measurement roughly equivalent to 30m.

polemarch – senior military position. In Athens this was the army commander, whereas in Sparta the *polemarch* commanded a *mora*, unless a king was not present in which case one *polemarch* would command the whole army.

polis (plural *poleis*) – Greek city-state.

proxenos – a citizen of one *polis* who had been selected to represent the interests of another *polis*.

satrap – a governor of a Persian *satrapy*.

satrapy – a province within the Persian Empire.

Sciritae – An elite force within the Spartan army, consisting of 600 men, drawn from the *perioeci*.

Spartiates – full citizens of Sparta.

stade – unit of measurement roughly equivalent to 180m, or 6 *plethra*.

stoa – roofed, public walkways, which most often surrounded the *agora*.

strategos (plural *strategoi*) – military commander. In the Athenian system the *strategoi* made the tactical decisions, not the *polemarch*, who was the figurehead of the army.

tresantes – a social subgroup of Spartiates. The name means the 'tremblers', or, more simply, cowards. The name denotes those Spartans who had been punished for running from the battlefield, or at least being perceived to have run from the battlefield. They were held in social contempt and very low esteem.

Key to Battle Maps

The following symbols are used on the battle maps throughout this book.

Due to the different characteristics of the sieges discussed in this book, each siege map comes with its own key.

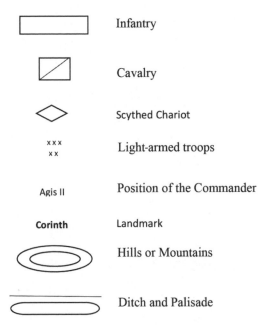

Infantry

Cavalry

Scythed Chariot

Light-armed troops

Position of the Commander

Landmark

Hills or Mountains

Ditch and Palisade

Part I

The Peloponnesian War

A fter 479 BC, and the successful repelling of the last Persian invasion, Greece became a political battlefield, with Athens at the fore expanding its power and authority. By the 430s, Athens had accumulated a vast alliance of small *poleis* who were duty-bound to them, known as the Delian League. It was an alliance that was tantamount to an empire. Only the strongest of *poleis* could resist their overtures, many of whom joined a looser alliance with Sparta, known as the Peloponnesian League.

As Athens looked to expand further afield, tensions rose with the powerful Peloponnesian *polis* of Corinth. This tension had come to the fore because of Corinthian interests in the north-westerly region of Greece, and a former colony of theirs called Corcyra. Corcyra had the second largest navy of the Greeks and formed an alliance with the largest, namely Athens. Fearing that the Athenians would reinforce the islanders' navy, Corinth acted and fought the largest naval battle Greece had ever witnessed, the battle of Sybota (433 BC).

Corinth claimed victory against the Corcyraeans on the day, butchering any survivors they found, but once an Athenian fleet joined the fray Corinth refused to continue hostilities through fear of breaking the peace accord between the two states. According to our main source, Thucydides, this was the first of two main complaints that induced Corinth to finally go to war with Athens.

Athens had become increasingly suspicious of Corinthian intentions and there was one very major and volatile area for Athenian-Corinthian diplomatic discord. It was a town to the very north of Greece, on the isthmus that connected the Pallene Peninsula to Chalcidice, called Potidaea. Potidaea had been founded by Corinthian settlers and so considered Corinth its *metropolis* (mother-city), but on the other hand it was a tribute paying ally of Athens in accordance with its membership of the Delian league – so both *poleis* laid claim to it.

Athens began with some harsh demands: they ordered the southern city walls to be burnt to the ground, they demanded that Potidaea gave hostages to Athens as a sign of good will, and they told them to dismiss the Corinthian magistrates from the town and to refuse the next appointees that Corinth would send (as Corinth did every year).

The Athenians had an added concern that Potidaea might in some way serve as a large, remote base for resistance against them. Its location lent itself to being influenced by the Macedonian King Perdiccas II, who was trying to resist the uprising of his younger brother, Philip, and another Macedonian ruler, Derdas. Philip and Derdas had already secured the support of the Athenians, forcing Perdiccas to try and re-direct Athenian attentions by invoking a war. He first tried to elicit the Peloponnesian states into war by going straight to Sparta, but when this did not work he set his sights on the Thracian tribes around him, as well as the Greek inhabitants of Chalcidice, and encouraged them to revolt.

For all of these reasons Athens began preparations to send a force of 1,000 hoplites on 30 ships, led by Archestratus, even before they had heard from the Potidaean envoys the response to their demands. Potidaea's representatives were unable to persuade the Athenians to revoke their demands, and further envoys had been sent to Sparta and Corinth to confirm their support should Athens attack. So, even though Athens refused to back down, the support shown verbally by Sparta and Corinth was enough for the Potidaeans to feel secure in their position and join the Perdiccas-inspired revolt of Chalcidice. At Perdiccas' request the Chalcidians abandoned most of the coastal cities and refortified Olynthus, which was to stand as the real base of the revolt. Thus, after defeating the confederate army outside the walls of Potidaea, Athens became embroiled in a two-year siege, beginning a conflict that would engulf Greece for over twenty-five years, on and off.

From the outset of the conflict the battlefield tactics were shown to be fluid and at times quite innovative. At Olpae (426/5 BC), the Athenian general, Demosthenes, utilised light-armed troops in an ambush position to attack a stronger Spartan-led force that opposed him. The tactic had pre-empted the plans of Eurylochus, the Spartan commander, who had placed his strongest troops on the left wing, rather than the more customary right wing, to attack the position of Demosthenes directly. This Spartan plan to attack the 'head of the snake', as the later Theban general Epaminondas is said to have so eloquently described it, was repeated over fifty years later by the Thebans at Leuctra (371 BC).

At Delium (424 BC) we see, for the first time, the massing of the Theban phalanx, where they chose a much deeper formation and chose to sacrifice the width of their battle lines. This gave the Thebans a greater staying power, with more ranks to call upon. We also see the use of the oft-ignored cavalry, whose appearance caused panic within the ranks of the Greek phalanx – when it was used effectively. Finally, the redeployment of horse during battle shows the level of tactical control still available to the Greek commanders as they fought shoulder to shoulder with their men, or conversely it shows how well they planned the battles.

During the Thracian campaign of Brasidas (424–422 BC), which culminated in the Battle of Amphipolis, we see the importance of the wider diplomatic issues that surrounded a Greek campaign. Brasidas was given *carte blanche* to form alliances and wage war with whomever he wished, without the need for authorization from Sparta. But at times this diplomatic need tore him away from his objectives. Brasidas was a great tactician who could use innovations with devastating effect. Most interesting was his implementation of a flamethrower during the siege of Torone (424/3 BC) which had ostensibly been seen for the first time during the siege of Delium, following the battle in that same year. Brasidas' pre-emptive ambush/sally from the walls of Amphipolis shows us an ability, like Demosthenes at Olpae, to second guess the actions of the enemy and exploit their weaknesses with good preparation and planning.

Finally, at the First Battle of Mantinea (418 BC), the issues of dissent and social pressures become self-apparent. The Spartan king, Agis II, felt obliged to fight a battle he had intended to avoid because of the stigma that was already being placed upon him for his (previously failed) military endeavours. The battle saw numerous mistakes being made and attempts to exploit them by both sides; showing the chess-like nature that hoplite battle could take. It also reveals one quirk of Greek warfare to its fullest: both armies were prone to veering to the right as they marched. This battle was the first time we can see this habit being counteracted tactically, by Agis and his trained Spartan troops.

Chapter 1

The Battle of Olpae (426/5 BC)

The Background (Thucydides, III.91–105; Diodorus XII.60.1–6)

By 426 BC the Peloponnesian war had spread throughout Greece, but most of the conflict so far had consisted of naval battles or else within the medium of siege.[1] But this year saw a shift in ambitions from both the Athenian and the Peloponnesian sides. A shift that was perpetrated by one man's pursuit of glory followed by his desire for forgiveness. This man was a young Athenian general, Demosthenes.

The summer of 426 BC saw a more confident Athenian strategy come into fruition. After securing their position in Mytilene, which had risen in a bloody revolt the year before, Athens looked to push the war out of Attica. They sent out two fleets, the first was sixty ships strong and under the command of Nicias, whose primary goal was to force the small island of Melos into submission; a task that sounded simpler in theory than it turned out in practice.[2] Resorting to the common Greek military tactic of raiding, Nicias devastated the Melian countryside. However, the people of Melos were unmoved. The Athenian fleet then decided to go back to the mainland, landing at Oropus, directly north of Athens. From this position Nicias began to ravage the Tanagran territory, before defeating a force of Tanagrans who sallied from their city to try and stop them. With this minor victory Nicias decided to return back to Athens, wreaking havoc on the Lorian shore along their way.

The second fleet was under the joint command of Procles and none other than Demosthenes. With a force of thirty Athenian ships they were travelling around the Peloponnese and headed towards the western frontier of Leucas and the Acarnanian coast. When Demosthenes landed in the territory of Leucas he orchestrated a successful ambush of a guarding garrison at Ellomenus, giving him a foothold in the region from which to prepare an escalation of the conflict. He set his eyes firmly on the eponymous city of Leucas and, after receiving reinforcements from the Acarnanians, Zacynthians, Cephallenians and Corcyraeans, he instigated a policy of agricultural destruction similar to Nicias. As in Melos, however, this did not have the desired effect because the Leucadians had no intention of leaving their walls to fight against such a vast and superior army. Demosthenes was thus urged by the Acarnanians to try a different approach and exploit the geographical phenomena on which Leucas was situated.

Leucas was a peninsula, connected to the mainland by a very narrow isthmus. The Acarnanians advised Demosthenes to build a small wall across this isthmus, which would isolate the Leucadians and allow them to be sufficiently weakened so that they would either surrender or else be taken with greater ease. If Demosthenes had not succumbed to the lure of even greater glory, this could have been the first major victory of his career.

Within Demosthenes' army was a contingent of Messenians from the Athenian colony of Naupactus. They succeeded in convincing Demosthenes that the size of his army could be put to better use by conquering the region of Aetolia. This in turn would then make it easier for the Athenians to secure the central mainland of Greece.[3] Demosthenes was quickly convinced. He had visions of using this victory to increase his army size, using his new Aetolian allies. This would enable him to march on Boeotia without the need for support from Athens.[4]

The Athenian fleet set sail away from Leucas, to the dismay of the Acarnanians, leaving with a slightly reduced force that consisted of Cephallenians, Messenians, Zacynthians and 300 Athenian marines.[5] The fleet landed in the territory of the Athenian allies Ozolian Locris, to the east of Naupactus. They set up base at Oeneon. Demosthenes hoped that his army would swell with his allies in Locris, who would meet him during his march inland; these warriors had the added benefit of being similarly armed to the Aetolians and also had many years' experience fighting them.[6]

Demosthenes marched his army with great confidence, taking the towns of Potidania, Krokyle and Tichium with ease. His aim was to penetrate north until he reached the Ophionian settlements. If he could not convince them to submit to him, he would return to Naupactus and regroup before heading back out on a second expedition. The only drawback to this plan was that Demosthenes' success thus far was not due to his military superiority, but because the Aetolians, aware of his plans, had simply avoided contact with him. As soon as the Athenian army had entered Aetolia, the many tribes of the region began to amass a joint force, with men coming from the furthest depths of the rugged Aetolian wilderness, all with the intent of removing this enemy from their land.

None the wiser, Demosthenes was cajoled into action by the counsel of his Messenian troops, who were now joined by the concurring voices of his own advisors. No longer content to wait for his Locrian allies to join him, Demosthenes ordered his men to march on as fast as they could towards Aegitium and storm its walls.[7] The inhabitants fled the city, moving into the hills that surrounded it, and beyond. As quickly as the hills emptied of refugees they filled again, flooded by the confederate army of the Aetolian peoples. The soldiers descended upon Demosthenes' men from every side, hurling their javelins as they ran. Faced with this onslaught, the Athenians had only two options: retreat or engage if they wanted to survive. They tried to chase down the Aetolians, but they could never catch them. As the hoplite line retired, the darters attacked once more. This ebb and flow characterized the battle for a long period of time, with the Athenians worse off in both positions as attacker and defender.

The only saving grace for Demosthenes' army was their own contingent of archers who were able to drive back the Aetolian advances with their arrows. With one accurate javelin this advantage was swiftly lost; the captain of the archers was killed and with him went the bravery and cohesion of the archer unit. The Athenian infantry were left exposed and, as the repetition of advance and retreat took its toll, they finally turned and fled.

This rout was an even greater disaster. With no guides to show them the way, the hoplites ran themselves into gullies and unknown woodland, weighed down by their equipment.[8] The lighter-armed Aetolians were much quicker in their running and were soon making short work of the panicked masses. Those Athenians who had entered the woods would fare worst: as the trees were set alight and the woods were burnt to the ground - with them inside. It is not known how many died that day, but 120 Athenian hoplites were killed, as well as Demosthenes' colleague Procles.[9] A truce was called so that the dead could be collected, after which the Athenians returned to Naupactus and then boarded their ships back to Athens, all except Demosthenes who feared the home reaction to this disaster of his own making.

By the coming of autumn, the Aetolians had convinced the Spartans to help them and attack Naupactus. An army of 3,000 hoplites, made up from a mixture of Spartan allies, was sent under the command of the Spartan officer Eurylochus.[10] The army met up at Delphi and received assistance from the Ozolian Locrians, who guided the army through their territory.[11] On arrival in the land of the Locrians, Eurylochus took the towns of Oeneon and Eupalium, both of whom had refused to help. He arrived in the territory of Naupactus, where he was joined by an Aetolian force; this joint army laid waste to the surrounding countryside and took control of the un-walled suburb of Naupactus itself.

Eurylochus had moved fast and was devastatingly efficient, but his movements had not gone unnoticed. Demosthenes, who had remained in the vicinity of Naupactus, had seen what was about to happen and proactively headed west into Acarnania to muster military support. It was not easy to convince them, as they still felt betrayed by Demosthenes over Leucas, but they finally agreed and sent him with 1,000 hoplites with whom he entered the walls of Naupactus. As commander of this small force, Demosthenes successfully rebuffed the Peloponnesian army.

Eurylochus decided against trying to storm the city, knowing what a folly that would be, and dispersed his army. They did not return to the Peloponnese, as one might have expected, because the people of Ambracia, to the north of Acarnania, had approached Eurylochus with a proposition. Help them to attack the region of Amphilochia, starting with Amphilochian Argos, and then together they could take Acarnania, which would give Sparta a strong set of allies in the centre of Greece.[12] It was not an offer that Eurylochus could turn down, so he encamped his men in the south-western tip of Aetolia, on the border with Acarnania, and waited for instructions.

The Ambracians stalled until winter before they finally marched out against Argos with a strong force, which included 3,000 hoplites. Entering Argive territory, the army took control of a hilltop stronghold near to the coast of the Ambracian Gulf, called Olpae. It was a good, strong position within two and three-quarter miles from Argos itself. The Acarnanians marched north quickly, part of their force was to help relieve their allies at

Argos whilst the remainder of their army camped at Crenae in Amphilochia so as to cut off the army of Eurylochus coming from the south, which was expected to join the Ambracians any day. Furthermore, the Acarnanians sent for Demosthenes, who they wished to lead them in this battle for survival.

On hearing that the Acarnanians intended to cut off the Spartan general, the Ambracian army at Olpae sent a message back home asking for more reinforcements, just in case Eurylochus could not reach them. For his part, Eurylochus mustered his men together and departed when he first got wind of activity in Ambracia. His army quickly traversed the wintery lands of Acarnania, which had left no army to resist him. As he entered Amphilochia and Argive territory, he waited until nightfall when, under a cloak of darkness, his army passed between the city of Argos and the army posted at Crenae, until he finally made it to his allies at Olpae.

The Battlefield

Very little is known about the battlefield of Olpae. It must have been between the coastal stronghold at Olpae, and the inland city of Argos, as we know that Eurylochus' march was heading towards the city. We are told that the Spartan army reached Metropolis, the most likely candidate for which is between the modern towns of Krikelo and Loutro, directly east of Olpae and directly north of Argos.[13] If this was the case then the terrain would have been rugged and difficult, as well as high up in the hills.

A great ravine separated the two armies whilst they were encamped, and as the Spartans were on the offensive it can be fairly deduced that it was they who crossed it before the battle lines were formed.[14] The hilly and shrubby terrain was enough to hide the tactical ploy used by Demosthenes, and must be considered to have been a frustrating barrier for the clean deployment of a phalanx.

The Armies

Thucydides does not give specific figures for the armies once they had arrived at the battlefield, and neither were any numbers given for the individual groups that comprised each army at any time in the run-up to battle. A few pieces of information are important though. First and foremost among them: the Acarnanian army under Demosthenes was outnumbered and could be comfortably outflanked.

We are told that the Ambracians had invaded the area with a force of 3,000 hoplites but some had been left to guard Olpae, giving us an army of maybe 1,500–2,000 hoplites. Eurylochus had marched on Naupactus with a joint force of 3,000 hoplites; if he incurred any losses we are not told about them and they would most likely have been small. As he was in allied territory it is not unreasonable to assume that any losses of men could have been simply replaced by locals, so it seems probable that he had a force of a consistent strength. In total, the Ambracian-Peloponnesian army would have totalled 4,500–5,000 hoplites, and an unknown number of light infantry and archers.

For the Acarnanians we have no figures, other than the 1,000 hoplites that were sent to reinforce Naupactus, but we are never told what happened to them; nor do we know how strong an army was held by Argos. We are told by Thucydides that the Acarnanians received help from 20 Athenian boats that were patrolling around the Peloponnese, but they were most likely involved in the blockade of the stronghold at Olpae rather than in the battle itself. Even if they were in the battle, one ship could hold somewhere in the region of 30–50 hoplites each – giving a possible force of 600–1,000. But the only non-Acarnanian troops mentioned in the battle narrative are a corps of Messenians (200 hoplites) and only a few Athenians (60 archers), which are just as likely to have been remnants of Demosthenes' own entourage. Due to the ease with which the Peloponnesians could outflank Demosthenes' army, 3,000–3,500 seems a realistic figure for his army.

The Battle (Thucydides III.106–112)

At Olpae, Eurylochus did not waste any time. At daybreak, he marched his newly swollen army towards Argos, encamping at a little town called Metropolis.

Demosthenes soon arrived in Amphilochia with twenty Athenian ships and his modest force of hoplites and archers. The fleet was put to immediate use in the Gulf, blockading the remaining Ambracians at Olpae whilst the Acarnanians camped at Crenae had marched on to Argos. In Argos,

Demosthenes and the Acarnanian generals rallied their men together and marched out to face the might of Eurylochus' army.

As the Peloponnesian army came into sight just outside of Metropolis, Demosthenes ordered the camp to be set up; placing his army to the south of a ravine that skirted around the town. For five days and five nights both armies did nothing; they just waited. Demosthenes must have been getting anxious. The longer he waited the more likely it was that Eurylochus would receive reinforcements from Ambracia. However, he knew that he was outnumbered and needed to be in a defensive position to have any chance of success.

Fortunately for him, Eurylochus was equally anxious to get past this enemy and move on to the more pressing need to besiege Argos.[15] On the sixth day the Peloponnesian army crossed the ravine and formed up into battle order; Demosthenes was ready for them.

Demosthenes knew his Acarnanian army was outnumbered and decided to use the uneven terrain to his advantage. Placing himself on the right wing with his Messenian hoplites, supported by his Athenian archers, Demosthenes intended to face the traditionally weaker left wing of his enemy with his Messenian and Athenian troops. The rest of his army was then made up of the Acarnanian hoplites and the Amphilochian light-armed troops. All, that is, except for a reserve force of 400, made up of Acarnanian hoplites and light troops whom he placed forward of the battle line, off to the right of Demosthenes' own position.[16] These men were hidden in a sunken road that had been overgrown with bushes; their sole objective was to let the Peloponnesian army pass them by, unnoticed, and to attack their left wing from the rear after the mêlée had begun.

Eurylochus was unaware of any such danger and set his forces up with an extended line. He saw the numerical advantage and was intent on outflanking Demosthenes and surrounding him in the process. Interestingly, Eurylochus placed himself and his strongest troops on the left wing so that he could extend beyond Demosthenes' right.[17] Next to him were the Mantineans who would serve as the 'real' left wing unit, whilst Eurylochus began his flanking manoeuvre. The rest of his army was a polyglot mix of Peloponnesians and Ambracian allies extending to the right.

The two armies approached one another. Eurylochus' unit began to extend left, drawing with him the Mantineans to make first contact with the enemy line. The battle lines clashed together and the men were gripped in the furore of combat. Eurylochus had succeeded in his flanking movement and with a prearranged signal called for his unit to pivot on an axis and begin to enclose around Demosthenes' helpless Messenians.[18]

It was the point of no return for Demosthenes. The concealed Acarnanians broke from their hiding place and charged headlong into the back of Eurylochus. From the sky rained javelins before the panicked, open lines of the Peloponnesian wing were struck at full speed by the hoplite reserve. The impact was as devastating as it was immediate. Acarnanian spears were used and dropped, as swords were quickly drawn and the cream of the Peloponnesian army was cut down.

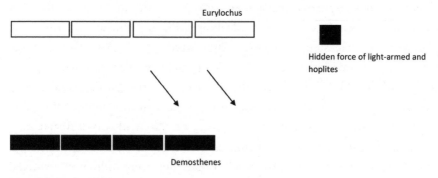

Map 1.1: Battle of Olpae, phase 1.

On the right wing the Ambracians were having greater success, having defeated the Acarnanians and now chasing them off the field towards Argos. When they returned from their pursuit they saw the great tragedy that was occurring: Eurylochus had been killed, his forces were running in panic and his allies had already routed at the sight of the ambush. The whole Peloponnesian–Ambracian force had broken ranks and raced west to Olpae without discipline or order. Only the Mantineans were able to retreat in any semblance of formation and would have suffered fewer losses because of it. The chase continued until nightfall, with the Peloponnesian army suffering heavy losses along the way.

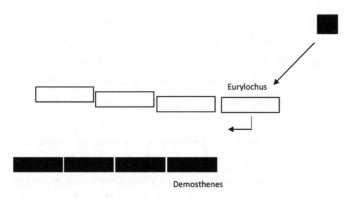

Map 1.2: Battle of Olpae, phase 2.

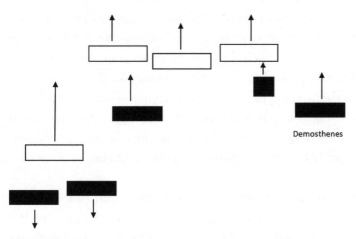

Map 1.3: Battle of Olpae, phase 3.

The next day saw a new Spartan take command of the army, Mendaius.[19] He took stock of the devastating defeat and its effect not only on his army's numbers but on their morale as well. How would he be able to stay and defend a siege at Olpae now that the Acarnanians had cut off his escape route by land and the Athenian fleet by sea? He had but one choice to save Sparta's reputation and the alliance of the Peloponnesian states. He had to betray the Ambracians in exchange for safe passage back home.

A parley was called with Demosthenes to request a safe retreat and the recovery of the dead. Demosthenes agreed to allow the dead to be collected but publicly refused a safe retreat. In actuality, Demosthenes and the Acarnanians gave permission for Mendaius to leave with the Peloponnesian contingents of the army. The reasoning for this was twofold: firstly, it left the Ambracians isolated from any Peloponnesian support; secondly, it discredited the Spartans and their allies as self-serving and treacherous to their allies.

Whilst the dead were being collected, Demosthenes received word that a new Ambracian army had been sent to join those at Olpae – but they did not know that a battle had already occurred.[20] Demosthenes sent a strong division ahead to set up ambushes for this new army whilst he saw the Peloponnesians on their way home.

He did not have to wait long. Whilst out in groups of twos and threes, ostensibly to gather herbs and firewood, the Peloponnesians began to pick up their walking pace as they went further and further from Olpae. The Ambracians who had joined them in their foraging began to chase after them to try and catch up. Seeing the enemy running like this, some of the Acarnanians mistakenly thought they were all trying to escape and began to pursue them. Emotions were running high and, whilst the Acarnanian commanders tried to stop their men by telling them it was authorized, the soldiers did not believe them. Some even threw javelins at their own commanders!

Eventually the soldiers realized their mistake and allowed the Peloponnesians to go, relishing instead in the mindless slaughter of the isolated Ambracians who had strayed too far from Olpae. In this simple act alone, the Ambracians lost 200 of their men.

Meanwhile, to the north of Metropolis, the Ambracian relief force had arrived at Idomene, a city that consisted of two lofty hills just off the northeast coast of the Ambracian Gulf. Unbeknownst to them, the advance force sent by Demosthenes had occupied the taller of the two hills at nightfall, after the Ambracians had set up camp on the smaller one. Demosthenes made a forced march from Olpae through the night taking half of his army with him through the lowlands, whilst the remainder of his troops went through the Amphilochian hills.

As dawn broke Demosthenes began to advance on the Ambracian camp, placing the Messenians at the head of his army so that they would confuse the sentries by speaking in the Doric dialect that the Messenians shared with the Spartans.[21] Demosthenes exploited the ignorance of the Ambracians and the pitch darkness that hid the true identities of his men from the guards. It was in this way that Demosthenes descended upon the camp, killing the Ambracians as they still slept.

The camp was awash with slaughter; only a few could escape. Those that did ran to the hills only to find the roads occupied by more Acarnanians and Argives. The Ambracians did not know where to turn, they just ran in any direction that they saw was unguarded. In doing so they fell into each ambush that Demosthenes' advance force had set. Some even jumped out to sea in the hope of reaching the Athenian ships, preferring to die at the hands of them rather than their hated rivals of Argos. Only a small handful survived the carnage to return to Ambracia.

The Aftermath

The impact of this defeat on Ambracia was devastating. Thucydides does not even report the figures for the dead that his source gave him because he does not think anyone would believe him.[22] It is not unrealistic from what he does say, to deduce that the Ambracians lost almost the entirety of their fighting force in just a matter of days. They were so depleted that the Acarnanians and Amphilochians were advised that they could take the city without any need to strike another blow. In the end, they decided against it for fear that Athens would use it to dominate the area and become worse neighbours than the Ambracians.

The spoils of victory were split between the parties. No less than a third of the spoils were given to Athens, which were unfortunately lost in their voyage home. Demosthenes had finally redeemed himself after the disastrous campaign in Aetolia, and he personally took home 300 sets of armour as booty, which he in turn presented to the various temples in Attica.

Agreeing a pact based on defensive, rather than offensive, unity, the Acarnanians forged a treaty with the Ambracians that finally brought an end to their war. For Athens, however, their war with Sparta was only just warming up.

Chapter 2

The Battle of Delium (424 BC)

The Background (Thucydides, IV.53–57, 66–77; Diodorus XII.65.1–67.1)

Athenian confidence was running high. The year of 424 BC saw a weakened and humble Sparta refusing to take the field as they cowered from Athenian maritime aggressions. Athens had seen great victories at Pylos and more recently at the island of Cythera, leaving Laconia at the whim of their raids.[1]

Sparta was in a panic. They anticipated regular Athenian raids into their lands and sent garrisons of hoplites to many points throughout their coastline where Athens was most likely to attack. They felt so insecure with their situation that they established a cavalry force of 400 horses and a standing force of archers to allow for a mobile response to any raiding. Sparta had prepared itself for a territorial siege and it had no intention of taking to the field any time soon. Even these preparations did little to ease Spartan worries, with one Spartan garrison near Thyrea, on the east coast of the Peloponnese, venturing against a raiding party before quickly running from the sight of a group of Athenian hoplites. Before long the city of Thyrea was raided, burnt and pillaged by the Athenians. They captured a small group of prisoners, including Aeginetans who were put to death, as well as the Spartan commander Tantalus.[2]

With a reluctant Sparta unwilling to continue the raids on Attica, Athens was able to consider its own land-based campaign in the territories of their neighbours.[3] By the start of the summer an opportunity appeared that allowed Athens to begin this expansion when a popular party in the city of Megara conspired to let them inside the city gates.[4]

This popular party uprising had seen a significant shift of power within Megara, with some of the most influential leaders of the former regime sent into exile. These exiles had not gone far, settling a few miles to the north at

Pelgae from where they raided the Megarian countryside to put pressure on the popular party. On their own, these raids would have been easily dealt with – the exiles had not amassed in any great numbers – but they coincided with an uncoordinated, but simultaneous set of raids by Athens who had taken it upon themselves to harass Megara twice a year.

The leaders of Megara were at their wits' end. The constant raiding caused unrest within the city, with some loyalists of the exiles calling for their return – preferring to remove one of the raiding forces rather than continue dealing with both. Through fear of civil unrest, coupled with fear of the oligarchic faction being allowed back into Megara, the Megarian leaders decided upon another option of opening negotiations with the Athenians.

Liaising with the Athenian commanders, Demosthenes and Hippocrates, it was arranged that the Athenians would take the long walls which connected Megara with its port harbour of Nisaea, thus preventing any Peloponnesian support being sent to the city that way.[5] Once they had secured the walls and harbour, they would set their attentions upon the main city which, it was assumed, would capitulate with little resistance.[6]

The Athenians split their forces between the two commanders. Hippocrates took 600 hoplites to the island of Minoa, lying off the coast of Megara, whilst Demosthenes had a force of Plataean light troops and a mysterious, mobile force of young Athenians called the *peripoloi*, set up nearer to Megara at the shrine of Enyalius.[7] They waited on the island for a few days, blockading the harbour but ostensibly having no ambitions to leave Minoa.

During this time, members of the popular party began a ruse in which they were granted passage outside of the main gates to carry out a rowboat under the cover of darkness. It was believed that these men were carrying out their own raids, marauding the Athenians in their camps. It ended every morning as they brought the boat back on top of a cart, dragging it back within the walls without raising any internal suspicions. On the set day, with daylight breaking, the gates were opened in expectation of the boat with the cart already in place under it. The Athenians had already left their island and lay waiting for their chance. Seeing the gates fully open, they ran at full speed to reach them before they shut again; a process that was successfully slowed by the positioning of the cart. Whilst the Athenians were running, the Megarian conspirators, still with their boat in tow, killed the guards, giving the ambush a clear path through the gates.

Once the long walls were secure, and the small Peloponnesian garrison was removed, it was time for the Megarian leaders to uphold their side of the plot.[8] Within Megara they fed upon the agitation and fear of the citizens. They called for the army of Megara to march out and fight the Athenians in battle, planning as they were to open the gates and allow the Athenians to enter before the Megarian army had even left the city. The conspirators anointed themselves in oils so that they could be distinguished by the Athenians when they entered, saving themselves from any slaughter that may ensue. But at the last minute they were betrayed from within their own ranks. One of the popular party members revealed the plan to the opposition party, who swiftly put a stop to the plans for battle. Increased security on the city walls and gates ruined any chance the Athenians had of entering the city by subterfuge.

The Athenian commanders looked instead to cordon off Nisaea by building a wall and encircling it. Within two days they had almost completed the wall, and this was enough for the garrison in Nisaea. They surrendered to the Athenians, giving up their arms and paying a ransom for themselves, whilst the Spartan commander and any other Laconians in the garrison were left to the discretion of Athens. Now that the harbour town and its long walls had fallen into the hands of the Athenians, it was just a matter of time before Megara would likewise capitulate.

Northwest of Nisaea, just up the coast from Corinth, lay a Spartan army led by Brasidas.[9] When he heard news of the breaching of the long walls between Nisaea and Megara, Brasidas swiftly called for Boeotian support whilst he marched a mixed Peloponnesian force through the Corinthian Isthmus to Tripodiscus, a town that lay between Pegae and Megara. Before he even arrived, Brasidas received the harrowing news that Nisaea had fallen. Changing tack he decided to act before the Athenians realized that he was in the area. Taking an elite group of 300 men from his soldiers, they marched to Megara and invited the people to let his small unit in. He was refused on the grounds that the Megarians did not believe he would be any better for them than the Athenians. They decided to wait and see which of the two armies won when they had battled it out.

Brasidas returned to his full force and was joined the following daybreak by the Boeotian support he had requested. The combined army numbered 6,000 hoplites and a cavalry force of at least 600 men.[10] A short battle ensued that day as the Boeotian cavalry caught the Athenian light troops off guard, driving them back to the sea. They were swiftly countered by the Athenian horsemen, who successfully killed the Boeotian cavalry general. But ultimately, no victor could be decided and both sides claimed victory.

Following this skirmish, Brasidas formed up the bulk of his army in full array as a challenge to the Athenians. The Athenians reciprocated, but neither side was willing to risk battle, and possible defeat.[11] After a long stand-off, the Athenians duly withdrew. Seeing this, the pro-exile Megarians wasted no time and proclaimed Brasidas as victor, throwing open the gates to allow him entry. With the Athenians seemingly beaten, the popular party members quickly became scarce through fear of retribution for what amounted to treason. This gave space for the exiles to return and the old oligarchy to be reinstated. When the exiles returned they took an oath to not take any vengeance for what had happened in the past. However, they promptly ignored this oath by calling to hold a review of the hoplites and subsequently killing about 100 men who had opposed them. After this, they rounded up known conspirators who communicated with Athens and offered them to the public for a verdict; they were subsequently condemned and executed. With this bloody status quo in place, Brasidas released his allies of their obligations and returned to his own preparations for an invasion of Thrace.[12]

For Athens this was not a major setback, they had not incurred any losses and Megara was never theirs to begin with. They quickly redirected their attentions away from the Peloponnese and turned to their oldest nemesis – Boeotia.

Demosthenes and Hippocrates had already received the request from individuals within Boeotia for Athenian assistance, individuals who wished to change the constitutions within their cities to a democracy. With their attentions now available, the two commanders devised a simple plan with which they would subdue the entire region. Their primary goals were to take and consolidate three areas: the harbour town of Siphae on the Bay of Crisae to the west, the town of Chaeronea to the north, and to the east the sanctuary of Apollo at Delium. By taking these places simultaneously the Athenians wished to prevent the Boeotians from uniting their forces, as the various *poleis* would have been unwilling to send men away from their land whilst an enemy force was encamped in their territory. These three areas would become the bases for subsequent raids into Boeotia and would also become a safe haven for any insurgents who wished to cause revolt in the region.[13]

With the plans laid out, Hippocrates set about building his army. Demosthenes was sent to Naupactus with forty ships to raise an army with the Acarnanians and their allies. He would then sail to Siphae to be let in by the internal conspirators who had first called for help. Hippocrates stayed in Attica and raised a force there, waiting for the allotted day for the coordinated attacks to begin.

The day of reckoning fell in the beginnings of winter. Demosthenes sailed to Siphae as arranged, only to find the gates of the city firmly shut. The plot had been discovered by a man called Nicomachus, who informed the Spartans, who in turn informed the Boeotians. Before Demosthenes had even arrived, support had flocked throughout the land of Boeotia, and the areas of Siphae and Chaeronea had been reinforced.

With Demosthenes helpless to intervene, Hippocrates continued with the plan not knowing what had occurred. He had raised his Athenian army and marched to Delium as he was meant to. On their arrival at the sanctuary of Apollo, the men dug a trench around the temple using the earth removed to form the basis of a wall. In to this wall were thrust stakes, bricks from the nearby houses, vines from the consecrated grounds. Anything they could get their hands on was irreverently dismantled and thrown onto the ramparts. Once these were up, the soldiers built a few wooden towers to reinforce gaps that existed in the sanctuary's own walls.

From start to finish, this enterprise took three days, after which a small group was left to complete the building work under the command of Hippocrates, whilst the remainder of the army would return home. They marched over a mile east from Delium before the majority of the light-armed troops left the hoplites in an encampment while they carried on home to Athens.[14]

All the while, the Boeotians had caught wind of the invasion and mustered their forces together at Tanagra. They marched to Delium as fast as they could, but when they saw the bulk of the Athenian hoplites in their camp it was quickly apparent to the Boeotian leaders that they were too late, Delium had been taken.

The Battlefield

The exact location of the battle is still a mystery, and the landscape is only described in regard to its impact on the tactics involved in the battle. So, we know that the terrain was very hilly, and it was from one of these hills that the Boeotians would launch their attack. We also know that between the two battle lines ran ravines on either side, creating a narrow theatre for combat – maybe only 800 yards across. This alleviated any fears of being outflanked by either side.

The Armies

The Boeotian army consisted of 7,000 hoplites, over 10,000 light troops, 1,000 cavalry and 500 *peltasts*. As a confederacy, Boeotia's army was commanded by a committee of eleven generals called *boeotarchs*. Thebes was the most powerful *polis* in the region so they contributed the largest proportion of men; in turn they held four of the *boeotarch* positions.[15]

In keeping with their position, Thebes was given pride of place on the right wing; the centre was made up of the Haliartians, Coronaeans and Copaeans; and the left wing held the Thespians, Tanagrans and Orchomenians respectively. On both flanks were placed the cavalry and light-armed troops. Whilst the majority of the army conformed to a standard formation of eight to twelve ranks deep, the Thebans had a different tradition of fighting and set their lines at twenty-five men deep. Such a formation was designed to outlast the enemy with densely concentrated manpower and superior reserve numbers to call upon, but its narrower frontage could also leave the hoplites vulnerable to flanking manoeuvres. This danger was nullified at Delium by the narrow battlefield.

The Athenian army had an equal number of hoplites, set up in lines eight men deep. On each wing sat an unspecified number of cavalry, most likely of similar strength to the Boeotians.[16] The Athenian weakness derived from their lack of light infantry, an area of the army in which the Athenians had not yet created a regular unit.

The Battle (Thucydides, IV.90–101.4; Diodorus XII.69.1–70.6)

With the sight of the Athenian army encamped outside of Delium, ten of the *boeotarchs* agreed that battle was unwise as the army in front of them was no longer in the official boundaries of Boeotia.[17] However, the one remaining *boeotarch*, Pagondas of Thebes, vehemently disagreed. Pagondas believed that victory was a real possibility and called upon his men to avenge the sacrilege that had befallen the temple of Apollo.[18]

With an impassioned and influential speech, Pagondas successfully convinced the Boeotians to march on the Athenian camp. The army broke up their own camp and marched off in the late afternoon, stopping to arrange their lines behind the screening of a large hill before the final descent onto the chosen battlefield.

Hippocrates, who was still at Delium when the Boeotian army first mustered, heard of their advance and sent word to the body of his army to form into battle lines. Hippocrates set out to join the main army, leaving a small cavalry force of 300 to remain at Delium with instructions to guard the fortification and join the battle if a good opportunity arose.

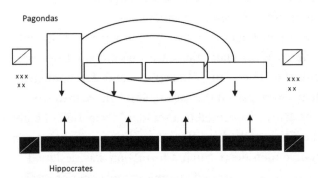

Map 2.1: Battle of Delium, phase 1.

As the Athenians set up their battle lines and Hippocrates began the customary pre-battle speech, he was interrupted by a low humming. The hum grew louder and louder until the full force of the Boeotian *paean* rang in the ears of Hippocrates' men, looking up to the hill in front of them they could see the Boeotian lines in full force. This quick and unexpected appearance sent shock waves through the Athenian lines but their shock was soon forced into action as Pagondas ordered the Boeotians to descend the hill and attack.

Hippocrates showed no concern for the landscape, ordering his men to meet the enemy on the hill. The two lines walked to within javelin distance and as the Boeotian *peltasts* threw their darts, the Athenians charged down the shield wall in front of them. The crash of shield against shield reverberated through both phalanxes as a stubborn mêlée ensued.

On their right, the Athenians quickly gained the upper hand. Whilst Boeotian units began to abandon their posts, the Thespians were left isolated and encircled by the dominant Athenian hoplites. Within the slaughter all identification became lost, with many Athenians being cut down by their own men, having been mistaken for enemies in the fog of war. The fleeing wing of the Boeotians raced toward their more successful right wing.

On the Theban right (the Athenian left), the deeper Theban lines were gradually pushing the Athenians further and further back but, even with the early death of Hippocrates, the Boeotian advance was not as fast as Pagondas may have hoped.[19] He had to cause a distraction to the Athenian's victorious right wing before it moved to outflank him, or else all would be lost in the blink of an eye. Two squadrons of cavalry were sent around the hill behind the Boeotians' own lines, appearing on the Athenian right flank as if out of nowhere. To tired and over confident Athenian eyes, the appearance of the cavalry was almost certainly like a new army coming to join the battle and sent panic through their ranks.

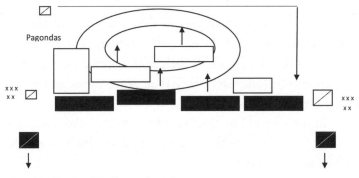

Map 2.2: Battle of Delium, phase 2.

With their attentions split, the Athenians could not resist the mounting Theban pressure, which finally burst through their lines and sent the Athenians into a chaotic rout. They fled in all directions: some ran to Delium, others to Oropus, anywhere they could run as long as it was away from the pursuing Boeotian cavalry.[20]

The cavalry was boosted by the late arrival of a contingent of Locrian horsemen which joined in the pursuit of the damned hoplites. In a scene that would more fittingly be described as a hunt, the Athenians were cut down and massacred in their droves. Their saviour came in the guise of nightfall, which brought the cavalry hunt to a speedy end, allowing more fugitives to escape than would have otherwise.

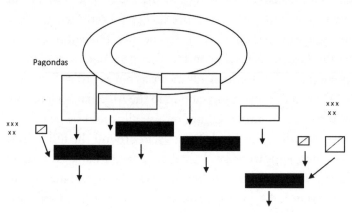

Map 2.3: Battle of Delium, phase 3.

The Aftermath and Siege

The following day saw a mass Athenian exodus from Oropus and Delium with the exception of a garrison left at the fortified sanctuary. The Boeotians set up their trophy, took their dead from the field and stripped the Athenian bodies, all in accordance to custom, after which their army moved to Tangara to plan the attack on Delium itself.

The Athenians sent their herald to request the retrieval of the dead, also as custom dictated, but were met with a staunch refusal which shook the Athenian sensibilities to their core.[21]

The argument was simple: the Athenians had befouled consecrated ground by fortifying the temple of Apollo and using a sacred water supply for their own personal uses, which negated the need for the Boeotians to fulfil their sacred duty to return the dead. The Athenians countered this claim by arguing that there was nothing more sacrilegious than the improper care for the fallen.[22] Neither side could concede, so the impasse left everything as it began, with the Boeotians finalizing their preparations for a siege.

The Boeotians knew that they were not yet equipped for a storming of the palisades, so they sent word to the Malian Gulf to call upon more light-armed troops and slingers. With this reinforcement of missile troops, combined with an extra 2,000 Corinthian hoplites who had arrived shortly after the battle, the Boeotians felt confident enough to march on Delium and attacked the fort.

The fighting was ferocious, with the Boeotians trying any which way they could to scale the walls and simply force their way in. With no end in sight, an unnamed Boeotian came up with a new idea: why not burn the Athenians out? To enact such a simple plan, they produced an ingenious contraption that can only be described as a primitive, yet giant, flamethrower.[23]

This weapon was made by the dissection of a large beam, which they hollowed from end to end and then plated most of the way along with thin plates of iron. The two halves were secured back together tightly, creating a very long and rigid tube running its whole length, with an added iron tube projecting at what would become the back end. From the front end was hung a cauldron by way of metal chains. This was laid across a number of carts and moved up to the walls of the fortifications. Placed at the point of maximum damage, directed at the section of the walls primarily constructed with wood and vines, the cauldron was filled with lighted coals, sulphur and pitch and was duly set aflame by a set of giant bellows.

Fire shot forth from the giant flamethrower and immediately ignited the walls around the sanctuary. The sight of the flames would have emptied the ramparts, and the searing heat quickly became too much for the defenders. They could not stay in the fort anymore – they had to flee. As the temporary walls crumbled before them, the triumphant Boeotians were able to sweep up and capture a few Athenian stragglers, taking control of their sanctuary once more.

With the siege brought to a close, the Battle of Delium was finally concluded. The Boeotians were victorious but still lost over 500 men; the Athenians lost 1,000 men including their leader Hippocrates (and an extra 200 were captured after the siege), and an unknown but significantly large number of light-armed troops were killed on their journey home.[24]

The Athenian defeat was a setback to their ambitions but it was by no means a tragedy. Sparta was still loathe to leave the Peloponnese; Athens still held sway over the seas. The only actions they needed to keep an eye on was a Spartan-led polyglot force under Brasidas, who was heading towards Thrace and the Athenian-held city of Amphipolis.

Chapter 3

The Battle of Amphipolis (422 BC)

The Background (Thucydides, IV.70, 78–88, 102–V.3; Diodorus XII.67.3–68.6, 72–3)

Whilst Sparta, having lost control of Pylos and Cythera (425 BC), was unwilling to proactively engage in the war with Athens, they were under a torrential and relentless series of raids from the Athenians and Messenians alike. This timid approach was alien to the Spartan ethos and one commander in particular was looking for a way to re-engage in the war.

The opportunity arose in the summer of 424 BC, when the peoples of Thrace and the king of Macedonia, Perdiccas II, sent a message to Sparta asking for an army to be sent that would aid the Chalcedonian cities in their timely revolt against Athens.[1] Perdiccas had a second, and much less altruistic, reason for wanting a Spartan presence; he intended to use them to subdue a rival king, Arrhabaeus of the Lyncestians.[2] The Spartans were not willing to send a fully-fledged army so far from their own territory, not with a potential *helot* revolt on their hands. So whoever was chosen to command the army would need to raise it almost from scratch, using Thracian and Macedonian money.[3]

A young Spartiate by the name of Brasidas jumped at the chance for action and volunteered himself for what was most likely his first campaign as the sole commander of an army. He was an admired and decorated soldier, who already boasted a distinguished military record. He had been present at the defeat in Pylos and was hell-bent on restoring Spartan prestige.[4] The Spartan authorities did not leave him unaccompanied. They chose to deal with two problems simultaneously: they armed 700 *helots* as hoplites and sent them with Brasidas as he entered the northern Peloponnese in search of more recruits.[5]

After his successful intervention at Megara, Brasidas was able to finalize his plans and begin his long march north into Thrace.[6] With his own army of 1,700 hoplites, he had autonomous power to make decisions that would otherwise have needed authority from Sparta.[7] He had permission to fuse his own alliances, wage his own battles and negotiate with whoever he wanted. As long as he was victorious and it cost Sparta nothing, he was given free rein.

No tradition survives of his march from Corinth, where he massed his men together, to Heraclea in Trachis on the northeast coast of Greece, so it must have been an uneventful one. When his army arrived in Heraclea, Brasidas sent word to his friends at Pharsalus in Thessaly to request an escort through their lands. By the time he had arrived in Melitia, in Achaea, he was met by five escorts from surrounding towns, including the *proxenos* from Chalcidice. Brasidas and his army were well supported, their mission was very popular in the region, but the act of taking an armed force through un-allied lands required a very delicate touch of diplomacy which the Spartans were not especially famous for. During his march through Thessaly in particular, Brasidas needed to keep his wits about him. His team of escorts could only protect him so much, and they were not far out of Melitia before they met resistance.

As Brasidas' army marched north toward the River Enipeas and prepared to cross they were faced with a small group of influential Thessalians. They forbade this army to continue through their lands uninvited and unannounced.[8] Brasidas' escorts jumped to his, and their own, defence saying that they were not forced into being escorts but were in fact acting as friends should when they receive an unexpected visitor. Brasidas added that he had come as a friend to all Thessalians, reassuring them that his army was not intended for them but was here with the sole intention of fighting the Athenians. He added, with a touch of manipulative brilliance, that he knew of no reason why Thessaly would not allow a Spartan army through as he knew of no conflict between the two states which would instigate such restrictions, but if they wished he would not continue his march.[9]

The Thessalian faction left the river, most probably to amass a stronger force, so Brasidas took the advice of his escorts and made for Pharsalus post-haste. In just a single day his army had covered over 20 miles, but he gave them no respite as he pushed them further and further north until they left the hostile lands of Thessaly and entered the territory of their patron, Perdiccas. It was only when they reached the small town of Dium, sitting on the slope of Mount Olympus, that Brasidas and his men could recuperate from their long march through the height of the Greek summer.

Brasidas' arrival in Macedonia sparked a great enthusiasm from Perdiccas, who saw his chance to finally inflict some damage upon his old rival Arrhabaeus. Rather unfortunately for Perdiccas, Brasidas was a pragmatist at heart and knew that he needed as many allies as possible to overthrow the Athenian influence in Thrace. This truth was not shared by Perdiccas, or perhaps he just did not care, and in a petulant fury he chastized Brasidas for reneging on his original promise. He demanded that Brasidas use his army to subdue the Lyncestians, if for no other reason than Perdiccas was covering the costs for half of the army and expedition. Even in the face of having his finances cut, Brasidas held firm. He entered into negotiations with Arrhabaeus before finally agreeing not to invade. Perdiccas was true to his word and revoked much of his funding for the army, deciding he would only cover one third of the costs from then on.

Leaving the ever-cooling reception of Macedonia behind him, Brasidas quickly marched on into Chalcidice. Here he was joined by a confederate delegation of Chalcidians to help persuade more cities to join the revolt against Athens. Their first destination was the Andrian colony of Acanthus, which lay on the east coast of the peninsula.[10] Brasidas arrived just before the start of the grape harvest, the importance of which was enough to make even the most cynical of Acanthians willing to let Brasidas enter the city and open discussions.

Brasidas used his unique skills of blending overt diplomacy with underlying threats, mixed in with some blatant lies, to manipulate the discussions in his favour. He began with a similar emotional exploitation to that he used with the Thessalians, proclaiming that the purpose of his army was the liberation of all Greeks. He similarly stated that he was surprised to see the gates of Acanthus shut. Were they not allies of Sparta? That was what the Spartans had believed, he lied. Brasidas speculated that maybe the Acanthians thought that the Athenians would easily defeat him. Yet the Athenians had not felt able to fight him whilst at Megara with the same army he now had, he lied again.[11] Brasidas then went on to guarantee Spartan respect for the independence of Acanthus, promising not to interfere with their own internal affairs.[12]

Following all of this glowing rhetoric, Brasidas finished his speech with a cold hard truth that cut through all of the niceties and the lies: if Acanthus refused this 'offer' he and his army would lay waste to the surrounding farmlands and destroy the harvests. After rebuttals were heard from leading members of the popular party, the Acanthians were left to vote in a secret ballot. Unsurprisingly, they voted to join in the revolt of Chalcidice, a decision that was quickly followed by Stagirus, another colony of Andros.

As the summer turned to winter, and the Athenians were embarking on their Delium campaign, Brasidas had turned his attentions away from invoking more revolts and onto dealing with the Athenian presence in the region. The large city of Amphipolis was an Athenian colony situated in a U-bend of the river Strymon. It had its own harbour town, called Eion, which sat at the mouth of the river, just under 3 miles south of the city. As the Athenian stronghold in the area, Brasidas knew it needed to be taken. But this city, with strong walls and full stores, was in a powerful defensive position to defy a siege.

Brasidas' army set out from Arne, in Chalcidice, in the depths of winter. With blustering storms and snow in the air, Brasidas was gambling with the lives and the loyalty of his men in the hope that it would catch the Amphipolitans unawares. If Thucydides is to be believed, Brasidas forced his men to march through the storm anywhere up to 40 miles in just twenty-four hours. Arriving at the crossing of the Strymon in the dead of night, Brasidas took the lightly guarded bridge with ease and pushed on into the suburbs of the city. With speed and surprise as the greatest weapons at his disposal, Brasidas was handicapped in his attempts to take the city. He had no real means to seize the walls by force and was reliant upon internal dissidents to betray the city.

As Amphipolis woke to the devastation beyond their walls, the streets were in chaos as panic overran reason in the minds of the people. It was said after the fact that if Brasidas had decided to storm the city there and then he would have met no resistance. Brasidas chose instead to plunder the surrounding areas, exploiting the atmosphere of fear within the city to try and force subjugation without any more bloodshed. This plan backfired in so far as it galvanized the public resolve to resist. The gates were never allowed to be opened by the traitors and the Athenian Eucles sent word to his joint commander, Thucydides, for support. This is the very same Thucydides whose account is our main source for the Peloponnesian War.[13]

Thucydides received the message on the nearby island of Thasos and returned with his 70 ships and soldiers.[14] He headed either directly to Amphipolis or to the Thracian mainland in the search for more military support before he would approach Brasidas. However, Brasidas could not wait. The more time that passed the more resilient the Amphipolitans would become. His only chance was to capitalize on the fear of the citizens and offer terms – and generous terms at that.

Brasidas declared that all defenders, Athenian and Amphipolitan, were able to keep their property and retain their full rights as citizens, whilst those who did not want to stay were given a five-day window to collect their property and depart without fear of harm. The decision was a simple one and the city soon surrendered to Brasidas and his small army.

When Thucydides finally arrived he saw that his worst fears had materialized. Amphipolis had fallen to the enemy while under his authority, and Athenian power was significantly dented in the region. In a last gasp attempt at resistance, Thucydides harboured at Eion and reinforced the harbour town. His actions were just enough to stop Brasidas from removing Athens' foothold in the north. The Spartan-led army attempted a dual assault of the town by land and sea but the Athenians held firm and repelled them.

With the fall of Amphipolis, Brasidas became a magnet for resistance to the Athenians, as more and more cities from the region flocked to his banner. His success could not be ignored. Even Perdiccas returned to Brasidas' side, hoping to ride the crest of his influence. Back in Athens, the news was met with alarm and grave concern for not only the loss of the city, nor the loss of resources, but the manner of Brasidas' terms.[15] By offering such generosity to the inhabitants of Amphipolis, other cities would not fear the ramifications of surrender anymore. Surrender was now a much more beneficial option than resistance. Athens quickly sent out garrisons to support the remaining towns still loyal to their cause.

For Brasidas, this victory was largely ignored by his motherland. Wanting to consolidate his position in the Thracian hinterlands, he implored Sparta to send reinforcements but they refused to support him. It was never their intention to extend the war with Athens; they wanted to use the incursions to the north to apply pressure on Athens to agree to a truce.

Brasidas had no time to dwell on the rebuff. If he was going to secure the future of his army it would have to lie in the camp of the revolting Chalcidian cities. Without a moment's rest, Brasidas began a grand tour of Chalcidice, recruiting cities to his movement. Anyone that resisted had their lands ravaged. After garnering the support of the cities in the Acte Peninsula, south of Acanthus, Brasidas was invited to march on the city of Torone, which was garrisoned by an Athenian force.

Mimicking his tactics at Amphipolis, Brasidas marched his army through the cold winter's night, arriving outside the city before dusk had even broken. His army stopped a quarter of a mile from the walls, resting at the temple of the Dioscuri, whist they waited for their allies inside the walls to give them the signal.[16] With the people of Torone still oblivious to Brasidas' presence, the traitors beckoned the army in.

Brasidas first sent a small force of twenty lightly armed men. By the time they reached the walls only seven had the courage to continue on their mission. These few were slipped in through the sea wall and made their way up to the garrison who held the highest post in the city, killing them to a man. Outside of the walls, Brasidas had sent an advance force of 100 *peltasts* ready to charge into the city once the gates had been opened. His entire plan rested on speed and the exploitation of the Toronaeans' fear.

As the Toronaean traitors finally cut through the bar of the gate, they directed some of the *peltasts* into the marketplace by a postern, thus striking panic into the hearts of the citizens. With all havoc breaking loose, a pre-arranged fire signal was lit and the remaining *peltasts* were brought through the main gate, attacking the market from a second direction.

With the signal ablaze, Brasidas ordered his men to advance, cheering loudly as they ran towards the gate and poured through. The main bulk of his forces did not waste time in the marketplace; Brasidas led them straight to the highest point of the city and began to systematically secure the place from top to bottom.

The assault was so fast and so unexpected that Brasidas had already entered the city before many of the citizenry knew what was happening. Fifty Athenian soldiers had been caught asleep in the market when the *peltasts* first arrived. Through a hastily formed fighting retreat they managed to extract themselves to a fort in the south of the city, called Lecythus, where a larger Athenian force was already preparing the defences.

As daylight fell upon Torone, Brasidas had secured the main part of the city, with only the fort left to subdue. He called to the Toronaeans within Lecythus to come out without fear of retribution and he offered the Athenians a truce with the freedom to leave Torone. The offer was refused but the defenders did ask for a day's truce to collect the dead. Brasidas gave them two days, giving him more time to prepare for the inevitable siege.

As the truce expired, Brasidas began his day-long assault of the fort, but his men were beaten back with every wave. With the arrival of day two, Brasidas unveiled his secret weapon. He had constructed a flamethrower, most likely of a similar design to that used at Delium.[17]

The Athenians had set up defences to counteract such a weapon, they had built a temporary tower on top of a house from which they would throw down water.[18] However, the weight of the water, stones and the multitude of men was too much for the unstable structure. When the tower crashed to the ground, many of the defenders thought that the walls had been breached and fled to their ships. Seeing the enemy in such confusion, Brasidas moved his men in, taking the fort and killing anyone they found.

With the resounding victories of Brasidas capping off a disastrous end to Athens' year, 423 BC saw Sparta and Athens agree to an armistice. This treaty was not enough to deter Brasidas from his plans and, contravening the new peace, he encouraged two more cities to revolt against Athens. Brasidas was no fool, he knew these actions would have consequences so he prepared the cities of Scione and Mende for the inevitable Athenian retribution.

Just on the cusp of the Athenian attack, Brasidas made the inexplicable decision to leave Chalcidice and join Perdiccas in his second invasion of Lyncestis.[19] So, whilst he was campaigning in the west, with little success it might be added, Mende came under attack from an Athenian force of 50 ships and over 1,700 men under the command of Nicias.

On the first day the Mendean force, numbering only 700 hoplites, was able to repulse the attacks but as the siege wore on for the next two days anxieties were running high in the city. The Peloponnesian garrison was quickly becoming unpopular and, when their commander knocked a member of the popular party unconscious for refusing to be part of a sortie, this anxiety quickly turned to rebellion. The people of Mende turned on their own garrison and quickly routed them, those that survived the attack found refuge in the citadel.

The city in disarray, Nicias launched an attack once more only to find the city gates already opened. His army entered as if it had taken the city by storm and began to massacre the inhabitants whilst their horrified commanders attempted to regain control. With the city taken and the massacre finally stopped, Nicias offered terms to the Mendeans that would let them retain their citizen rights.[20]

With Mende secured, Nicias quickly moved on to Scione, winning a battle and investing the city in siege. As the siege works were in construction, Nicias received word from Perdiccas. The Macedonian king was now reeling from his failed invasion of Lyncestis, for which he blamed Brasidas, and wanted to negotiate an alliance. Nicias was amenable, but righty suspicious of this turncoat, setting him a challenge to his new loyalties. Sparta had finally sent Brasidas reinforcements under the command of Ischagoras, Perdiccas was to stop his advance through Thessaly and Macedonia.

With the machinations of an experienced politician, Perdiccas manipulated his influential friends in Thessaly to make a stand against the Spartan army. The Thessalians were so resolute and formidable in their opposition to Ischagoras that he refused to even march into their lands. He sailed on with two companions to meet up with Brasidas in his secondary capacity to inspect the state of affairs in Chalcidice. Once Ischagoras arrived he immediately betrayed the promises of Brasidas and placed his two companions in command of Amphipolis and Torone, removing any illusion of the cities maintaining their independence.

The year of 423 BC ended with an ambitious but ultimately unsuccessful attempt by Brasidas to take the city of Potidaea under the cloak of darkness, but even in the wake of this failure the year had been very profitable for the Spartan general.

The following year saw an end to the official armistice and with it the Athenian general, Cleon, began to apply pressure on the Athenians to send him to Chalcidice. He wanted a strong army to remove Brasidas from the area and, with it to secure the vital resources which Athens relied upon from that region. The assembly agreed and authorized Cleon to take a force of 1,200 Athenian hoplites and 300 cavalry, with an even larger force of allies, along with 30 ships.

Unlike the Spartan armies, Athens had a strong sense of security on the sea so Cleon quickly landed at the besieged town of Scione to acquire a few more soldiers from the Athenian force there, before sailing on to Torone. On arrival, he found deserters from the city that informed him of Brasidas' absence and that the city was grossly understrength. Cleon made short work of storming the fortifications, killing some of the garrison and enslaving the women and children. With Torone secured, Cleon moved his army onwards, around the peninsula of Mount Athos and on to Amphipolis.

Meanwhile Brasidas had been marching an army to support Torone, but he arrived too late. Just four miles from the city walls, he received a messenger that informed him of the city's capitulation and the capture of over 700 men, including the Spartan commander Pasitelidas. Brasidas had no choice but to retreat back, and anticipating Cleon's next target, he marched his men back into Amphipolis.

The Battlefield

The battle was fought outside the walls of the city itself. Amphipolis was located in a u-bend of the River Strymon so that it was protected by water on two sides. The Athenians had begun to construct a 'long wall' which connected the river at two points running north to south. This was not completed when Brasidas took control of the city and it was under his guidance that the wall was finally finished. The city walls were circumnavigated by a road which would have followed the river and branched off to the north toward the hills.

To the northeast of the city is a hill now known as Hill 133, which is the strongest candidate for what Thucydides called a 'strong hill'.[21] It was here that the Athenian army were situated and the attack occurred, atop the western plateau of Mount Pangaeon. As the Athenians fled, they headed south parallel to the long wall, the terrain of which was rugged and hilly.

As a battlefield, it flies in the face of modern assumptions regarding hoplite warfare: there was no open ground, nor a flat plain on which to set up an orderly phalanx.

The Armies

Brasidas had a conglomerate force of allies under his command: 2,000 hoplites, which would have included the majority of the 1,700 hoplites he brought with him on his original voyage; 300 Greek cavalrymen; 1,500 Thracian mercenaries; 1,000 *peltasts* from Myrcinus and Chalcidice; and an unknown number of Edonian cavalry and *peltasts*. This gave Brasidas a force of over 6,500 men. Whilst he was not considerably outnumbered by Cleon, Brasidas was concerned about the capabilities of his men – they were nowhere near the elite standards of the Spartan armies he used to serve in, nor were they comparable to the forces held by the Athenians.

The exact size of Cleon's number is not known, but we do know that they did not outnumber Brasidas' army, or at least not by any considerable amount. Alongside his original force of 1,200 Athenian hoplites and 300 cavalry, plus his original number of allies that more than doubled the army numbers, Cleon recruited more and more allied/mercenary forces of *peltasts*, cavalry and light-armed troops whilst in Thrace.[22] With an army of 6,500-plus men, Cleon would have derived great confidence from the calibre of his Athenian hoplites who would have formed the core of his battle plans, as well as the local elite forces from Lemnos and Imbros.[23]

The Battle (Thucydides, V.6–11; Diodorus XII.74)

On his arrival at the mouth of the River Strymon, Cleon set his base up at Eion and went about trying to consolidate the surrounding area while awaiting the arrival of his allies. When Brasidas heard of Cleon's arrival, he took a force of 1,500 men with him and watched from a hill called Cerdylium to the southwest of Amphipolis. The remaining force readied themselves within the city walls, under the command of Clearidas.

Inside Eion, Cleon was beginning to struggle with the morale of his men. The inactivity that came from waiting for reinforcements began to reflect badly upon Cleon as a leader. It was perceived as a weakness or, worse, a fear for Brasidas. The waiting became too much and contingents from the Athenian army began to branch out from their central control.

One group decided to head straight for Brasidas' position of Cerdylium. Lacking confidence in their ability to take the craggy high ground by headlong attack, they surrounded the hill with a stone wall to prevent Brasidas from being able to leave, hoping to starve him and his men out. Brasidas' men began to panic, imploring Brasidas to attack the Athenians before it was too late but he ignored them. As they asked again and again, Brasidas refused to move, stating that he knew when the best time for battle would be. The wall went up with great speed and, just as it was nearing completion, he finally ordered the advance through the last remaining passage to the bottom of the hill. Through the confined space, Brasidas' men forced their way, utilizing the cramped conditions to negate the numerical advantage held by the Athenians. With very few losses on his part, Brasidas had inflicted the first bloody nose upon his enemy.[24]

As the days passed and Cleon's men grew further discontented, he decided to make a move. Relocating his army, he marched them north beyond the walls of Amphipolis and camped once more atop Hill 133. From here he could properly survey the city before he would return to Eion and plan the inevitable siege. As he scanned his eyes over the walls of the city, he thought about how empty the battlements looked and how it was a missed opportunity not having brought any siege engines with him – he could have taken the city there and then.

Little did he know that Amphipolis was not empty but abuzz with the adrenaline-fuelled excitement of armed men that precedes battle. Brasidas had marched his small force back into the city and began to organize his plans. He knew that his men were not capable of beating this Athenian force in a fair fight. He would have to use other means of winning the day.

Brasidas was not going to miss such an opportunity. He selected a force of 150 hoplites that would remain with him in the north of the city, whilst the rest moved to the Thracian gate in the eastern wall with Clearidas. Brasidas wanted to exploit the element of surprise to its fullest, and this relied on the Athenians seeing nothing of the full strength available to him.

All was not going to plan for Brasidas though. His movements down from Cerdylium had been seen, and word was given to Cleon that a large army was present by the Thracian gate, meaning that a sally was imminent. Cleon had no intention of fighting a staged battle before his allies arrived, so, believing he had time on his side, he signalled the retreat south toward Eion. Ordering his left wing to lead the retreat he became frustrated by their lack of speed and rushed to lead them, whilst ordering his right wing to wheel round, exposing the unshielded side of their formation towards Amphipolis.

Brasidas was watching intently, and the moment he saw the change in direction from the spears and helmets of the enemy he acted quickly.[25] Calling for the north gate to be opened, his small force ran from the walls up the road into the hills, rushing directly toward the very heart and centre of the army. The Athenians were in a panic, the sheer audacity of the attack combined with their disorganized ranks was enough to make the centre rout without a fight.

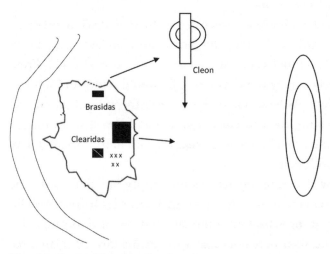

Map 3.1: Battle of Amphipolis, phase 1.

As Brasidas led the line crashing into the enemy, Clearidas ordered the Thracian gate thrown open and over 6,000 men poured from the city and into the old left wing which led the retreat. Cleon was being attacked on both sides and his men were suffering in the confusion that arose from the speed and aggression of the attacks. It did not take long before the left wing followed the actions of the centre and collapsed into a rout; Cleon died in this rout, chased down and killed by a Myrcinian *peltast*.

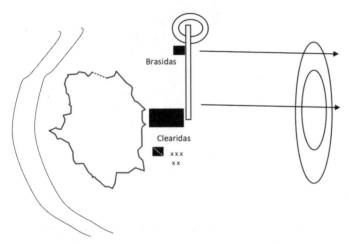

Map 3.2: Battle of Amphipolis, phase 2.

Brasidas tried to push on his advantage and turned his small unit onto the Athenian's right wing. During this offensive, Brasidas received a fatal wound but, unperceived by the Athenians, his men were able to drag him from the field before it buoyed the enemy's morale. The only section of the Athenian army able to make a stand was the right wing, which formed a solid formation on the hill, repulsing the waves of attack coming against them.

With no fortune from the infantry assaults on the hill, Clearidas ordered the cavalry and *peltasts* to harass the small, defiant unit. The Athenian right had no response to their missiles and soon fled after their comrades into the hills and toward Eion. With the whole army in flight, the battle turned into a hunt, with the advantage resting solely with the fast-moving Amphipolitan *peltasts* and cavalry, until the Athenian hoplites could find safety in the hills.

While the Athenians ran back to Eion, Clearidas returned to the battlefield and erected the victory trophy. His army had only lost 7 men, but it had taken over 600 enemy lives, including Cleon's. [26] The battle had been a resounding victory but it came at a grave price.

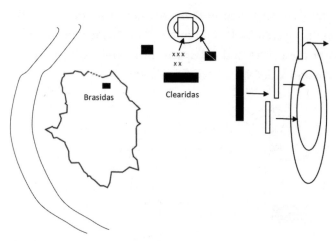

Map 3.3: Battle of Amphipolis, phase 3.

The Aftermath

After Brasidas fell in battle, he was dragged back into the walls of Amphipolis where he held on to life, waiting to hear news from the battlefield. A messenger was sent to inform the city of the Athenian rout and, with victory ringing in his ears, Brasidas was able to release his final breath in the knowledge that his legend had been cemented in the history of his beloved Sparta.

Clearidas brought the army back into Amphipolis and, in full armaments, they buried their commander in a tomb at the front of the *agora*. This spot became the focus of a hero-cult dedicated to the man the Amphipolitans appointed their new founder of the city – replacing the true founder, Hagnon the Athenian.

For Athens this defeat, alongside the defeat at Delium, was too much for them to consider continuing the war. Similarly, the Spartans were still trying to recover from their embarrassing defeat at Pylos and no amount of success in Chalcidice was enough to compensate for this. A ten-year peace was finally agreed and, although in fact it only lasted seven years, this gave both sides time to recover from their tragic losses.

Chapter 4

The First Battle of Mantinea (418 BC)

The Background (Thucydides, V.49– 65)

By the year of 420 BC the supposed peace of Nicias was already beginning to falter. In just the short amount of time that had passed since its inception, discontent was brewing as the various sides neglected to fulfil all of their agreements. These broken promises allowed for the dissemination of internal dissent, with citizens of Sparta and Athens beginning to question the new status quo which the peace dictated. 420 BC was a year of political wrangling and the drawing of allegiances over and over again. Whilst Sparta and Athens never reneged on their alliance, they were not above trying to steal each other's support and security. Athens even went as far as signing a 100-year treaty with three Peloponnesian *poleis* (Argos, Mantinea and Elis), forming a very threatening confederacy so close to Spartan lands.

This year held the Olympic Games, but in a political twist the authorities of Elis accused the Spartans of breaking a previous Olympic truce by sending an armed force into the town of Lepreum.[1] Sparta was subsequently banned from joining this year's festival and from offering sacrifices at the temple of Zeus. The action was so shocking, and the ban considered so insulting, that the games were tinged with a constant fear of Sparta arriving with an army and forcing their right to give due sacrifices – but these fears never materialized. Emotions were running very high and Greece had become a veritable touch paper, waiting for the slightest spark to ignite deep running feuds.

In the following summer that paper was finally lit as war broke out between Argos and the small *polis* of Epidaurus, which lay on the coast due east of Argos. Argos' aggression was made under the pretext of religious sensibilities, but a more likely cause was that it benefited the Argive alliance with Athens.[2] By taking Epidaurus, Argos would secure a direct route for Athenian reinforcements from the island of Aegina to their own city.[3]

At the same time that Argos was planning its assault on Epidaurus, Sparta had put together its own secret force under the command of their King Agis to march out and oppose them. But it was forced to turn back before crossing beyond the Spartan frontiers due to the results of their sacrifices which discouraged any imminent military action.[4] Instead, they sent word to their allies to be ready for action after the month-long Carneia celebrations.

Argos pounced on this delay and, three days before the end of the Carneia, they marched upon Epidaurus and raided the surrounding lands. The Epidaurians were caught in a spin. They quickly sent off messengers to their nearest allies calling for help, but many used the religious holiday as an excuse not to act. Whilst a few did march to the Epidaurian border, they did not cross into Epidaurus to assist them and instead remained inactive.

Once the Carneia had come to an end, Athens called a meeting of embassies at the city of Mantinea where Corinth challenged the Argive aggression in Epidaurus. Argos was required to withdraw from Epidaurian lands, which they agreed to do, but they very quickly returned as the talks of peace in Mantinea showed no signs of progressing. Epidaurus was left isolated whilst Argos ravaged a third of their lands. Sparta tried to send another army in support but they once again received poor omens and were forced to return home. The Athenian commander, Alcibiades, had also marched an army 1,000 strong to aid the Argives against the prospective Spartan threat, but once the news reached them of what had happened he soon retreated.

That winter saw a daring move by a small garrison of 300 Spartans, under the command of Agesippidas, who were covertly transported into Epidaurus by sea, avoiding detection by the patrolling Athenian fleet. With this small set of reinforcements, the hostilities between Argos and Epidaurus became slightly more even handed, with small-scale raids and ambushes affecting them both equally.

With the coming of summer, 418 BC, Sparta finally acknowledged just how dire a situation Epidaurus was really in. Not only was its own independence at risk but the actions of Argos had left the Peloponnese in disarray between those allies who supported it, those who opposed, and the remaining disillusioned. Sparta had to act quickly before the discontent spread and Spartan authority was all but lost in the region.

King Agis was given command of the full Spartan force available, including a strong contingent of *helots*. He also called upon his allies from the Peloponnese and Boeotia to march with them against Argos, to be part of an army which was the finest that had ever been seen in Greece.[5] Argos kept a close eye on proceedings, calling upon their own allies to send reinforcements but they decided not to force any action just yet.

Once Argos received their allies in full they finally marched out to confront Agis' purely Spartan force before it met up with their allies at Philius. The Argive army cut them off at Methydrium and prepared for battle, but Agis evaded them by night and took his army north to meet his allies. The Argives were not despondent, they quickly marched back to Argos and then up the Nemean road, where they anticipated Agis would march down, but once again they were outmanoeuvred.

Agis split his force into thirds: he sent the Spartans, Arcadians and Epidaurians by a more difficult and much steeper road into Argive territory; the Corinthians, Pellenians and Philiasians were sent by another equally difficult road; whilst the Boeotians, Megarians and Sicyonians were the only elements to march down the Nemean road, with the role of holding their position and opposing the Argives if their army turned to attack Agis' two descending forces. Agis had not set his army up to evade the army of Argos, he had dictated his own military invasion of Argive territory and the result was emphatic.

The plains of Argos were swiftly ravaged by the two mobile contingents working in tandem. By daybreak, the army of Argos quickly scrambled into a forced march from just outside Nemea, rushing back down the Nemean road toward their mother city, where they were confronted by the Corinthian-Pellenian-Philiasian guard.[6] The fighting was brief, with minimal losses on either side before the Argives continued moving on into the plain to confront the Spartan army that was laying their lands to waste.

Agis' Spartans had only the Arcadians and the Epidaurians for immediate support, having sent the Boeotian-led force back to Nemea to discern what the Argive army was planning – knowing nothing of their march and subsequent skirmish along the road. Once the Boeotians arrived outside

Nemea and fully assessed the situation they prepared for battle and began to march back toward Argos.

Agis could not have planned this any better. His enemy was threatened on three sides and all three forces were slowly pressing in for the kill.[7] To make matters even better, the Argives knew nothing of the Boeotian army and actually believed that they held the advantage with the Spartans pinned up against the walls of their home city.

As the armies moved ever closer and battle was imminent, a surprising call of parley was honoured from the Argive army. Two men from Argos, a general called Thrasylus and the Spartan *proxenos* named Alciphron, approached Agis and implored him to call off the battle and for all complaints to be dealt with by fair arbitration, after which a treaty could be arranged.[8]

The two Argives had absolutely no authority to make such arrangements and, as strange as it may sound for a king, neither did Agis. Yet the agreement was struck and a truce was granted for a period of four months. Agis immediately withdrew his army without giving any explanation, neither to his own men nor to his allies. Whilst they did follow, as they were required to by their own laws and customs, they were vocal in their disgust for this inaction. This ignoble retreat in the face of fair battle was beneath men of their strength and courage. In effect Agis had taken their prospective honours and glory from them.

The Argives were equally furious with Thrasylus, believing that he had allowed Agis to escape when he was faced with certain defeat at their hands. As the army of Argos returned to the city walls they stopped in the empty river bed of the Charadrus, in the traditional spot where all of their military trials were held, and stoned Thrasylus. Thrasylus only saved his life by escaping and finding sanctuary by a nearby altar.[9]

Following the trial, an Athenian force finally arrived to support Argos. This comprised of 1,000 hoplites and 300 cavalrymen under the command of Laches and Nicostratus, with an ambassador to speak to the people of Argos, called Alcibiades. The Argives initially asked the Athenians to turn around and go home because they were afraid of breaking the truce in place with Sparta. Whilst Argos tried to hold firm, their Mantinean and Elean allies forced them to allow the Athenians to bring their message before the people. Alcibiades' message was simple and effective: Argos had no right to make a truce without the agreement of their confederacy, and now that the Athenians had arrived the war could continue immediately.

The argument was not refined but it worked. All of the allies marched upon the town of Orchomenus and placed it under siege, the aim being to free a number of hostages who had been placed there by the Spartans. The siege did not last long. Orchomenus was in no position to resist due to its weak walls, so they quickly capitulated under the agreement of releasing the hostages that they held, and joining the Athenian–Argive confederacy.

With Orchomenus secured, the allies decided upon their next target. Whilst the Eleans pushed hard for Lepreum, the Mantineans called for a direct assault on Tegea, an idea that was supported by the Argives and the Athenians.[10] The Eleans were furious and left the allies to attack Tegea without them, something the confederates quickly arranged to do with the help of Tegean traitors.

For Agis, the decision to not engage in the battle outside of Argos was still haunting him. As his army arrived in Sparta, after the cessation of the four-month truce, he was still being publically blamed for wasting such an opportunity. Once news arrived about the loss of Orchomenus this public bitterness turned into rage, with an unprecedented reaction from the Spartan people who decided to fine him 10,000 drachmae and intended to burn his house to the ground. Agis threw himself on the mercy of the Spartan officials. He promised to make up for his poor military service and agreed that if he failed to atone then they could do whatever they wished with him and his property. They agreed and Agis was left with his wealth intact, but they subsequently passed a law that forced upon him a council of ten advisors from whom he needed consent to lead any army out of the city.

Word arrived in Sparta from Tegea, they were threatening to join the Athenian–Argive confederacy if a relief force did not arrive quickly to help in their resistance. Sparta did not wait to find out if the Tegean threat was an honest one. They quickly marched an army from the city in unprecedented numbers, including a strong force of *helots*. They headed north into the land of Arcadia, calling on their remaining allies from the region to follow them towards Tegea. The Spartan army stopped at the town of Orestheum and sent home one sixth of their strength, the oldest and youngest elements of their army, to guard the city whilst they continued their movements northeast to Tegea.

Sparta had already sent word to Corinth, Boeotia and other allies calling on their support once more, but it was very short notice and they were marching through enemy lands, so they took much longer to arrive than expected. The Spartans were not going to wait in Tegea for everyone to arrive; as soon as the Arcadians joined them, they moved on towards the lands of Mantinea. Basing themselves near the local temple of Herakles they began to ravage and plunder the surrounding lands.

The Battlefield

The temple of Herakles has not yet been found in the archaeological records, so the precise location of the Spartan camp and therefore the battle site is not strictly known. As it so happens, the battle itself was not impacted by any geographical obstacles, and the only description given by Thucydides is that this was fought in the plains outside of the walls of Mantinea.

As Agis had marched his army directly from Tegea, it is fair to assume that the temple was situated to the southeast of the city. To the east of the camp was a hill range stretching north, and to the south may have been the Pelagus Woods through which the army would have marched to get to the water course which Agis had redirected.[11]

The Armies (Thucydides, V.67–68)

Thucydides' account of the Spartan army at Mantinea is confused to say the least.[12] His confusion seems to come from Spartan terminology where he mistakenly describes the units as *lochoi* rather than *morai*. A simple mistake to make but it creates a statistical nightmare as one *mora* was made up of two *lochoi*, meaning that if we take Thucydides' very detailed breakdown of the army at face value we end up with half of the value that he seems to have meant.

Thucydides' literal figures for the entire army comes out at approximately 6,000 men, but we are told that it was noticeably bigger than the Argive confederate army who could realistically have put up to 10,000 men in the field, this obviously does not add up.[13] If we take Thucydides having made a mistake as a fact, then there numbered somewhere in the region of 8,000 Spartan troops alone. This 8,000 was made up of just over 6,000 Spartiates; over 1,000 freed *helots* including those veterans from Brasidas' campaigns (Brasideans); and 600 of an elite force known as the Sciritae. We do not know how many men were supplied by their allies, but it seems unlikely to have numbered more than 3,000 as the big powerhouses from Boeotia and Corinth had not arrived in time. In total this army would have numbered in the region of 11,000 hoplites.

The battle order placed the Sciritae on the left wing, next to whom were the freed *helots*. After them came the bulk of the Spartan force, followed by the allies of Heraia, Mainalia and Tegea. On the far right wing was a small contingent of Spartans. Agis would have been placed in the centre of the army and surrounded by his corps of 300 *hippeis*, a bodyguard force that always stayed with the king in battle. A small force of cavalry would have flanked the lines on either side along with the light-armed troops.

Thucydides did not give the numbers for the Argive confederate army except for an elite fighting force of 1,000 Argives who were counted separately from the rest of the forces of Argos.[14] We do know the battle order adopted but the numbers attributed are guesstimates.[15] On the left wing sat 300 Athenian cavalry flanking the 1,000 Athenian hoplites, led by Laches. Next in line were the troops from Orneae and Cleonae, then 3–4,000 Argives, next to which lay the 1,000 picked Argives, then a small number of Arcadian allies and the right wing was held by 3,000 Mantineans. Orneae, Cleonae and the Arcadian allies would not have supplied any great number of men, maybe 1,000 in total; this gives an estimated strength of 9–10,000 hoplites. Added to this are the light-armed troops, including slingers, which either flanked the formation or else formed a loose line out in front.

The Battle (Thucydides, V.66–75; Diodorus XII.79)

It was whilst encamped at the temple that the Spartans were finally spotted by the Argives, who quickly countered the threat by taking a strong position atop a nearby hill and forming into their battle lines. The Spartans were undeterred. Agis was in command and he had to prove himself to the

Spartan people, even if it meant advancing on such an indomitable position. He ordered his men to march up to the Argive army and, as they moved within the range for javelins and slingers, he is said to have been berated by an older soldier who accused him of trying to cure one evil with another, that is, trying to undo his earlier dishonour by wishing to condemn his men to an unwise engagement.

Agis decided at the last minute to call his men into a retreat and fall back into Tegean territory. He calculated a different way to deal with the Argive army, a way in which he could draw them from their natural stronghold and face them on the equal plains. Agis ordered the diversion of a river which was renowned for the damage it could cause in both Tegean and Mantinean lands, knowing that such an act would force a counteraction.[16]

The Argive men were furious at what they perceived as another failing of their commanders. Agis had drawn his army within killing distance only to retreat without opposition. Argive emotions were running high once more and they directed their ire toward their generals. Half-stunned by the whole situation, the Argive generals gave in to popular demand. They ordered the army's descent from the hill and headed to the plains below, where they camped and prepared for their imminent assault of the Spartans the next day.

As the dawn finally broke, the confederates rose early, hoping to descend on the Spartans whilst still in their camp. What they did not know was that the main force of Agis' army was not in camp but was still returning from the river they had been diverting. For the Spartans, the sight of the enemy having not only descended from the mountains but in full battle array caused shock, and they quickly formed into their own battle order. Agis took control of a difficult situation. Utilizing the full hierarchy of the Spartan army he brought calm to his men through the authority of his military officers.[17]

With both battle lines in order, the confederate commanders began to expound words of encouragement to their men, calling on their sense of duty and honour. For the Spartans, rhetoric was often considered a waste of time and in this case the men chose instead to sing their songs of war, reminding each other to remember what he had already learnt in his upbringing.

Once the order to march was given, the Argives and their allies advanced in furious haste, filling the air with song and battle cries that betrayed the fear running through their veins.[18] The Spartans were the complete opposite. Marching forward in silence but for the flute players that gave the army its marching rhythm, allowing them to remain in step without breaking their order.

As the two armies moved closer and closer together, Agis spotted the inevitable drift in his enemy's lines. As men in the phalanx become more and more frightened they would squeeze closer to the man to his right, trying to find more cover behind his shield. This would make the entire line prone to drifting to the right. In this case the Mantineans were on course to completely outflank the Sciritae, whilst the Spartans would outflank the Athenians. Agis was afraid of being outflanked so he ordered the Sciritae and the Brasideans to push out to match the furthest positions of the Mantineans. As this would leave a gap in the left wing, Agis then ordered two *polemarchs*, named Hipponoidas and Aristocles, to fill it with one of their *lochos* each.[19] The order was refused.

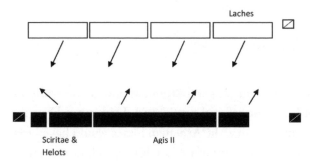

Map 4.1: First Battle of Mantinea, phase 1.

Agis' fury must have been palpable, but he did not have time to stew on the matter, combat was imminent and there was now a hole in his lines. He quickly sent another message to the Sciritae ordering them to return to their original position, but time had finally run out. The Mantineans powered into the loose lines of the Sciritae and broke them quickly, with the Brasideans following swiftly behind them. With the breach opened fully, the Arcadian allies and picked Argive troops poured through and surrounded a section of the Spartan force, driving them into a full rout back to their wagons, killing some of the guards there.

Whilst the Spartans were floundering on the left, the centre was a completely different story. The strong cohesion of the lines made light work of the main body of Argos' fighting force. The Spartans moved forwards as their enemy fled. Argives, Cleonaeans, Orneans and Athenians, all were fleeing at the sight of the Spartan might. Many did not even wait to trade blows, they simply ran at the thought of it. In the chaos of the rout many were trodden to death under foot, all in the fear they could be caught by their enemy.

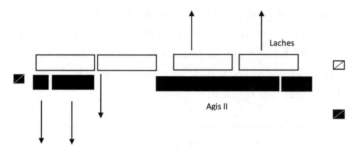

Laches

Agis II

Map 4.2: First Battle of Mantinea, phase 2.

A remaining corps of the Athenians was left stranded and at the whim of their assailants, they had been cut off and outflanked. Had it not been for the intervention of the unsung cavalry, the Athenian losses would have been catastrophic. Agis saw through the euphoria of such resounding victory as he looked to the flight of his left wing. Seeing their distress and impending destruction, Agis called for the rest of his army to advance in support of that wing.

The Mantineans stopped their pursuit of the Sciritae and, seeing the mass of bodies coming toward them, broke into a disordered rout. The elite force of Argives did not flee and Agis had other designs for them. He wished to purge himself of his earlier failings and he intended to kill every one of these picked men to do so. Having them surrounded, Agis was set to fulfil his intentions but for the intervention of Pharax, one of the appointed advisors that accompanied him. Pharax forbade him from continuing the fight against men who had given up all hope of life, as a way of learning about valour.[20] An escape route was left in the surrounding formation and the picked Argives were able to escape without any great loss to their numbers. The Spartans did not pursue the routing confederates for long, having fought hard for a long time they were not inclined to pursue a defeated army.

With the battle over, the Spartans set up a trophy at the head of their fallen adversaries, stripped the bodies before they allowed the confederates to collect them, and collected their own dead to take back to Tegea where they were buried. The Argives, Orneans and Cleonaeans lost 700 men in total, whilst the Mantineans lost 200 and the Athenians 400, including their commander Laches.[21] Little is known about the Spartan allies' losses, and Thucydides does not seem to trust the Spartan figure of 300 dead.

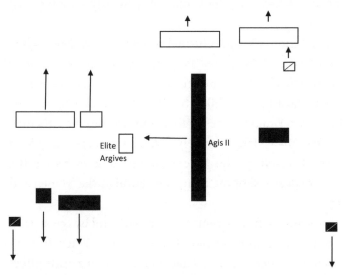

Map 4.3: First Battle of Mantinea, phase 3.

The Aftermath

As a victory, Mantinea brought Sparta little more than a small boost to their diminished military record. This was a battle that Sparta did not have to win as much as they could not lose it, but it did little to affect the wider Hellenic conflict.

Ostensibly this battle reaffirmed Spartan control over the wider Peloponnese, but it did not last long. Argos was made to renounce its pacts with Athens, Elis and Mantinea and sign a new treaty with Sparta. Argos forced Athens to abandon Epidaurus and join with the Spartans to establish an oligarchy in Sicyon. This joint force of 2,000 men then turned their attention back onto Argos and subdued the democracy there, replacing it with a pro-Spartan oligarchy of its own.

By the summer of 417 BC this oligarchy had been overthrown by the popular party in Argos. Sparta did not send an army until the winter, by which time the Argives had courted the help of the Athenians and also built long walls to their harbour in case they became blockaded by land. Agis led a Spartan force that went and destroyed the newly built walls, but they did not try and take Argos by force. Agis chose, instead, to return to Sparta via the Argive city of Hysiae, which they took and subsequently massacred all of the freemen.

Following this minor action, Sparta returned to its inaction. Meanwhile Athens used the First Battle of Mantinea as a springboard to reinvigorate their expansionist tendencies. In the summer of 416 BC, the Athenians sent a fleet of 38 allied ships, hosting over 3,000 hoplites, to the Spartan colony on the island of Melos. After raiding the Melian countryside, the Athenian generals opened negotiations which ultimately failed and a siege was put in place. Following internal treachery, the Athenians were able to breach the defences of Melos, put to death all of the men, and sell all of the women and children into slavery.

Athenian power was growing from strength to strength and by the start of 415 BC they felt able to plan a major campaign that would open a new front in the Peloponnesian conflict. Athens made a decision that would greatly affect the outcome of the war and begin their own demise – they voted to send an army to Sicily and start a war with Syracuse.[22]

Part II

The Spartan Hegemony

In 404 BC, following the Spartan victory over Athens in the naval battle of Aegospotami, the Peloponnesian War came to an end, and the great Laconian *polis* took its position as the superior power in the Greek world. The Delian League was broken up and Athens was put under new governance, led by a Spartan-backed oligarchy, called the rule of the 'Thirty'. This began the period of Sparta's hegemony.

The hegemony was never a harmonious rule. Sparta failed in its promise to liberate the Greek states, many of whom felt they had simply replaced one powerful and intervening *polis* with another. When Sparta began hostile relations with Persia (c.401 BC), Sparta's own unpopular status in Greece became a target of sabotage for the Persians. By 394 BC, the Persians were able to force the Spartan king Agesilaus to abort his plans to invade the heart of the Persian Empire by causing unrest on the Greek mainland.

The year 394 BC began a tumultuous period for Sparta, a period which coincided with a dramatic loss of fully-fledged Spartans (Spartiates). This forced them to rely more and more on mercenaries, allies, and the wider community of Laconia. But, in spite of this, Sparta had just won a hard-fought Corinthian War (395/4–387 BC), a war which saw some of the greatest battles fought during the period. This victory was followed by a sustained campaign to consolidate Spartan power and control in Greece.

By the start of the 370s Sparta was in its strongest position, and when the opportunity came to occupy the acropolis in Thebes, it was one that was taken with glee. The occupation of Thebes began the Boeotian War (378–372/1 BC), a conflict which Sparta began with great success but ended with defeat in one of the most decisive battles of the classical Greek world, the Battle of Leuctra.

The year 371 BC saw the upturn of the Hellenic status quo, with a new order in Thebes taking up the mantle as the strongest *polis*. The next nine

years saw a period of Theban ascendency which witnessed the very soil of
Laconia become marred by the marching footsteps of an invading army for
the first time in centuries.

For all of the Theban gains, they were never able to take Sparta, nor
were they able to control the uneasy Greek alliances that they had formed
to consolidate their power. By 362 BC a coalition of forces came together
to resist Theban expansion and fought a great battle at Mantinea, which
brought an end to Theban designs for hegemony.

During the hegemony period, warfare undertook an important shift.
Simultaneously, the reliance upon mercenaries as opposed to citizen troops,
combined with the weaknesses that were becoming inherent in hoplite
battle, allowed for a new Hellenic order to become apparent. Once the
monopoly that Sparta held over effective military training was broken by the
introduction of these professional mercenaries, and the further introduction
of elite fighting units (*epilectoi*) from various *poleis*, the old party lines of
Greek politics could be redrawn.

At the Nemea (394 BC) Sparta exploited the 'known rules' of hoplite and
phalanx battle tactics. The Spartans encouraged a dominant display by
dragging their own left wing further in as they marched, exposing them
to the strong Theban contingent ahead of them. The enemy then lost their
formation and became weak. The Spartans enacted a manoeuvre which had
their right wing curve inwards as it marched on the Athenians in front of
them. This move resulted in the outflanking of the enemy before contact
was even made, the Spartans then exploiting the broken lines with an
unprecedented level of discipline, order and tactical manipulation. The
result was nothing less than a resounding triumph for the Spartan army,
and showed just how much of an advantage having a professional army really
was.

In the same year, the Spartan king and general extraordinaire, Agesilaus,
returned early from a triumphant campaign in Persian-held Ionia to help
resist the rise in anti-Spartan feeling. The Battle of Coronea reveals a tactical
ploy which forced contact in the centre of the lines rather than either wing.
This bulge in Agesilaus' lines stopped the momentum of his enemy and
allowed his elite forces to join a mêlée already in action, rather than be part
of its inception. What we also see at Coronea is the danger of arrogance

on the field. Agesilaus was being garlanded in victory by his men on the right wing, whilst his left wing was still being driven from the field by the Thebans. Agesilaus then allowed his personal hatred for Thebes to influence his tactical thinking, choosing to face them head-on rather than wait and fight them from their unshielded right-hand side. The result was a bloody victory for Sparta, with the incurring of unnecessary losses, just to appease the king's own arrogance.

In 392 BC, the Spartans infiltrated the Long Walls of Corinth and prepared for the most unique of all of the battles from the classical Greek period. Once the small Spartan army entered the walls it fortified its position, entrenching itself within the tight battlefield, and building a stockade. The Spartans were preparing for a strong defensive action, and placed a cavalry reserve behind the lines to act in the best interests of the army as the battle progressed.

The Spartans' momentum during the Corinthian War was cut short by the shocking Battle at Lechaeum, just outside the walls of Corinth. The Athenian commander Iphicrates used his force of *peltasts* to exploit the cumbersome and slow moving nature of the Spartan hoplite over an open plain. The result was a masterstroke of tactical nous, which brought the ever growing reputation of light-armed troops right to the front of Greek military thought. Not since the campaigns of Demosthenes in the 420s had light-armed troops been utilized to such a devastating effect. Furthermore, the effective annihilation of a Spartan *mora* sent shockwaves through the Hellenic world.

By 371 BC and the Battle of Leuctra, Sparta's time at the top finally came to an end. The military powerhouse was Thebes, who had learned the lessons of hoplite warfare from the Spartans and implemented them against the old masters. What the Theban commander, Epaminondas, achieved was not innovative but audacious. He replicated the tactics of the Spartan commander Eurylochus at Olpae (426/5 BC) by putting his strongest forces on the left wing and directly targeting the main commander of the enemy ahead of him. This tactic was reinforced by the Theban tradition of having a very deep formation, giving the Thebans greater resources to call upon as the attrition of the battle in that isolated area wore on. Finally this battle saw the emergence of the Theban *epilectoi*, the Sacred Band, as a powerhouse of hoplite battle, after they successfully pushed back the greatest Greek warriors known to date.

Thebes refused to learn from the political mistakes of the Spartans and repeated many of them, causing the formation of a coalition against them. The subsequent Second Battle of Mantinea revealed the precarious nature of military power in the Greek world. Epaminondas was lauded by our sources for avoiding an early battle against the coalition in favour of attacking an empty Sparta. This commendation from ancient Greek writers comes even though the mission was an unmitigated failure and the Theban commander had squandered the momentum he had gathered through his campaign in the Peloponnesian region. By the time his army approached Mantinea he faced a united army that was prepared to fight him.

At the Second Battle of Mantinea we see the impact a joint force of cavalry and light-infantry could have on the proceedings of battle. We also see the same tactics the Thebans used at Leuctra, but within this battle it becomes apparent how much of their previous glory had come from a glimmer of luck. The Theban advance seemed unstoppable, but for the concerted Spartan effort to kill Epaminondas and deprive the Thebans of their talismanic leader. As he fell, the Theban advance stopped in its tracks and they refrained from trying to take control of the battlefield. This left the outcome of the battle open-ended, and resulted in a bizarre ritual where both sides accepted victory and defeat at the same time.

Chapter 5

Battle of the Nemea 394 BC

The Background (Xenophon, *Hellenica*. III.1, Pausanias, III.9.1–12)

Following the failed rebellion of Cyrus the Younger, Persian eyes resettled on the Greek outpost to the east of their empire, Ionia.[1] Tissaphernes was rewarded by the Great King for his service during the revolt and was given Cyrus' old *satrapy* to be included with his own. He wasted no time in laying his claim and demanded that the Ionian cities pledged their loyalty to him. The Ionians were not so willing to bow down. They refused on two grounds: firstly, they wanted their freedom from Persian control; secondly, they were understandably nervous of a backlash with Tissaphernes as their *satrap* after refusing him support against Cyrus. The Ionians knew they would not be able to resist on their own and called to the Greek mainland for help, directing their pleas to Sparta.

The year 399 BC saw Sparta send over a modest force to support the Ionians, with its commander Thibron to act as governor.[2] After a summer season of strong defensive measures, followed by small attempts to exert Spartan influence throughout Ionia and south into Caria, Thibron was replaced as commander by another Spartan called Dercylidas.[3] Dercylidas was a very shrewd man, he was nicknamed Sisyphus for good reason, and he quickly grasped the importance of local support.[4] Contrary to Thibron's policy of allowing his army to take what it wanted on the march, Dercylidas stopped his men from doing any harm through allied lands.

He headed north, into the lands of the *satrap* Pharnabazus, in an attempt to call over the Greek-held cities of Aeolis to join the Ionian desertion. Whilst he did meet some resistance from centres such as Cebrene, Scepsis and Gergis, his advance north was a simple one. In just over a week, he had taken control of nine cities and, with winter approaching, decided to exploit this advantage by entering negotiations with Pharnabazus. The message was clear, his offer was either peace or all-out war. Pharnabazus was shocked by the speed of his losses and was equally afraid that the fortification of Aeolis was done with intention of attacking his own homeland Phrygia. He unabashedly agreed to a peace.

Dercylidas spent that winter in Bithynian Thrace fighting alongside his Odrysian allies against the Bithynians, and for the following year he kept his men to the north, around the Hellespont, in an attempt to help protect more Greek cities, before being called back to deal with an uprising of exiled Chians who had besieged Atarneus (in Aeolis).

By 397 BC Sparta had decided to reinvigorate the Ionian cause and pressure the Persians to free the Greek cities. After receiving ambassadors from the Ionian cities, Sparta became convinced that the only way for the Greeks to regain independence was to go on the offensive against Tissaphernes. They ordered Dercylidas to attack the heartland of Tissaphernes' *satrapy*, Caria, with a Spartan fleet led by Pharax in support.

Their plan was hatched too late. The two *satraps*, Tissaphernes and Pharnabazus, had already joined forces in an attempt to rid them of the Ionian problem. After Dercylidas had crossed into Caria he sharply crossed back, following the joint Persian force over the River Maeander.[5] The Greek force was surprised whilst on the march but, with the prospect of battle imminent, neither side was willing to engage. Dercylidas was not confident in his army's capabilities, many of whom had already run in fear before the battle lines were even formed. Tissaphernes was likewise reticent. He ignored the war-mongering of Pharnabazus and meditated on the strong show of force and ability the Greeks had shown at Cunaxa only four years earlier. He chose instead to call a parley and enter negotiations, the result of which was a resounding victory for the Ionians who had their autonomy reinstated in exchange for the removal of the Spartan army and their governors.

If Sparta thought that this was the end of matters they were sorely mistaken. The year 396 BC brought with it news that the Great King was assembling a huge fleet in Phoenicia. No one knew against whom this fleet was going to be sent, but the Spartans did not want to take any chances. Famed commander Lysander convinced the Spartans to send a force of 8,030 hoplites under the command of the king, Agesilaus.[6]

Whilst he met a few minor setbacks in the two years he spent in Asia Minor, Agesilaus caused absolute chaos for the Persians. His methods were unpredictable and his foresight infallible: when they set an ambush in Caria, he invaded Phrygia; when they sent a strong cavalry force to pepper the army, he turned the tables and took control of their camp; when they tried to tie him up in diplomacy by pretending to ask for peace, he just marched on Phrygia again.[7] The situation got so bad for the Great King's representative, Tithraustes, that he changed tack and sent an envoy to Greece who successfully bribed the men of Thebes, Corinth and Argos to attack Sparta as a grand alliance.[8] The bribe itself would not have been enough to stimulate a war, but it would have enticed the politicians to which it was handed to exploit underlying hatred of Spartan authority that was simmering within their communities.[9]

To start a war against Sparta was no easy feat. Thebes decided it needed to happen in an indirect manner or else Sparta would be reluctant to release its alliances. The Thebans convinced the Locrians to tax land that was disputed between themselves and Phocis, knowing as they did that this would lead Phocians to start a conflict. For protection against this aggression the Locrians looked to the strongest allies, Thebes, who in turn attacked Phocis. Phocis could not handle the might of Thebes on its own and looked to Sparta for support. Sparta could not pass up the chance to fight the Thebans, who they felt held disdain for Spartan rule.

Once the Spartan army was on the verge of invasion, Thebes sent for Athens to join them in an alliance, something Athens agreed to in the hope of regaining the power they held only two decades before. The Spartan army was split in two under the command of Lysander and their other king Pausanias. Lysander quickly moved and laid siege to the city of Haliartus but was quickly routed by a Theban army outside of the walls. Lysander was himself killed in the fighting and the Spartan force was hunted down by the Theban victors. As the chase grew in fervour, the Spartan hoplites began to exploit the narrowing roads and uneven ground to launch small counterattacks, killing over 200 men in the process. The Thebans were crestfallen as they saw so many of their brethren fall to javelins and rocks.

The following day, which saw the arrival of an Athenian force, Pausanias called for negotiations with the Theban commanders in which he asked for a truce to recover the dead. This was granted under the condition that he would immediately remove his army from Theban lands, something Pausanias was all too ready to agree to.

On his arrival home Pausanias was accused of capital crimes, such as failing to arrive on the arranged date for a coordinated attack with Lysander, refusing to fight for the bodies of the fallen and for an earlier crime of releasing the democratic faction in Athens. To make matters worse, he did not even turn up to his own trial and was subsequently sentenced to death, causing him to quickly flee to Tegea, where he died most likely in the 370s.

Sparta was at a loss. Having discovered the true extent of the Persian-funded alliance against them, they had no one else to turn to. They had to recall Agesilaus.

Agesilaus was going from strength to strength in Asia Minor. His exploits in Phrygia forced Pharnabazus to agree a meeting and subsequent truce with the Spartan. For the *satrap* this was relief from the constant threats he posed; for Agesilaus it opened up his options exponentially and he had eyes for one thing alone, the glory of defeating the Great King himself. It was whilst he was planning his own invasion that the Spartan envoy arrived. After informing him of the situation at home and that his orders were to return as soon as possible with his army, the envoy left Agesilaus without a choice.

After he convinced his Asiatic allies to join him in his new venture he set about maintaining, and even strengthening, the army he had amassed over the two years in the region. A major stumbling block was that the Asiatic Greek soldiers were not enthralled by the idea of going abroad and leaving their homes behind. Agesilaus anticipated this apathy and offered prizes to the city that could provide the best army, the mercenary commander that could send the best force of hoplites, archers and *peltasts*, and the cavalry commander who could furnish his force with the best horses and riders. The incentive was strong enough that Agesilaus was able to leave behind a force of 4,000 to maintain a defence of the area, without concern for the numerical loss.

With Agesilaus on the march, Sparta was soon to receive much-needed reinforcement and leadership. But his journey would take months, and time was not on Sparta's side. They had to make a move, they had to go on the offensive and show that they were not a cowering shadow of their former selves. The Spartan *ephors* mobilized their army and put it under the command of Aristodemus, who was the guardian of the new child-king Agesipolis.

In the words of Timolaus of Corinth, Sparta was like a river – at its source it was quite small, but as it got further away other rivers would flow into it and make the current flow that much stronger.[10] The danger for the Theban allies was in Sparta's ability to accumulate allies as they marched. With this in mind, they intended to confront them as near to Sparta as possible. As if to prove Timolaus right, by the time the Thebans and their allies arrived at the Nemea River to the west of Corinth, Aristodemus had arrived at Sicyon with allies from Mantinea and Tegea.

The Spartans moved quickly, heading north to the coast of the Gulf of Corinth, going via the town of Epieikia. A skirmish ensued, with light-armed troops hurling their javelins and doing great damage to the Spartan army as they tried to descend onto the coastline. Once they had descended they were able to march through the plain unopposed as they destroyed the land with fire. The Boeotian alliance withdrew behind the Nemea River and set up camp with the river in front of them. As the Spartans marched toward the river they spotted the camp opposite and chose to pitch their own, stopping just over a mile from the banks of the Nemea.

The Battlefield

The location of the battle was on the western side of the Nemea, the side on which the Spartans were camped. It would have been fought in front of their camp, which was roughly one mile away from the river, and it would have been on open ground. The sight of the river was distorted by overgrown trees and shrubs but the battlefield was most likely unencumbered with such obstacles and would have been several hundred feet wide.[11]

The Armies (Xenophon, *Hellenica*, IV.2.16–17; Diodorus, XIV.83.1)

The Spartan army was made up of 6,000 Lacedaemonian hoplites, led by Aristodemus, 3,000 from Elis and its neighbours, 1,500 Sicyonians and 3,000 from Epidauros, Trozen, Hermione and Halieis.[12] In addition to this

Xenophon states they had 600 Spartan cavalry, 300 Cretan archers and over 400 slingers from the countryside of Elis. Unfortunately, Xenophon does not remain consistent in his description of the army as he fails to mention the Tegean and Mantinean forces that we know joined the Spartan army on the march, and a contingent from Pellene.[13] This makes estimation very difficult, with academic conjecture ranging from a few thousand extra to as many as 9,500 more hoplites. A few clues are available in the battle itself, namely that the Tegeans were pitted against 2,400 Athenians on their own, which is not something that was really possible without a similarly sized force. Mantinea was capable of producing a similar number of men, but because we do not know how many were supplied by Pellene, then a conservative estimate of an extra 5,000 seems prudent. This gave the Spartans a fighting force of approximately 18,500 hoplites, or just under 20,000 all in.

The opposing force is described as containing 6,000 Athenian hoplites, 7,000 Argives, 5,000 Boeotians, 3,000 Corinthians, and 3,000 from Euboea.[14] In addition they had 800 cavalry from Boeotia, 600 from Athens, 100 from Chalcis and a further 50 from Locris; as well as an even larger number of light-armed troops from Corinth, Locris, Malis and Acarnania. This gave a fighting force of 24,000 hoplites, 1,550 cavalry and then the light-armed troops on top of that. This was a phenomenal army at their disposal.

A small issue arises in the account of the battle given by the much later source Diodorus. He does not dwell long on the battle but gives the overall participating figures as being 23,000 foot for the Spartans, and 15,000 for the Boeotian alliance. For the Spartan figure to be anywhere near reconcilable with Xenophon an additional 9,500 hoplites needed to be found, which as we have seen is most unlikely. There is the distinct possibility that Diodorus got the figures the wrong way around, as his numbers do pretty much conform to Xenophon's assessment when they are reversed. In this instance Xenophon seems to be the more reliable source of information and this narrative will work from his figures, with the aforementioned adaptations.

The Battle (Xenophon, *Hellenica*, IV.2.18–23; Diodorus, XIV.83.2)

Battle plans had been drawn from both sides; before the Spartans had arrived at Sicyon the Boeotian allied commanders were already discussing tactics and phalanx depth. They knew that the greatest threat was to be encircled. Whilst this would not normally have been an issue for the larger army, it is possible that there were reservations over the Boeotian force that had already shown at Delium that they were inclined to fight in a much deeper, and therefore narrower, formation.[15]

Due to the conglomerate nature of the allied army, the prestigious role of commanding the right wing was rotated (most likely each day). The Boeotians were said to have been against affirmative action whilst they held the left wing, knowing that they would have faced the strongest Spartan force that held their right flank. But once they were moved to the right wing, opposite the Achaeans, they were eager to engage.[16]

The signal was given to cross the river and form into their battle order. Whilst the rest of the army set out as originally planned, in ranks sixteen deep, the Boeotians did as was feared and took up a much deeper formation.[17] They then began the forward march, purposefully veering to the right with the intent of outflanking the enemy's left flank. The entire army followed suit. The Athenians on the left flank were forced to follow so as to keep the line from separating, but also staying aware of the danger of their own encirclement.

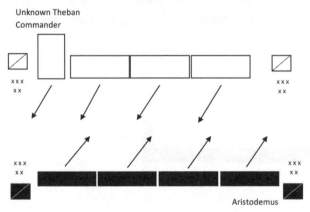

Map 5.1: Battle of the Nemea, phase 1.

Their march remained undetected, screened as they were by the overgrown landscape nearest the river. The Spartans had no knowledge of their presence until they heard the almighty *paean* being sung by 24,000 voices. This left no doubt in their minds and they quickly gave the order for everyone to arrange themselves for battle.

The formation had been pre-arranged, a precaution that allowed for a very fast deployment to occur. The Spartans took their position on the right flank, with the Tegeans alongside them, and orchestrated an identical move to the Boeotians. The word was passed along the lines that each soldier should follow the lead company, and the Spartans duly marched their army forward, edging to the right with purpose as they did so. The simultaneous tactical moves meant that the Spartan force ended up with only six of the ten Athenian tribes facing them, the other four were now in line with the Tegeans.[18]

As the armies marched toward each other, gaps began to show but the Spartans halted their advance when they were around 200 metres away and sacrificed a goat to Artemis Agrotera, as they supposedly did before any engagement. This was not necessarily a tactical decision but it would have the effect of allowing the lines to become re-ordered before the final charge.[19] With the customary sacrifice complete, the Spartans charged their army forwards. As they ran, their far right began to curve inwards so that at the point of contact the protruding force of elite Spartan soldiers pivoted around the corner point of the Athenian line, creating a battle line that now ran along the enemy's front and then folded in along his left flank, forming an L shape.[20]

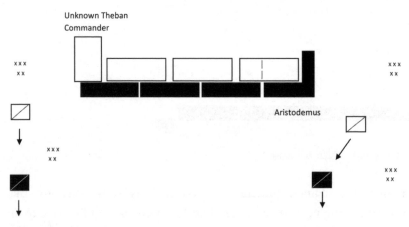

Map 5.2: Battle of the Nemea, phase 2.

As the mêlée ensued, the Spartan allies did not fare well, with only the men of Pellene refusing to move from the spot they were given, choosing to fall where they stood rather than run. By contrast, the Spartans themselves made very short work of the six Athenian tribes opposing them, killing many men in the process. The ease of their fight allowed them to proceed without any disruption to their own line through injuries or losses. The men forming the 90 degrees and original Spartan wing were now all able to work their way through the vulnerable flank of each contingent they met, rolling up the enemy line towards the centre.

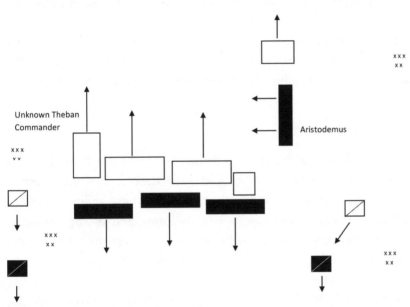

Map 5.3: Battle of the Nemea, phase 3.

The other four Athenian tribes were victorious against the Tegeans, and so they were not in the Spartans' line of sight. Instead, Aristodemus' men moved straight on to the Argives who were returning from their own pursuit of their foes. The commander in charge of the extreme right flank of the Spartan force wanted to wheel his army a further ninety degrees so that it would be facing the Argives head on, meaning that they would be facing the original rear of their enemy's lines. It is said that someone shouted to him that he should simply allow the Argives to run past as they were, and attack them on their undefended side (i.e. their unshielded right). The result was catastrophic. Argives fell in their droves, while the rest, powerless to resist, ran for their lives. With ruthless efficiency the Spartans swiftly moved on, hitting the Corinthians and Boeotians likewise, before falling upon the hapless Thebans returning from their blood-fuelled pursuit of the Achaeans.

The fleeing allies headed for the security of Corinth but after the first wave of survivors were admitted the remainder were callously shut out. Left to fend for themselves, they returned to their camp by the river. With the battle over and night beginning to fall, the Spartans marched to the spot where the battle first began and erected their trophy, bringing proceedings to a formal end.

Xenophon does not tell us about the figures of the dead other than 8 Spartans.[21] For a set of figures we have to turn to Diodorus who claims the Spartan force lost 1,100, whilst the Boeotian alliance lost 2,800 men.[22]

The Aftermath

With the large Boeotian allied force defeated, Sparta was buoyed by the reclamation of their military prowess. Add to this the benefit of the returning army under the command of Agesilaus, a man whose military exploits in Asia had no doubt become the talk of the town, and the Spartans had nothing but a strong and bright future to look to. Whilst the full army was disbanded, one *mora* was sent to join Agesilaus at his expected rendezvous on the outskirts of Boeotia.

Whilst the Battle of the Nemea was a pre-emptive, defensive action for Sparta against the Boeotian alliance, Agesilaus was en route to carry out an offensive campaign that took the battle right into the heart of Theban lands.

Chapter 6

Battle of Coronea 394 BC

The Background (Xenophon, *Hellenica*, III.3.1–3; Pausanias, III.9; Xenophon, *Agesilaus*, 1; *Hellenica Oxyrhynchia*, XXI. 1–4)

With a moderate force of 8,030 hoplites, Agesilaus' campaign in Persia (396 BC) was not going to be an easy one.[1] This military action was not even his own idea, it was one encouraged upon him by his former mentor, friend and political ally Lysander.[2] Lysander had been instrumental in the deconstruction of Athenian influence when the Peloponnesian War came to a close. Many of the Asian Greek cities had been implanted with Lysander-approved *decarchies* (governments run by ten men) who were pro-oligarchy, anti-democracy, and preferably pro-Lysander. These *decarchies* had subsequently been dissolved by later Spartan action, and Lysander wanted them reinstated.

For Agesilaus the concerns of political machinations, outside of Sparta itself, were of little interest to him. His concerns lay in the more practical elements of military action and the necessary piety needed to garner support from the gods. Once he agreed to lead the expeditionary force he made demands for relevant provisions, which included six months' worth of grain supply, after which he presumably intended to establish his own long-term supply. Now that he felt fully prepared, he performed all the necessary sacrifices before sending messengers to all of his allied cities. He informed them of how many men to send him and to wait for him at Geraistus in Euboea, whilst he set out for the town of Aulis in Boeotia.

Agesilaus wanted his final sacrifice to be made at Aulis because it was here that the legendary king Agamemnon had sacrificed his own daughter before he headed to Troy.[3] His intention was to sacrifice a hind but he wanted his own soothsayer to perform the rite rather than the relevant Boeotian official. This demand caused such great offence that his rituals were interrupted by the officials, and the remainders of the sacrifice were thrown from the altar.

In a fury born from devout piety, Agesilaus called on the gods to witness the sacrilege afforded to them and stormed out of Aulis, heading straight to Geraistus without any more sacrifices being given.[4]

Having finally joined his army, Agesilaus had them board the ships and head to Ephesus on the Ionian coast. On their arrival they received a messenger sent by Tissaphernes enquiring as to why they had landed in Asia. Agesilaus did not mince his words, he declared his mission was to ensure the autonomy of all of the Greek cities in Asia. Tissaphernes was not greatly concerned but, rather than face a Greek force unprepared, he played for time. He advised a truce, under the pretence that he would contact Artaxerxes, the Great King of the Persian Empire, for approval of Agesilaus' request; he even went as far as to suggest that the king would approve the cessation. The truce was made and both leaders agreed to not act with deception, nor to do any harm to the enemy territory during the set period of three months.[5]

Contrary to his oath, Tissaphernes did not send the Greek demands to Artaxerxes but, instead, requested a large force be sent to aid him in removing this new threat. When Agesilaus was informed of the deception he continued to observe the truce regardless, something Xenophon considered to be indicative of his honourable and pious personality.[6]

With the truce in place, Agesilaus had time to address civic issues in the Ionian cities who were still in disarray following the political upheavals forced upon them. What should have been quite a simple issue was complicated by the presence of Lysander. Not only did Lysander have supporters in Asia, as well as a long-established authoritative relationship over Agesilaus, but he held the polar opposite personality to the Spartan king, which made him the object of many supplicants. Agesilaus was a calm-mannered man, known for his self-control and an emotional spectrum not usually associated with the Spartan image. Lysander was a different kettle of fish. He was a harsh and often violent man, who utilized the laconic habit of using very few words whilst speaking.

While Agesilaus noticed Lysander's growing influence, he did nothing to curb it at first. This influence soon grew, resulting in Lysander being habitually followed by throngs of hangers-on. All wanted their voice heard by the most powerful Spartan who could take their pleas straight to the ear of the king. Agesilaus may have been appreciating the quiet this afforded him, but the thirty other Spartiates with the king were less impressed. They complained to Agesilaus that Lysander's actions were tantamount to acting like a king, something which was unlawful in Sparta.

Agesilaus knew he had to act and did so with a calm and authoritative manner that defined his military career. Very simply, he refused the request of any man brought to him by Lysander. They were not aggressively refused nor were they refused an audience, but soon the word got out that Lysander was no longer able to influence the king. Lysander saw what was happening and requested to be sent away from the king due to the dishonour that was being shown to him. Agesilaus agreed and sent him to the Hellespont, where Lysander persuaded the Persian *satrap* Spithridates to revolt from the Great King, an act which mended the fractured relationship between the Spartan king and his former mentor.

Whilst this was transpiring in Ionia, Caria was abuzz as Tissaphernes finally received his reinforcements from Artaxerxes. Now feeling confident of his military strength, the *satrap* demanded that Agesilaus leave Asia or face a war. The threat was very real, and the Spartiate commanders that had joined their king were noticeably concerned at the sheer size and power of the force at Tissaphernes' disposal. Agesilaus on the other hand was left smiling, and thanked the Persian envoys who delivered the threat. To Agesilaus' mind, Tissaphernes had finally revealed himself to be a breaker of oaths and had made the gods his enemies, thus making them allies of the Greeks. With war now imminent, Agesilaus wasted little time in preparing his men for the campaign. He called on more Asian Greek cities to send troops, and he also sent word to the cities that stood between him and Caria to prepare marketplaces for his army.[7]

For Tissaphernes, the advantage lay solely at his feet – not only was his army far greater, but he also had a strong force of cavalry, whereas Agesilaus had very few mounted troops. The plan unveiled itself to the Persian. He knew that Agesilaus would be furious at his earlier deceptions and would head straight for the heart of Tissaphernes' power, Caria. The problem lay in the fact that the Carian terrain was not well suited to cavalry tactics, so Tissaphernes wanted to head the Greek army off at the Maeandrian River valley with his horsemen, while his infantry continued on to Caria.[8] With his plan in place, Tissaphernes was ready to deal a major blow to Greek morale, but he had made one vital mistake in his estimations. Agesilaus was not a man run by his emotions, and Caria was not the only region he could attack to make a significant impact upon his enemy. Whilst the Persians were marching fast to prepare for the supposed attack, Agesilaus redirected his troops from their march to Caria in the south, heading them straight for the lands of Phrygia to the north.

Utilizing the element of surprise, Agesilaus' army marched almost unopposed, falling upon cities as they went, subduing them to his authority and claiming phenomenal quantities of loot. His army faced one minor setback outside the town of Dascylium where it was faced with a superior cavalry force, which his own meagre horsemen could not hope to overcome. After finding all of his sacrifices unfavourable, Agesilaus refrained from taking to the field again until he had established for himself a far better cavalry arm.

It was not until the spring of 395 BC that Agesilaus mobilized his army once more in Ionia, turning the city of Ephesus into a workshop of war as he encouraged competition between all forms of soldier in his army, offering prizes for the best of each, and filling the city with military craftsmen.

A year had passed since Agesilaus had first embarked on his mission, so in accordance with Spartan customs the thirty advisors that left with him were duly replaced by a new batch from Sparta. As they were naïve to the campaign thus far, Agesilaus decided to blood them as quickly as possible. He announced that he would lead the army to a high impact area in his enemy's territory by the shortest land route possible. When Tissaphernes heard this he assumed that this was a bluff. Gambling that Agesilaus would finally attack Caria under this blanket of subterfuge, he set his army up once more at the Maeander plain. But Agesilaus was not bluffing, his intentions were exactly as he said. He needed these rookies of the Persian sphere to learn as quickly as possible and so headed northeast to the city of Sardis.

For three days the Greek army marched unabated, but on the fourth day a Persian force of cavalry finally appeared. The cavalry ordered their baggage train to cross the Pactolus River, to set up camp, whilst the bulk of the force spied that the Greeks were greatly dispersed in their search for plunder and food, and quickly descended upon them, slaughtering many.[9] Agesilaus spotted it all too late, but sent out his own cavalry to quell the killing before it became a massacre. When the Persians spotted the Greek cavalry they drew together into a tight, deep formation and awaited battle. Agesilaus' chance for a resounding victory was now. He had not fared well against the might of the Persian horse, but this was his best opportunity as the Persians had not yet received any infantry support. After an unsuccessful charge from his own cavalry, he followed it up with a charge from his youngest group of hoplites, and *peltasts*, supported by the rest of his army. This proved too much for the Persians who quickly gave way and were routed. The Greeks fell upon the Persian camp and took over seventy talents worth of money, they also captured some camels which Agesilaus evidently became well known for.[10]

The defeat outside of Sardis was the last straw for the Great King. He sent a representative called Tithraustes to the city to have Tissaphernes beheaded under the charge of betrayal. Tithraustes used this removal of the *satrap* to urge Agesilaus to leave Asia and promised that the Greek cities would become autonomous once more, only having to pay a tribute to the Persians as they had done before. Agesilaus could not agree to the offer himself and sent word to Sparta for an official response. Tithraustes accepted this delay but requested that the Greek army attack the territory of Pharnabazus, as repayment for him taking vengeance upon the enemy of the Greeks. Agesilaus had little choice but to agree, but he demanded that the Persians supplied his army with all of their necessary provisions. Once this was agreed upon, a fee of thirty talents no less, Agesilaus sent his army north once more into Phrygia.

Arriving at the fall of autumn, Agesilaus set about causing chaos for Pharnabazus by burning the countryside and plundering many of his cities.[11] He soon received word from Spithridates – the Persian *satrap* so recently turned by Lysander – and under his recommendation formulated an alliance with Otys, the king of Paphlagonia. Whilst this further secured support for Agesilaus in the Hellespont region, more importantly Otys was persuaded to offer a force of 1,000 cavalry and 2,000 *peltasts* to Agesilaus' army.

With winter approaching Agesilaus had concerns about his army's provisions. He moved them into the very centre of Pharnabazus' lands, at Dascylium where Pharnabazus had his royal residence. The move was both arrogant and bold, but the benefits far outweighed the risks for Agesilaus.

The surrounding area was filled with large villages awash with all of the provisions that Agesilaus needed, and held perfect hunting and fishing grounds. The Greeks got into the habit of foraging and, thanks in part to the excess available and in part to the lack of opposition they had faced in doing so, they became lax and careless in their manner. On one winter's day many of the men were out foraging when Pharnabazus appeared with a cavalry contingent 4,000 strong, and two scythed chariots that would have struck fear into the hearts of the isolated foragers.[12]

Many of the foragers spotted what was happening and banded together to form a makeshift phalanx, but Pharnabazus just sent in his chariots to do what they did best, cause chaos in enemy lines. The Greeks fell away to the awesome power of the bladed chariots, leaving the Persian cavalry to cut down over 100 of them, whilst the rest fled to the safety of Agesilaus and the bulk of the army.

The Greeks quickly got their revenge within a few days, falling upon the Persian camp at dawn and taking unprecedented quantities of plunder. Agesilaus had not organized this raid and when the army returned to him, he found a great dissent within his forces as the Asian contingents had been robbed of their share of plunder by their Hellenic counterparts. Spithridates and the Paphlagonians abandoned the Greeks and moved on to Sardis which was held by a sympathetic *satrap* named Ariaeus.

This recent debacle caused Agesilaus much grief. A large portion of his force had just left because of a needless show of Greek arrogance. When he was offered the opportunity to call a truce with Pharnabazus, to be brokered by a mutual guest-friend, he jumped at the chance. A truce was declared and in the spring of 394 BC Agesilaus moved his army south to camp on the plain of Thebe. He brought together all of his available forces, including new recruits from the many friendly cities he had passed on his march, planning his own *anabasis* into the heartland of the Persian Empire and directing his aggression upon the Great King himself.[13]

With his plans coming together and his forces ready to march, he received unexpected word from Sparta – it was under attack from the Boeotian alliance and needed him home as quickly as possible.[14] Agesilaus was understandably upset, all of his hopes of glory and honours were to be taken from him. But he called his allies together and promised that, in return for their help in

Greece, he would return to Asia and resurrect his grand campaign to free the Greek cities. They all voted to help him.

The soldiers themselves were less willing to join this expedition, far from home as it would be. It was a war for mainland Greece, it was no concern of theirs and did not help them protect their families in Ionia. Agesilaus knew he could not convince them through clever speeches, instead he incentivized the supply of the best troops. He offered prizes to the cities who could provide the best army; to the mercenary commanders that would fit out the best company of hoplites, archers and *peltasts* respectively; and to the cavalry commander which furnished his regiment with the best horses and cavalrymen.[15]

After crossing the Hellespont, Agesilaus marched his army by the same route that Xerxes followed during his invasion in 480 BC.[16] They headed west, following the Thracian coast of the Aegean Sea, and they were passing through Chalcidice when Agesilaus heard of the Spartan victory at the Nemea.[17] They continued through Paeonia, before turning south and following the Aegean coastline down into Thessaly.

Through Thessaly, the army was harassed by the allies of the Boeotians as they passed the cities of Larissa, Crannon, Scotoussa and Pharsalus. The Thessalian cavalry was such a threat that Agesilaus ordered his army to march in a hollow square formation and split his cavalry in half, with one contingent covering the front and the other the rear of the square. The Thessalians were less inclined to fight such a strong hoplite formation, whilst the Greeks at the same time were understandably cautious in pursuing any cavalry they chased off, lest they lose their defensive formation and expose themselves to counterattack. The stalemate was finally broken by Agesilaus when he recombined his cavalry force and ordered them to attack the Thessalian horsemen, without giving up the pursuit. The tactic worked and the Thessalians fled in a panic, with a few killed and many more captured. Agesilaus was especially pleased with this relatively minor victory because the Thessalians were said to have been the very best cavalrymen in Greece.

The rest of the march through Thessaly passed without harassment and they soon arrived on the borders of Boeotia. On the 14th of August, Agesilaus heard news of a naval defeat for the Spartans near Cnidus against a joint Greek and Persian naval force.[18] The Spartan commander was gravely concerned about how the news of this defeat would affect the morale of his own men. In a master stroke of group manipulation, he declared to his men that the Spartans had won the battle but had sadly lost the *navarch* Peisander.[19] He then made the relevant sacrifices as if it were for the victory, and he even sent pieces of the sacrificial victim to his men to eat, so that all could share in this great 'win'.

With morale at its highest, Agesilaus was ready for anything the Boeotian allies could throw at him, and they did not disappoint.[20] In preparation for what Xenophon described as a battle 'quite unlike any other in our time', the Boeotians and their allies brought their forces to the border town of Coronea.[21]

The Battlefield

The battle was fought on the plain of Coronea, to the west of the actual city. The lack of description in the sources implies that it was a nondescript plain, flat with no obstacles to mention. To the southwest lay Mount Helicon, which sat behind the Boeotian allies, and to the northeast lay the River Cephisus, which lay behind Agesilaus' men.

The Armies

Frustratingly, for a battle at which he was present, Xenophon provides very little in the way of specifics: most notably he does not give any figures regarding the relative sizes of the two forces.[22] All that we are told is that the two armies were evenly matched, with equal cavalry numbers and possibly equal hoplite forces, but that Agesilaus had considerably more *peltasts* present.[23]

Agesilaus had at his disposal the remaining veterans from the original 2,000 freed *helots* which he took to Asia, now battle hardened and very disciplined. To add to this he had a full Spartan *mora*, which had been sent by sea following the victory at the Nemea, and also half a *mora* which was stationed at the nearby city of Orchomenos, giving an invigorating boost of 1,680 Spartans.[24] In addition he had the support of his allies from Asia Minor; some hoplites were deployed from the nearby cities of Orchomenus and Phocis; and we are told that he also had the remnants of the Ten Thousand, the Greek mercenaries who had fought for Cyrus during his revolt in 401 BC, under the command of the Spartan general Herippidas.[25] The overall hoplite force may have numbered somewhere in the region of 15,000.[26]

The Boeotian allies contained a strong, Theban-led Boeotian army of 5–6,000 hoplites, joined by what was likely to have been a strong force from nearby Athens of 5–6,000 hoplites.[27] The Euboeans also resided nearby, so they may well have sent a strong force in the region of 3,000. Forces from Argos and Corinth are harder to judge because they had just sent 10,000 between them to the Nemea, but that battle had been fought in close proximity to their own lands and it cannot be assumed they chose to send such a strong army far from their homelands. The remaining allies were the Ainianians and the Locrians, who could possibly have supplemented the numbers enough to compensate for the smaller contingents from Argos and Corinth, giving the entire hoplite strength of the army at roughly 20,000 hoplites.[28]

There would have been a large force of light-armed troops and *peltasts* for both armies. However, because we know that Agesilaus had considerably more *peltasts*, combined with the fact that we know he was not outnumbered, raises the question of just how many light-armed troops did he have? The cavalry numbers are not given but a modest force of 1–1,500 is a realistic figure for both armies. This would give the Boeotian allies a force of around 21,000 hoplites and horses and an unknown number of light-armed troops. If the Spartans had a force nearing 16,000 with horsemen, Agesilaus would have needed *peltasts*, skirmishers, slingers and archers that far exceeded 5,000 in number.[29]

The Battle (Xenophon, *Hellenica*, IV.3.17–21; *Agesilaus*, 2.9–14; Diodorus, XIV.84.1–2; Plutarch, *Life of Agesilaus*, 18.1–19.1

Agesilaus moved his men southwest, away from the River Cephisus and formed them into their battle order. He personally held the right wing with his reliable Spartan troops, and the Orchomenians held the left wing. The enemy had likewise entered the field, with the looming shadow of Mount Helicon behind them. The Thebans took up the right wing, whilst the Argives held the left, opposite Agesilaus' men.

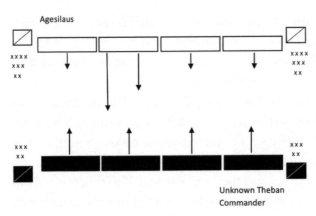

Map 6.1: Battle of Coronea, phase 1.

Both armies marched slowly toward each other across the plain. An eerie silence filled the air, with little more than the clinking of weapons and armour breaking the peace.[30] The gap in between shrank further and further until, at just a *stade* (about 180 metres) apart, the Thebans could hold back no more: the quiet calm that covered the battlefield was replaced with thousands of voices striking up the *paean* and beginning their run to close quarters.

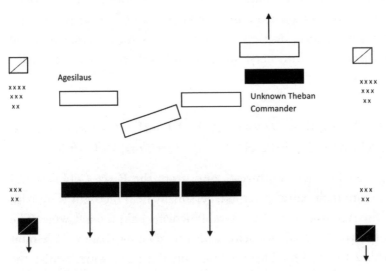

Map 6.2: Battle of Coronea, phase 2.

Agesilaus' men did not react but continued their march, probably slowing it down as they prepared for imminent contact. The Thebans were closing in on the Orchomenians quickly. When there was just 3 *plethra* (half a *stade*, 90 metres) separating them the army of Agesilaus finally began to act.

Herippidas led the countercharge from the centre right of Agesilaus' formation. His mercenary corps charged forward, followed by the Asian Greek allies swiftly behind. Agesilaus' own Spartans lingered back, creating a billow within the ranks, possibly designed for the strongest contingent to join the fray last and cause the greatest impact. The tactical ruse was not necessary. Already intimidated by the 'solid mass of bronze and red' that stood before them, the enemy line capitulated before contact was even made.[31] The Argives did not even wait for Agesilaus' troops to begin their manoeuvre, they turned and fled back to mount Helicon.

With their side of the field won with minimal bloodshed, the mercenaries had begun to crown and garland Agesilaus as the victor before they were interrupted with a report from the right wing: the Thebans had won the day, cutting through the Orchomenian lines and were now attacking the baggage train.

Agesilaus quickly restored his lines and sharply wheeled his men round to the left to head off the Thebans where they were. But the Thebans had been watching the Argive flight to the mountain and wanted to make good their own escape. This meant they had to fight their way back through the enemy lines to re-join their allies to the southwest. They drew their lines together in a solid formation and headed boldly forwards.

In a strange and shocking error of judgement Agesilaus decided against the more logical tactical decision, posited by Xenophon, of allowing the Thebans to pass through before falling upon them from behind.[32] Instead he led his men into the Theban lines head-on, fighting toe-to-toe and man-to-man.

Their shields clashed together, pushing one another as they attempted to find space in the mêlée. Spears splintered and shattered, replaced quickly by swords as the ordered combat of the phalanx descended into the chaos of a brawl. There were no cries of anger or anguish, just the sound of combat echoing in the ears of the fighters. Here, as Xenophon laconically put it, 'setting shields against shields they shoved, fought, killed and were killed'.[33]

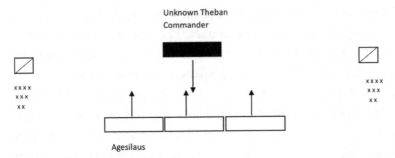

Map 6.3: Battle of Coronea, phase 3.

Whilst many of the Thebans broke through the Spartan ranks and escaped to Helicon, some were picked off in isolated groups and killed.

In the mêlée Agesilaus had been wounded numerous times, from a variety of different weapons, and had to be carried to his victorious battle lines.[34] In the midst of the celebrations he received word from some of his horsemen. Eighty fully armed soldiers of the enemy had taken cover in a nearby temple of Athena. Agesilaus ignored the pains of his wounds that fuelled a desire for revenge; remembering his piety he gave orders that the men were free to go where they wished and would come to no harm. He ordered his own personal mounted guards to escort them to safety, if the supplicants so wished.

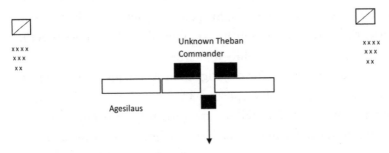

Map 6.4: Battle of Coronea, phase 4.

Xenophon's personal purview of the battlefield betrayed the carnage that this battle had wrought. The bloodstained earth served as a macabre bed on which lay the intertwined corpses of both friend and foe. Shields lay shattered upon the floor, pieces of spears and bare daggers littered the area on the ground, sticking from bodies, and some were still clasped in the hands of fallen men. It was a horrific sight which stayed with Xenophon for the rest of his life.[35]

The following morning Agesilaus ordered Gylis, one of his Spartan commanders, to deploy the troops into their battle order, erect a trophy on the site, place garlands around the necks of every man in honour of the gods, and to have all of the pipe players playing their music in unison. Whilst these orders were playing out, a Theban representative came to request the customary truce and return of the bodies, which was granted, and the battle came to its formal end.

Diodorus is the only source that gives the body count, claiming that the Boeotians and their allies lost 600 men to Sparta's 350.

The Aftermath

The victory of the day was a symbolic one at best. Agesilaus had won the battle, of that there is no doubt, but the Thebans were by no means disappointed with the outcome.[36] Thebes' own contingent had not been defeated and, what is more, they had successfully broken through the enemy's lines not once but twice.[37]

Agesilaus did not attempt to follow up his victory with a powerful sweep through Boeotia; something that we might have expected if the victory had any impact, but alas it had not. The Spartan king headed to Delphi where he dedicated one tenth of the spoils, but he did not return to Theban lands.

A small force had been left under the command of Gylis, but he soon departed north to Phocis before he began an invasion of neighbouring Locris. The force met little opposition as they advanced and soon became complacent, with soldiers beginning to plunder any villages they fell upon. Believing the Locrians to be absent, the Spartans were unperturbed when a few began to appear in the early evening; these threw rocks and javelins at the Spartans, but were soon chased away without any real problem. As the evening turned to night the small Locrian disturbances became more frequent and, to make matters worse, they had taken to the higher ground where the Spartans could no longer chase them down.

As the darkness began to thicken, the Spartans were not just failing to repel the Locrian skirmishers, they were losing men in the process. The terrain sealed the fate of many. Uneven ground, allied with impenetrable darkness, caused many to stumble and fall, joined by many injured comrades who could not stand up to the constant missile barrage. The commander Gylis was killed in the night, as was a second high-ranking companion, two of eighteen lost that night. If it were not for the remaining soldiers back at camp finally joining the fray, all of the men may well have been killed.

The end of 394 BC should well have brought with it a reflection on some important lessons for Sparta: one regarding the danger of a densely formed Theban formation, the other the vulnerability of their soldiers against light-armed troops. But these lessons were either not picked up on, or just as likely, they were ignored.

Chapter 7

The Battle of the Long Walls of Corinth (392 BC)

The Background (Xenophon, *Hellenica*, IV.4.1–8; Diodorus XIV.86)

Whilst the Spartans had experienced two successive victories on the field, they were not in a position of strength from which to exploit them. After the loss of Gylis' men, the Spartan allied army was disbanded and Agesilaus sailed back home. Without delivering a killer blow to the Boeotian alliance, Sparta had achieved little in its attempts to curb the anti-Spartan feeling that was quickly growing.

In the year 393 BC the war was continuing. The Athenian commander Conon sailed to Greece with a portion of the naval force he had been given by the Persians.[1] His fleet raided Laconia and he occupied the island of Cythera, just off the south Laconian coast. He continued sailing up to Corinth and left with them an unknown, but presumably considerable, amount of Persian money before he headed back to Athens. While in Corinth, or back at Athens, Conon established a mercenary force which would remain in Corinth under his own control before he passed it on to the command of the Athenian commander Iphicrates.[2]

With this act, the Boeotian allies had established a base at Corinth from which they could orchestrate their resistance. In opposition to this, Sparta made their base at Sicyon, roughly 10 miles northwest of Corinth. The combat was minimal, consisting of raids and skirmishes. In fact neither side was particularly troubled by the aggressive stance of the other, except for the Corinthians themselves.

Corinth was bearing the brunt of the assaults: it was their land that was being ravaged, it was their crops which could not be harvested, and it was their citizens that were being made casualties. Corinthian grievances were not solely pointed toward their Spartan enemy; their own allies were as much to blame. Their allies had chosen to make Corinth their base, they could enjoy the comfort and safety of their homelands, and they could reap the rewards of their agricultural labours – leaving Corinth to suffer in the name of freedom.[3]

The allies underestimated one important aspect of Corinth; it was not as unified as may have perhaps been believed. Even before the end of 394 BC, Corinth had begun to show the dissension that existed with its walls. It cannot be forgotten that the Corinthian soldiers that fled from the Battle of the Nemea returned to the city to find looming gates shut in their faces and their entry initially refused.[4]

With anti-war sentiment growing amongst wealthy citizen groups, whom Xenophon calls the 'majority and the best' of the Corinthians, many gathered together and began to encourage each other to try and bring an end to the suffering of Corinth. Rumours of influential citizens advocating peace finally reached the ears of the Athenians, Boeotians, Argives and, perhaps more importantly, the Corinthians who were responsible for bringing Corinth into the war in the first place.

By 392 BC, this pro-war group's greatest fear was that the anti-war movement could lead to Corinth resurrecting its old alliance with Sparta, which would most likely result in their own individual exile or worse. Their plan was as efficient as it was gruesome. They intended to kill all of the anti-war leaders and they would use the cover of a religious festival to achieve it.[5]

The festival was that of Artemis Eucleia and, when the final day's celebrations were underway, the conspirators put their plan into motion. They headed to the *agora* and, when the signal was given, the chosen assassins of the group unsheathed their swords and attacked. The purge was frighteningly efficient. Each of the men had their given targets and brazenly attacked them whilst they stood talking and laughing with friends, or sat in the theatre watching a performance. They even killed judges as they sat in plain view.

When people began to realize the horror that was unfolding in front of them they descended into a panicked mob. The 'best' men amongst them, knowing they were the target of this attack, fled to the statues of the gods in the *agora*, or else to the altars. Even these sacred places of sanctuary held no safety for the hapless men, as they were swiftly struck down and left in pools of their own blood.[6]

One hundred and twenty men were cut down, most of them were the older members of the anti-war group. The younger members had not been in the *agora*, thanks to the suspicious nature of one of their group, Pasimelus, who had suspected such an act was going to occur soon. They had congregated at the gymnasium in the suburb of Craneion, located in a grove of cypresses which lay near to the city walls.[7] With the onset of violence and the arrival of some survivors the young men quickly ran south, fighting off any Argives or conspirators who got in their way. On they ran to the safety of the ancient citadel atop the Acrocorinth.[8]

While they waited in relative safety, they were perplexed by a strange omen: a capital fell off from its column without being touched by man, wind or earthquake. They turned to a seer amongst them who interpreted it to mean that they were not secure on top of the hill and needed to descend before it was too late. They knew that Corinth was no longer safe, so they fled the city walls and went into self-imposed exile.[9]

With the anti-war party succinctly dealt with, the conspirators entered into an isopolity agreement (a pact of shared citizen rights) with Argos and secured their position in power for the short-term.[10] To those in exile this arrangement appeared to be a betrayal of Corinth's sovereignty: in their eyes Corinth had become part of Argos.

Some of the exiles returned to Corinth, in response to the pleas of their families more than anything else. They were given the word of those in power that if they returned they would suffer no harm, and so they went home. But home had changed. The agreement with Argos saw an influx of Argive *metics* (resident aliens). It saw the removal of the boundary stones of Corinth, and it was even believed that the leaders were acting like tyrants.[11] The city was no longer the exiles' own, it had lost its identity and its way, and the returning exiles needed to do something fast.[12] The situation was a win-win, either they would become saviours of their city, freeing it from the shackles of oppression and foreign control, or they would die with the highest praises for such an honourable pursuit.

The situation in Corinth was dire, and any action needed to be both drastic and decisive to avoid any alarm. Two men, one being Pasimelus and the other a man named Alcimenes, were chosen for the job. They avoided detection as they snuck out of the city, swam and waded through the springtime swellings of the rivers to the west, and headed to the Spartan commander Praxitas, who was stationed at Sicyon.

On arrival at the Spartan camp, Pasimelus and Alcimenes offered Praxitas entrance to the Long Walls which stretch from the city of Corinth up to the northern port of Lechaeum. The Long Walls flanked either side of the road that ran to the port and kept this lifeline secure in case of sieges. By offering entrance to these walls, the men were offering Sparta a way to starve Corinth and all of its citizens.

The offer of such a brazen betrayal did not raise any suspicions from Praxitas. He trusted these men and began to make the necessary arrangements.[13] Spartan plans to extract a full *mora* from the region were quickly reversed and the force was put on alert, waiting for the opportune moment to strike. When the moment arrived, it was not just opportune but also beautifully symbolic.

Pasimelus and Alcimenes were soon given an assignment to guard one of the gates along the wall, a gate which faced toward Sicyon, a gate which was near to the site of the Battle of the Nemea – the very gate by which the Spartans had erected their trophy of victory only two years before.[14]

With his inside men on the gate, Praxitas arrived at the head of a Spartan *mora*, with a complementary contingent of Sicyonian troops and 150 Corinthian exiles. When the moment came to enter the walls, Praxitas became afraid of entering in full force in case he was walking into a trap. He chose one of his most trusted men to run a reconnaissance, who was subsequently taken on a quick tour of the interior vicinity by Pasimelus and Alcimenes. Everything the man saw was as it was meant to be so when he returned to his commander, Praxitas gave the order to enter the walls.

The Battlefield

The battlefield lay within the mid-space of the two parallel walls which ran over 2km apart from one another.[15] The lay of the land is not described in the battle narrative, but would have been relatively flat as it was mostly used for agriculture. Important physical features that impacted the battle were the ditch and stockade built by the Spartans; the harbour of Lechaeum to the north, which sat behind the Spartan line; and without doubt the most important feature, the walls themselves, which had steps up to the ramparts at frequent intervals.

The static obstruction of the walls restricted the entire sphere of combat and dispelled any hopes of tactical manoeuvring on a large scale. This forced the light-armed troops to play an almost redundant role in proceedings and the small amount of Spartan cavalry to be held back in reserve. At the same time, it was the wide gap between these walls which forced the Spartans to seemingly introduce revolutionary tactics into Greek warfare, by fortifying their position on the battlefield.

The Armies

If the Spartan *mora* was at full strength their contingent could have numbered anywhere up to 1,120 hoplites.[16] A small Spartan cavalry force was also there but no numbers are given by Xenophon. Apart from the 150 Corinthian exiles, we are not given any more numbers for the Sicyonians. However, as we know that they contributed somewhere in the region of 1,500 hoplites to the Battle of the Nemea, and as it can be assumed that they did not send as many men to this offensive mission, it is unrealistic to presume they sent more men than the Spartans.[17]

The confederate army against Praxitas consisted of the *peltast* mercenaries led by Iphicrates, alongside a force of Argive and Corinthian hoplites. As we are not given any concept of their strength, other than it must have greatly outnumbered the Spartan army, any figures given for this battle are speculative at best. But if we presume that the army of Praxitas was under 2,000 strong, inclusive of cavalry, then the confederate army must have numbered somewhere between 3–5,000 men to explain their rather brash and over-confident tactics.

The Battle (Xenophon, *Hellenica*, IV.4.9–13; Diodorus, XIV.86.3–6)

In the darkness of night the forces of Praxitas entered the open gate of the western wall. With the port town of Lechaeum behind him, Praxitas quickly surveyed the situation. His forces were too diminutive to create a battle order that would be protected by the walls on both flanks, and he was in no position to wait for reinforcements. Thinking on his feet, Praxitas ordered his men to dig a trench across the span of the two walls, using the excavated soil to build a rampart that stood behind the excavated ditch. Their position was still a precarious one, with a Boeotian garrison to their rear which defended the port of Lechaeum.

Amazingly, the Spartan position was not challenged for the day following their first sunrise in situ.[18] But as the second day dawned, the sound of thousands of men coming towards them would have made for an unsettling time for many. With the arrival of an Argive army, the Corinthians finally moved on the defensive position of Praxitas. The battle line they saw before them was thinly stretched behind its barricades: the Spartans were in the customary position on the right wing (by the western wall), with the Sicyonians next to them, and the Corinthian exiles holding the left wing (by the eastern Wall).

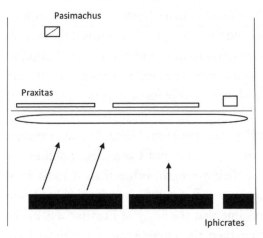

Map 7.1: Battle of the Long Walls of Corinth, phase 1.

The confederate force formed opposite the stockade with Iphicrates' *peltasts* nearest the eastern wall opposite the exiles. Next to them were the Argives, while the Corinthians held the left wing opposite the Sicyonians and the Spartans.[19] With the battle line formed, the Corinthians looked toward the stockade and saw just how superior their numbers were to the enemy ahead of them. They could not resist the temptation and quickly charged the siege works.

The Corinthians aimed their charge at the Sicyonians and crashed into the stockade, breaking parts of it in the process.[20] Before they had even begun their crossing of the ditch, the Sicyonians were routed and fled north to the sea. Pulling themselves from the ditch, the bulk of the Corinthians chased after the fleeing men, whilst their remaining numbers were being held by the Spartans.[21] The Sicyonians were cut down by the shoreline and a small massacre was about to begin.

The Spartan cavalry commander, Pasimachus, had been watching all of the proceedings from behind the ditch with the horsemen, who had been held in reserve. Once he saw the precarious position that the Sicyonians had landed themselves in, he ordered his small cavalry force to tie their horses to some trees and follow him. Rather than move to support them by the shoreline, he instead wanted to exploit the gap left by the Corinthians in the confederates' battle line.

As his force of volunteers moved toward the rampart, they picked up fallen Sicyonian shields. The Argives, as they spotted the men advancing, saw the sigma (Σ) symbol on the shields and felt little more than contempt for them. Pasimachus pressed forwards, exploiting the low expectations of the Argives as he closed quarters. The fighting was fierce as his vastly outnumbered contingent took many Argive lives, before Pasimachus finally fell alongside his men.

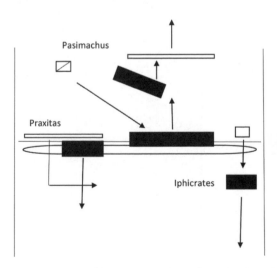

Map 7.2: Battle of the Long Walls of Corinth, phase 2.

The exiles of Corinth had much greater success against the lightly armed *peltasts*, who had been hamstrung by the confined spaces which restricted their greatest asset – mobility. The exiles slipped through the confederate lines and moved toward the city walls of Corinth itself. With the battle lines broken up as they were, and the Spartan force having successfully repelled the remaining Corinthian soldiers, it was time for the main Spartan force to act.

Praxitas had three choices: he could move to relieve the Sicyonian allies that were still being slaughtered to the north; he could try to somehow hold the stockade on his own but the Argives had by now begun crossing the ditch; or he could press ahead and cause absolute mayhem by appearing to take an offensive position. Needless to say he chose the latter.

The Spartan troops crossed the ditch and rampart and with tactical precision wheeled 90° anti-clockwise and marched parallel to it east, keeping the earthwork on their left at all times.[22] When the Argives saw what was happening they panicked and quickly rushed back from the rampart. As they ran, their right wing was intercepted by the Spartan march and the undefended side of the Argives was exposed to Spartan attacks. The impact was horrendous. As the Argives fell in droves on their right, their left wing closed together like a crowd and ran for the city. They ran into the Corinthian exiles and, realizing their peril, turned back and fled to the steps up the eastern wall.

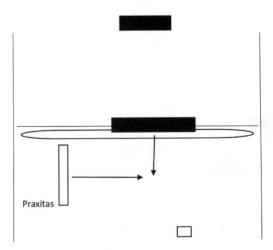

Map 7.3: Battle of the Long Walls of Corinth, phase 3.

Those who were able to escape fast enough, soon found themselves with nowhere to go. The Spartans were sweeping through the Argives, heading closer and closer to the eastern wall. Argives were being killed at the foot of the steps by the spears and swords of the exiles, or trodden under foot and suffocated in the commotion by their own comrades. The men on the wall were at a loss. They could not trust that the brutal killings that the Spartans and exiles were bestowing was not to become their own fate. With their hearts filled with despair they could do nothing but jump to their deaths, preferring to take fate into their own hands rather than give the Spartans and the traitors any satisfaction.

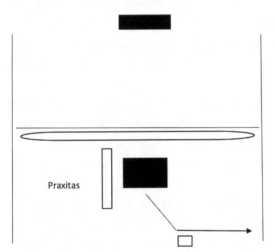

Map 7.4: Battle of the Long Walls of Corinth, phase 4.

For Praxitas' men, the battle had gone from a contest, to a hunt, to a slaughter. It was like a gift from the gods, as they were able to kill as many of the enemy as they wanted. Opposition had been completely abandoned, all that Sparta faced was a petrified mob with an exposed right-hand side. With the field taken, a part of the Spartan army headed north to deal with the Boeotian garrison at Lechaeum. Having watched the battle from afar, the Boeotians did not put up a resistance; some fled to the Long Walls where they were killed, and others climbed the roofs of the trireme sheds where they too fell.[23]

Losses are unfortunately not described in the sources, but Xenophon does paint a vivid image when he describes the bodies left on the battlefield:

so many fell in such a short time that the inhabitants, who were used to seeing heaps of grain, wood, and stones, saw instead on that day heaps of corpses.[24]

When the battle came to an end, the Corinthians and Argives called a truce with Praxitas to retrieve their dead.

The Aftermath

Reinforcements finally arrived for the Spartans and their position was secured. Praxitas ordered for part of the Long Walls to be torn down, he wanted a gap large enough to march an army through it. Once this was completed he marched his army east and took control of the towns of Isthmia and Crommyon. Before Praxitas disbanded his army he returned west and walled the small town of Epieiceia.

The Battle of the Long Walls was a resounding victory for the outnumbered Spartans; however, without taking the city of Corinth, Sparta once again refrained from pushing home their advantages. While the war did continue, it would no longer see the large citizen forces that had adorned classical warfare up to this point.

The following year of 391 BC saw Iphicrates at the head of an offensive campaign that terrorized the region of Arcadia. With the lack of Spartan presence, Athens was able to rebuild the Long Walls of Corinth, but Sparta soon responded with an offensive strategy. This saw Agesilaus ravaging the land of Argos and, by 390 BC, returning to the Corinthian Isthmus and causing havoc, without capitalizing on any of his victories.

Chapter 8

The Battle of Lechaeum (390 BC)

The Background (Xenophon, *Hellenica*, IV.4.14–V.10; *Agesilaus* 2.17–19; Plutarch, *Life of Agesilaus*, 21–22.2

The spring of 391 BC saw a continuation of the intent to control the area surrounding Corinth, from both the Spartan side and that of the confederates. Garrisons had been sent to reinforce the confederate-held city of Corinth, and to strengthen the Spartan position of Sicyon. Both sides had come to realize that the Corinthian War was becoming one of attrition, with no single battle capable of proving dominance in the region. So they resorted to employing more mercenary forces, stepping away from the traditional, citizen-based armies, which had commonly graced the battlefields for the past 100 years.

Iphicrates had taken his force of *peltasts* out of Corinth and had invaded the territory of neighbouring Phleious, which lay to the west-southwest. With characteristic precision, he set an ambush for the Phleiasian garrison by drawing it out in defence of their lands against a small group of *peltasts* who had begun to plunder. As the Phleiasians sallied forth from their walls, they did so unguardedly and without any thought for their own safety. Iphicrates' main force pounced on their laxity and killed many of them.[1] The small defeat was enough for the people of Phleious to cower in fear at the might of Iphicrates' band and, refusing to meet them in battle again, they called for a Spartan garrison to take control of the city.[2]

The Spartans did not have to stay long, because Iphicrates had no intention of simply terrorizing Phleious. His aim was to strike fear in the surrounding lands of Arcadia so he swiftly moved on, plundering the land and at times even attacking various Arcadian city walls. His utilization of terror tactics was so effective that no Arcadian hoplite force ever came out against him. But his troops were not invincible. The *peltasts* were likewise afraid of the younger Spartans who were using a simple tactic which, for many decades, had been put to great affect against both cavalry and *peltasts*: they would be sent out to chase off the *peltasts*, even killing some in the process.[3]

For the Spartans, a fear of Iphicrates' men was not one that they shared. For all of the contempt they felt for these spindle throwers, it was nothing compared to that which they felt for their own allies who could not even face Iphicrates in battle.[4] It was not just the Arcadians, the hoplites of Mantinea had likewise been bested in the field. Their hoplite lines had also given way after the initial hail of javelins, with many of them struck down as they turned their backs to run for safety. The Spartans would often mock them by saying they feared *peltasts* as children do the bogeyman.[5]

With Iphicrates looming large, the Spartans gave a show of force outside of Corinth. Marching a near-full strength *mora* out of Lechaeum with the Corinthian exiles, they made camp around the city walls, before returning to the harbour without any confrontation from Corinth.[6] The Athenians panicked, their greatest concern was the wide chasm that Praxitas had left in the Long Walls after his victory the previous year. With the wall compromised, Sparta had easy access into the Isthmus and into Attica itself, leaving Athens feeling very exposed, and this show of strength from Sparta was not helping matters.

The Athenians sent out a strong force of their own to escort stone masons and carpenters, with the express job of rebuilding the two walls as quickly as possible. The greatest threat to the construction work was the garrison in Lechaeum. To counter this the Athenians lay siege to the harbour, thus cutting off any exit they could have used.[7]

In a remarkable feat of human endeavour, the craftsman successfully, and according to Xenophon 'handsomely', rebuilt the western wall in just a few days. This gave them some respite as it was the wall facing the Spartan power base of Sicyon. So they slowed down and continued work on the eastern wall at a more leisurely pace.

During this period, Agesilaus was leading a rampaging attack through the territory of Argos. The campaign served little strategic importance, it was driven by the Spartan disdain for their historic enemies who, in their opinion, were taking pleasure in a war that was not affecting them at home. To counter this, Agesilaus successfully took the fight into their lands, ravaging and pillaging the Argive countryside. He then quickly turned his army of Spartan allies around and headed straight for Corinth.

On his arrival he captured the Long Walls once more. His mere presence was enough for the Athenians to abandon their siege of Lechaeum and return to the safety of Corinth. Moving in parallel to his army on land, Agesilaus' half-brother Teleutias supported him by sea. After taking control of the harbour and the moored Corinthian ships, Teleutias left there a small fleet of twelve triremes. Agesilaus subsequently disbanded his army of allies and marched his citizen forces back to Sparta, just in time for the festival of Hyacinthus in early summer.[8]

But the turn of the new year in 390 BC, and the end of the debilitating winter, brought with it word that Corinth had found a way of sustaining itself thus far without fear of Spartan intervention. Corinthian exiles informed Sparta that men from Corinth had placed their cattle in a region called Peiraeon, on the west of the Isthmus, due north as the crow flies from Corinth itself. But the situation was much worse than the herding of cattle and the sowing of crops, because the Boeotians and Athenians were using the region as an avenue through which to send troops to support Corinth. It needed to be closed and Corinth shut off from their allies.[9]

Agesilaus marched up to the Corinthian Isthmus in early summer. He took with him a strong army, whilst making sure that he maintained a strong force in Lechaeum. His army arrived in the Isthmus just in time for the year's Isthmian Games that were held at the sanctuary of Poseidon in Isthmia. Argives were present at the games and taking a leading role in the proceedings, something which was normally the position held by Corinth. On hearing of Agesilaus' approach the Argives fled in fear. They took the road past Cenchreae which was in sight of Agesilaus' main force, but he let them go. He continued to Isthmia and, finding both the sacrificial victim and the festival meals prepared but unused, Agesilaus set up camp in the sanctuary and allowed the Corinthian exiles with him to conduct their sacrifices and have their contests.

After three days had passed, Agesilaus moved his army north towards Peiraeon. On arrival he found the area heavily guarded by a strong force, including none other than Iphicrates himself, so he chose to create a ruse and draw the army out of the area instead. Waiting until after breakfast,

Agesilaus marched his men toward Corinth, aiming for the Acrocorinth on the southern side of the city. On arrival his Spartan army made camp and 'acted as if the city were being betrayed to him'.[10] The Corinthians were so afraid of a repeat of what happened two years earlier that they walked straight into Agesilaus' plan. They recalled Iphicrates from Peiraeon, who marched through the night bringing with him the majority of his *peltasts*.

Agesilaus knew when the *peltasts* had marched beyond his camp and so he quickly turned once more, heading straight for the relatively unguarded Peiraeon, arriving at the crack of dawn. Agesilaus continued on his path running past the hot springs that sat on the shoreline, at the foot of Mount Geraneia, whilst he sent a *mora* to spend the night on the crest of the ridge, so as to hold the highest grounds.[11]

When the people in Peiraeon finally saw the Spartan position, they realized they stood little chance of success, having already lost the high ground. They felt unable to defend themselves and instead fled to the Temple of Hera at the most western point of Peiraeon. Agesilaus took his time. Moving his army along the shore, while the *mora* on the ridge descended and seized the walled fort of Oinoe. By the time he reached the temple the refugees came out willingly, to allow Agesilaus to do with them whatever he wished. He handed to the Corinthian exiles any who were involved in the massacre which had taken place in 392 BC, whilst the rest were to be sold.[12]

Agesilaus had succeeded in taking Peiraeon, he could finally close off the corridor to the Peloponnese that Athens and Thebes were wilfully exploiting. He could strengthen the position of Sparta in the region, and he could subdue his enemies without fear of outside support. Many different embassies came to see him, especially from the Boeotians who were suing for peace – but Agesilaus simply ignored them. His hatred for Thebes had been long simmering, and this opportunity to revel in their discomfort, to force them to watch as he presided over the amount of goods and loot which had been obtained by his men, was hard to resist. His smugness could know no bounds. He held the power of almost half of the Greek mainland, and it was now just a matter of tidying up loose ends.

Agesilaus' frivolity was broken by the sound of a gasping horse and the sight of a red-faced horseman driving towards him, sweat pouring from the pair of them, galloping as fast as they could go. People tried to stop the man, asking what he had to announce, for only a messenger would push his horse as hard as this one. But he ignored them and headed straight for the king himself. As he neared Agesilaus he jumped from his horse and continued the run on foot. On entering the king's presence, his demeanour became decidedly downcast as he informed Agesilaus of the unthinkable: a Spartan army had just been defeated outside of the walls of Corinth, and what is more, they had been massacred.[13]

When Agesilaus had initially set out for Peiraeon, he had left part of his force in Lechaeum. Either as a part of this garrison, or in addition, Agesilaus left all of his hoplites who came from the Spartan village of Amyclae. It was custom for the Amyclaeans to be granted leave from their military duties so that they could return home to celebrate the festival of the Hyacinthia, no matter where they found themselves. As Agesilaus' campaign was due to run through the early summer it was deemed unnecessary to drag the Amyclaeans all that way, just to be sent home again.[14]

The garrison commander at Lechaeum was made aware that the festival was due to commence in a week's time and began his preparations.[15] He organized the allied troops within the garrison to guard the wall, whilst he marched out with a *mora* and the cavalry to accompany the Amyclaeans past Corinth and on to Sicyon.[16] The march would only take four or five hours at which time the *mora* would return to Lechaeum, leaving the Amyclaeans with the cavalry escort as far as they wished before the cavalry would likewise return to the harbour.[17]

As the Spartan escort moved out from Lechaeum, marching between the Long Walls and out onto the road which ran next to the Corinthian walls, they were unaware that they were being watched. The Athenian commander in Corinth, Callias, and his subordinate, Iphicrates, stood on the north-western corner wall of the city watching the *mora* begin its march. They knew that this day was coming and put into motion a tactical display that would expose the arrogance of the Spartans, and their limitations on the battlefield.

The Battlefield

The battle took place to the west of the Long Walls, inside the alluvial plain which gently slopes away from the hills to the south into the shore.[18] The road on which the *mora* was marching, and on which the attack began, ran west to east near to the hills before skirting around the walls of Corinth herself. North of the road lay a solitary, small hill situated 350m south of the sea, and about 3km west of Lechaeum.[19]

The wide expanse available in the plain could allow Iphicrates' agile *peltasts* to utilize their greatest asset of speed and manoeuvrability; but in turn it would make the perfect terrain for a cavalry countercharge. The hills to the south would give a strong vantage point to a reserve-hoplite position and in turn give the *peltasts* a secure point on which to retreat if the Spartans began to chase them. The only element at a disadvantage was the *mora* which was stranded on the road with little hope of preventing an outflanking manoeuvre; however, with the right support it should have been possible to make a relatively safe return to Lechaeum.

The Armies

The Spartan *mora* was under strength at roughly 600 hoplites, due in part to the loss of the Amyclaeans who they were escorting in the first place. The hoplites were accompanied by an unspecified number of *helot* shield-bearers, but they played no discernible military role in this instance. During the battle the *mora* was joined by the cavalry that formed part of the escort for the festival-goers. If the cavalry was at full strength it would have numbered somewhere between 100 and 120 men, and other than the poor performance of the cavalry itself, there is no reason to suggest that it was particularly undermanned.[20]

The Athenians in Corinth were split into two distinct forces. Under the leadership of Callias were the hoplites, whose numbers are unfortunately not described by the sources. It can by deduced that the presence of Callias, who was a *strategos*, shows an original force amounting to roughly 1,000 men. But, taking into account the long term presence of the hoplites in foreign territory, plus the restrained manner in which Callias acts during the battle, it seems likely that the hoplite force numbered somewhere in the region of 600–700 men.[21] The second force was led by Iphicrates, and consisted of his veteran *peltasts*. Once again, Xenophon does not give any figures for the *peltasts*, but we do know that Iphicrates' force was not at full strength as he left some of his men in Peiraeon. At the very least Iphicrates had 1,200 men, giving him enough strength to feel the confidence that comes with such an overwhelming numerical superiority.[22]

The Battle (Xenophon, *Hellenica*, IV.5.13–18)

Standing on their observation point atop the Corinthian walls, Callias and Iphicrates were in a prime position to watch as the *mora* marched west to Sicyon. Whilst it was no secret that the *peltasts* were based in the city, the Spartans felt no fear for them – after all, they had never been beaten by the mercenaries. For the two Athenians, the sight must have been one of great excitement. The Spartan religious calendar was no secret, and the *mora*'s march would have been a difficult secret to keep due to the size of the preparations. Callias had known for a few days what was going to happen, and it was finally time to execute their plan.[23] His faith in the junior commander would be tested to its fullest. This was likely to have been Iphicrates' own strategy but it took the strong hand of Callias to agree; so with the excitement of potential victory came the trepidation of utter defeat.[24]

The *mora* marched within 4 or 5 kilometres of Sicyon before peeling away from the escort and heading back east to Corinth. Their change in direction was quickly spotted by Callias and he gave the orders for the Athenians to march from the city and set up in formation on top of the hill to the west, looking down onto the road below.

The clear midday sky would have allowed the Spartans to spot the Athenians from quite a distance, but it did not deter them from their trajectory. Although an attack seemed imminent, they had little cause for concern from *peltasts*, and no Athenian hoplite force had defeated a Spartan counterpart outright – besides, the *mora* only needed to reach Lechaeum, it was not obliged to fight.

They continued their march with brazen vigour, exposing their unshielded right-hand side to the Athenians as the road moved parallel to their position on the hill. Iphicrates' men began to pepper the Spartan file with javelins, moving forwards within range and retreating after each throw. The Spartans did not panic, they turned to face the cliff with only a few losses from the first assault. The dead and wounded were quickly picked up by the shield-bearers and carried to Lechaeum, whilst the commander ordered the ten-year class in his *mora* (those hoplites in their first ten years of service, aged 20 to 30) to chase down the *peltasts*. These 150–200 Spartans drove the *peltasts* back, creating space for the *mora* as it slowly edged north toward the shoreline - or so they thought.

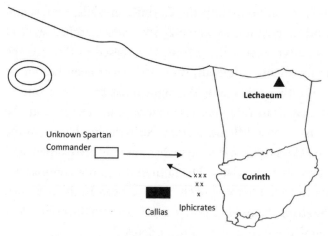

Map 8.1: Battle of Lechaeum, phase 1.

Iphicrates' men withdrew from the Spartan advance, drawing them into the empty space between the two forces and breaking any semblance of order they held as differing levels of fitness and verve meant that hoplites advanced at differing rates.[25] Weighed down by their arms, the Spartans had little chance of catching the lighter armed *peltasts* so they soon turned around to return to their lines. The plan had worked, and the *peltasts* wheeled round and chased down the stranded hoplites. Swarming around them in their isolated pockets, they hurled their javelins from all angles, killing ten and injuring many more in the process.

As the hoplites returned to the protection of the *mora*, the *peltasts* were able to recover their thrown javelins and begin the second attack on the Spartan formation. Utterly helpless and thoroughly outflanked, the Spartan commander ordered the fifteen-year class to charge forth. A hundred men chased after their assailants, but the *peltasts* retreated once again, drawing the Spartans into no-man's-land before they decided to turn back. Once their backs were turned, the men of Iphicrates pounced. Many more Spartans fell; some by javelin whilst others were likely wounded and finished off with a spear or sword, the *peltasts* took no prisoners.

Undeterred by their losses, the Spartans continued edging north and awaited the next attack. It was now that the cavalry attachment to the Amyclaean escort finally arrived, and with it came a new impetus to chase down the *peltasts*. As the younger Spartans charged them down the cavalry misunderstood their role, ruining any advantage they may have held. Rather than charge down the hapless *peltasts*, they chose to maintain a steady pace in keeping with the hoplites on foot, both in the attack and the retreat back to the *mora*. The result was that nothing had changed in the Spartan situation, except the extinguishing of hope.

Iphicrates' attacks became bolder with each successful wave, and the Spartans had already lost over a tenth of their fighting force, with more and more dropping before them. The commander was at a loss of what to do. His only chance was to regroup in a strong defensive position, but Lechaeum was still too far away. His eyes would have moved north to the small hill – that would have to do. The Spartan retreat was constantly harassed as more and more of them fell, and by the time they reached the hill it did not bring the solace they may have hoped for.

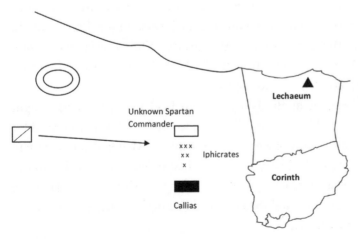

Map 8.2: Battle of Lechaeum, phase 2.

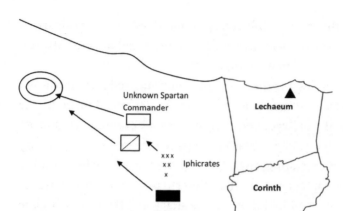

Map 8.3: Battle of Lechaeum, phase 3.

The men on the hill were in a state of despair, they had lost comrades in their hundreds by now, their enemy was untouchable, and the Athenian hoplites had finally begun to march forward to finish the job once and for all. Destruction was imminent and the men had only one option – to run.[26] When the Spartan commander that had been left in Lechaeum finally received word of what was happening, he sent out boats along the shore adjacent to the hill in the bid to pick up survivors.

Seeing the boats approaching, many of the men decided to head for them, flinging themselves into the sea in an attempt to get away from the *peltasts'* onslaught. Those who did not head north aimed instead for a direct route to Lechaeum, under the 'protection' of the cavalry. While this smaller group reached the harbour relatively unscathed, the bulk of the force incurred losses of another 100 men, or even more.[27]

With the final retreat of the boats back to Lechaeum, the long fought battle came to an end. That evening the *mora* would have been assembled for roll call and only then would the harrowing reality of what had befallen them come to light. At least 250 Spartan hoplites had fallen in the battle. Add to this the numner incapacitated by wounds (many of whom would later die from sepsis and gangrene), and the *mora* had lost nigh on fifty per cent of its fighting strength in one skirmish.[28]

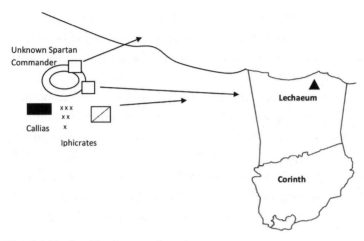

Map 8.4: Battle of Lechaeum, phase 4.

The Spartans sent the request to recover the dead, in doing so formally accepting their defeat, and the Corinthians left the city walls to erect their trophy.

The Aftermath (Xenophon, *Hellenica*, IV.5.8–10, 18)

Agesilaus tried his best to maintain his composure after hearing of the defeat. He quickly grouped his men and began the march to Lechaeum, taking with him the embassies from Thebes who now showed no signs of wanting peace, but instead appeared to gloat at Spartan misfortunes. Agesilaus showed them exactly how much had changed because of this battle by entering the Lechaeum plain and, leaving the trophy erect, cutting down and burning every tree he came across without any opposition from the forces inside Corinth. His point was obtuse, but clear: this defeat had done nothing to redress the balance in Greece. But he was wrong.

The impact on Spartan morale was hugely detrimental. When the news spread through the entire Spartan army there was much grieving, except among those who's sons died in the battle: in the standard Spartan practice, these men delighted in their honourable misfortune. The innate Spartan sense of superiority had been shattered by the lowest form of combat. Their best and finest could no longer stand up to the 'cowardly' *peltasts*. Agesilaus personally led the remainder of the *mora* back to Sparta, choosing to enter any city en route as late as possible and leaving just as early. He completely passed Mantinea during a night march to protect his men from seeing the joy in the eyes of the Mantineans.

Agesilaus was right about one thing, the battle itself had resolved nothing. The harbour of Lechaeum was still held by Sparta, and the continued fighting moved north of the Isthmus. The Corinthian War continued with renewed energy for a further three years, with Iphicrates in particular forging a great reputation for himself. It finally came to an end with Persian intervention and the signing in 386 BC of the King's Peace, also known as the Peace of Antalcidas, after the Spartan diplomat who negotiated the treaty in Asia Minor.

Chapter 9

The Battle of Leuctra (371 BC)

The Background (Xenophon, *Hellenica*, V.2.23–36, 3.27–VI.4.5; Plutarch, *Life of Pelopidas*, 5–20.2; Plutarch, *Life of Agesilaus*, 23–28; Diodorus, XV.20.1–3, 25–27.3, 52–53.2)

With the King's Peace in place, Sparta began to reassert its authority over the whole of Greece. Nowhere was the Spartan presence and power more keenly felt than in Boeotia, the seat of King Agesilaus' most hated *polis*, Thebes. In 382 BC, four years into the Peace, Sparta received envoys from the Chalcidice region warning of the growing power of Olynthus and requesting that the Spartans help their cities maintain their independence in accordance with the terms of the Peace.

The request was accepted by the Spartans who voted to raise a force of 10,000 men and send them against Olynthus. The organization of such a large force would understandably take some time, so they further agreed to send a smaller force of 2,000 men, under the command of Eudamidas, to establish a presence in the region immediately. The remaining troops would follow on later under the command of his brother, Phoebidas.

Unlike his brother, Phoebidas was not a shrewd, or even a particularly bright man. As he marched his men north he stopped and made camp near the gymnasium outside of Thebes. The presence of such a large Spartan force caused some consternation inside Thebes, which was itself politically volatile at this time. Two factions were at loggerheads with each other. One side was anti-Spartan and refused to have any dealings with them, the other, led by Leontiades, was pro-Spartan and quickly moved to woo Phoebidas. Leontiades offered the Spartan commander the greatest prize of all: help his party take power in Thebes and the city would happily subject itself to Spartan rule.

During the three-day festival of the Thesmaphoria, Phoebidas began to make a show of marching his army away from Thebes.[1] By midday the streets of the city had gone quiet, the time was right for Leontiades to make his move. He rode his horse out to the Spartans then led them straight into the city and into the acropolis (the Cadmeia) itself. With the Cadmeia fortified and garrisoned, Leontiades entered the Theban Council meeting in the market. He announced that the Spartans had taken the heart of Thebes, but that they had only come as enemies for those who were eager for war. Using this justification, Leontiades arrested his rival's leader whilst the remainder of his political opposition fled the city to the safety of Athens.

Although Thebes had been successfully taken, a small problem arose in Sparta – the entire enterprise was unendorsed by the Spartan authorities. It took the intervention of Agesilaus, and an appeasing speech by Leontiades, to convince the Spartan people that the taking of Thebes was necessary to stop the city from exerting control over the rest of Boeotia.[2] The Spartans were finally convinced and subsequently voted to keep the Cadmeia garrisoned, and to put the opposition leader in Thebes on trial, which ended in his execution.

For three years Sparta held the heart and soul of Thebes in its hands, and likewise pushed their own power to its zenith throughout Greece.[3] But the year of 379 BC saw a shift in fortune which the Spartans could not have anticipated, and which began the dismantling of their mighty pedestal.

Of the Theban exiles, one young man stood out above the rest for his rigour and his impassioned speeches of loyalty and honour. Pelopidas may have been one of the youngest in their number, but he felt courageous enough to chastise his elders for choosing to live under the rule of their protectors in Athens, and ignoring the plight of their mother city.[4] His constant appealing finally convinced the exiles of his words, and they began to make arrangements to overthrow the Spartans in the Cadmeia.

A group of the exiles, dressed as women, infiltrated the festive, night-time celebrations of the Theban chief magistrates and killed them whilst the magistrates were in a drunken stupor.[5] With this accomplished, they quickly moved on to the house of Leontiades who was likewise killed and his wife threatened to silence. By the time they entered the *stoa*, the small band of conspirators were met by the rest of their party who had lain in wait outside of the city. The men armed themselves with the weaponry and armour that had been left hanging in the *stoa* as spoils of earlier wars, and by breaking open the sword and spear workshops of the neighbouring vicinity.

The city was driven to chaos by the noise and the darkness. Nobody knew what was going on and the citizens of Thebes refused to join their would-be saviours until day broke and the truth of the situation finally revealed itself. Then, with enough manpower behind them, the exiles finally felt strong enough to face the Spartan stronghold of the Cadmeia.

The stronghold was being held by some 1,500 soldiers but, because they had failed to meet the exiles whilst their numbers were still low, the garrison was left at the whim of Theban action. Pelopidas set up a blockade of the acropolis and began to assault the position from all sides with unrelenting pressure. It did not take long for the Spartans to realize the severity of their position. They were heavily outnumbered and the Thebans were fighting with a zeal that they could not match. The Spartans arranged a truce which allowed for them to leave the city safely and with their weapons. The deal was one that the Thebans were all too pleased to agree to, as they were more concerned about the imminent arrival of Spartan reinforcements than with the decimation of a small Spartan garrison. As the garrison descended from the acropolis, the Thebans spotted some of the traitors who had allowed the Spartans in and swiftly killed them, before later killing their children as well.[6]

With the outbreak of this Boeotian War, Sparta looked for a speedy resolution through direct action. In 378 BC they sent an army, under the command of their other king Cleombrotus I, into Theban territory during the depth of winter. After setting up camp in Cynoscephalae, Cleombrotus remained stationary for sixteen long days before he left one third of the army under the command of Sphodrias, and returned home.

The presence of this Spartan army was a cause of great fear among the Athenians and the Boeotians. In Athens they put on trial the two commanders who had helped the Theban exiles reclaim Thebes, one of whom was executed while the other fled into exile. In Thebes a slightly different plan was hatched. Unlike Athens, the Thebans were not concerned with Spartan intent. They knew that Sparta hated them and would attempt an assault of the city at some point. Thebes' greatest concern was not fighting Sparta, but having to do it alone, and the actions of Athens certainly showed an attempt to appease the Spartans rather than confront them. Theban representatives went to Sphodrias and persuaded him to invade Attica and induce the Athenians to meet him in battle. The foolish commander was convinced of the plan, or at least well bribed, and declared that he would capture the un-gated Piraeus as well.

The Spartan force began to raid the countryside around Athens, and when word reached the city of their presence they immediately armed their forces. They also captured three Spartan ambassadors that were staying in the city. The ambassadors were just as stunned as the Athenians by the act of aggression shown by Sphodrias, and assured them that the attack was without Spartan sanction and that the idiotic commander would be tried and executed back at Sparta. When Sphodrias was recalled by the Spartan authorities, he refused the summons, and was put on trial *in absentia*, but amazingly he was acquitted.[7] This was enough for the pro-Theban groups in Athens to prove that the Spartans had commended the attempt on Athens, allowing them to convince the assembly that Athens needed to join forces with Thebes to stop the ever-present threat of Sparta.[8]

The year of 377–6 BC saw Sparta invade Theban lands over and over again, ravaging its countryside but never venturing for the killer blow. With the assistance of Athens, Thebes was able to distract Spartan attentions at sea and, after two years with no direct assault, they felt strong enough to march on their neighbouring cities and reform the Boeotian League under their direct control.[9] Thebes even managed to bloody the noses of their adversaries, defeating a larger Spartan force at the battle of Tegyra, ostensibly with the help of their newly created elite force, the Sacred Band.[10]

By the end of 375 BC, a shaky cease-fire was in place, initiated by the Athenians who were suffering financially at the expense of their alliance with Thebes.[11] But, by the start of 373 BC, hostilities had begun once more, with Athens back on the side of Thebes. The conflict focused on the north-eastern isle of Corcyra off the Molossian coast, which was a point of contention between Sparta and Athens due to its position of control in the eastern Ionian Sea.[12]

The Athenians had returned anti-Spartan exiles from Zacynthus back to their homeland of the west Peloponnesian coast, and the Spartans in turn decided to take control of Corcyra before the Athenians could build upon their position of strength. The Spartan commander, Mnasippus, landed a strong force of Spartans and mercenaries onto the island and blockaded the main city, also named Corcyra. The islanders quickly turned to Athens for help, and a strong force of seventy ships was sent in support, led by none other than Iphicrates.[13]

By the time Iphicrates reached the island in 372 BC, the situation had greatly changed. Mnasippus had grown arrogant and released many of his mercenaries from their duties. A Corcyraean force, seeing the weakened position of the Spartans, sallied from the city and attacked the enemy guard posts. A counter attack ensued but the Spartans were undone by the sheer ferocity of the Corcyraeans, and were forced into a hasty retreat to sea. When the Athenians did arrive, their only concern was an impending fleet of Syracusan ships which were on route to assist the Spartans, but Iphicrates launched a surprise attack and captured the majority of them.

With the island secure, Iphicrates looked south to Acarnania to keep his men active and prepared for war. After a short excursion in the region, he returned to Corcyra then took the fleet south to take control of the island of Kephallenia (modern Cephalonia). With Athens in control of the three major islands off the Ionian Sea coast, Iphicrates felt strong enough to begin preparations to take the war directly into Spartan lands. With his preparations under way, he most likely received word that all was not well in Athens and that his plans were to be put on hold.

While Athens had been fighting this war with Sparta, their supposed allies in Thebes had been expanding their control in Boeotia and had begun campaigning against long-standing allies of Athens such as Thespiae and Plataea.[14] Once Theban intent moved on to Phocis, Athens could no longer stand by and watch this blatant disregard for the autonomy of these cities, nor for the alliance as a whole.[15] In 371 BC, Athens sent envoys to Sparta in the pursuit of peace, and advised Thebes to join them. The envoys convinced the Spartans that a peace was in their interests; as neither side had yet been defeated there was no loss of face to be found in a truce.[16] The Spartans voted to negotiate a peace which called for all of the Greek cities to be autonomous, and for the external forces garrisoned in them to be removed immediately. Any city seen to break the autonomous right of another could expect the intervention of any who wished to aid the wronged party, but there was no obligation to act.

Every party present swore to the peace, including Thebes, whilst Athens and Sparta swore on behalf of their allies as well. The following day, the Theban leader, Epaminondas, asked for the wording of the Theban contribution to be changed from 'the Thebans swore' to the 'Boeotians swore', to reaffirm their control over the Boeotian League.[17] Agesilaus challenged the notion, asking if Epaminondas thought it fair that the Boeotian cities should be free of Theban control, for which he was rebuked – could the same not be said of the Laconian cities under Spartan control? Agesilaus was furious and demanded a direct answer: would Thebes free the Boeotian cities from their obligations? But Epaminondas simply sent the question right back, did Agesilaus intend to free the Laconian cities? The Spartan king had had enough, he struck the Theban name from the treaty and war was resumed.

For the rest of the Greek *poleis* peace was declared and any territory that had been acquired was swiftly returned. But Sparta was going to waste little time in attacking Thebes. Whilst they withdrew their forces from many of the cities they garrisoned throughout Greece, the Spartan Assembly sent orders to their King Cleombrotus to take his army from Phocis, lead it directly into Boeotia and induce the Thebans to battle.

It was expected that Cleombrotus would follow the same route that Agesilaus had many years earlier, heading through the narrow pass at Coronea. As soon as the Thebans received word of the Spartan march they mustered a force of 6,000 under the command of Epaminondas, and sent it to hold Coronea before Cleombrotus reached it. When Cleombrotus finally arrived near the pass and saw the Thebans holding such a strong position, he decided to turn his army around and march through the mountains to Thisbe, which lay due south of Coronea. From Thisbe he took another mountainous route, this time southeast to Creusis, where he captured the defensive wall and took control of twelve Theban triremes.[18] With Creusis subdued the Spartans marched inland into the territory of Thespiae and set up camp at Leuctra.

The army of Epaminondas would have received reports of the assault on Creusis and quickly marched to intercept the Spartan path to Thebes. Once they had arrived at Leuctra they saw the Spartan camp on the southern hills and chose to encamp on those opposite, only a short distance away. It had been just twenty days since the peace treaty had been signed and battle was about to commence once more.

The Battlefield

The plain of Leuctra was the perfect landscape for an even, pitched battle between two Greek armies. The land was level and extended between the two foothills on which the armies were camped to the north and south. To the east and west ran the rivers Asopus and Parmessus respectively, but the distance between them was so great that they formed no barrier to either formation. It is unlikely that the plain had any obstacle in place, such as woodland or marshland, because not one of our sources makes any mention of it. In fact the only obstacle described in the sources was a ditch that lay in front of the Spartan camp, but it was not on the field of battle.

In effect the battlefield was a blank canvas on which either army could set up as they liked, fight as they liked and arrange their tactics as they liked, without any physical factors in need of accommodating.

The Armies

The army of Cleombrotus was made up of 4 *morai*, giving a strength of almost 4,500 hoplites, plus the 300 Hippeis who travelled with the king: of these Spartans, only 700 were full Spartiates.[19] Each hoplite *mora* would have attached a cavalry *mora* of roughly 100–120 horses, giving a cavalry strength of 400–500 in total. In addition to their own regular forces, the Spartans were joined by a strong contingent of mercenaries: *peltasts* from Phocis, and cavalry from Heracleia and Phleious. It appears likely that the army consisted of allied forces, and while our main sources do not list them, we do know of a tradition from Arcadia that shows their begrudging presence, most likely as allies.[20] It seems equally likely that the Corinthians were also there in some capacity as allies. But, predominantly, Spartan allies were allowed to provide money in lieu of military service and, when that is combined with the lack of reference to them, it must be assumed that mercenaries vastly outnumbered the allies. The only realistic figure for Cleombrotus' army from our sources is given by Plutarch at 10,000 hoplites and 1,000 horses, which in light of the figures for the Spartan force means their mercenaries and allies needed to provide a further 5,000 men and 500 cavalry, which is not unrealistic.[21]

The Boeotian army of Epaminondas is not attested outside of one source, Diodorus, who numbers them as 6,000 hoplites under the command of 6 *boeotarchs* whilst they were stationed at Coronea.[22] This figure gives an even split of 1,000 hoplites per *boeotarch*, and when this army was met by a seventh *boeotarch* it revised the Boeotian strength to 7,000 hoplites of which 4,000 would have been Theban.[23] The Theban number included the elite force of 300 hoplites called the Sacred Band, led by Pelopidas, who were the only professional soldiers in the entire army.

The Boeotian cavalry strength is harder to deduce because it is not mentioned anywhere in the historical record. However, if we accept a 1:10 ratio, as described by *Hellenica Oxyrhynchia*, then they would have had nearing 700 horsemen.[24] With no allied forces to call upon, the Boeotians were outnumbered 3:2, but the Theban contingent numbered almost equally with the Spartan *morai* opposite them.

The Battle (Xenophon, *Hellenica*, VI.4.4–15; Plutarch, *Life of Pelopidas*, 23; Diodorus, XV.55–56; Pausanias, IX.13.4–12)

As they sat atop their hills, both camps were filled with trepidation – the omens were not good. The Spartans had a number of she-goats, which led their flock of sacrificial sheep, wiped out by wolves during the night, causing doubt to rear into the head of Cleombrotus. It was not until the close friends of the king began to warn him that inaction would be perceived as fear that he decided upon battle.

The Boeotians were likewise plagued by ill omens, but Epaminondas began to orchestrate his own omens to rouse their spirits. On the due-arrival of a few extra men from Thebes, he had their journey intercepted and a message was passed. It told them to bring word that the temple of Heracles was empty of its weapons, extolling a message of hope that the heroes of Thebes had come to join them in battle.[25] Epaminondas likewise gave sacrifice at the monument on the Leuctran plain, dedicated to two girls who had been raped by Spartans and had committed suicide because of the shame, followed shortly by their father who found no justice. But even this obvious attempt to evoke Theban hatred for the Spartans was not enough to convince all of the commanders to take to the field.[26]

The six *boeotarchs* met in conference to discuss what to do but there was an even split between those for and those against battle, with Epaminondas leading those wanting a confrontation.[27] With the arrival of the seventh *boeotarch*, who had finally arrived from Mount Cithaeron, the deadlock could be broken. He chose to side with Epaminondas, after a subtle word with the general beforehand, and the decision was made to stand and fight.

On the morning of the battle the camps had their morning meals and held their final councils, finalizing tactics and ensuring that all of the commanders knew what was expected of them. For the Spartans, this meal was washed down with a little too much wine, which awoke a false courage within them.[28]

When the meals were finished, both armies began to don their armour, erasing any doubt that a battle was imminent. In the Boeotian camp the merchants, baggage carriers and camp followers began to make haste and depart. Epaminondas opened an invitation to any soldier who did not want to fight, saying they could leave with the camp followers without fear of retribution, which a small group duly did.[29] As the group moved further and further away from the Boeotian camp they became isolated and were swiftly attacked by the *peltasts* and cavalry mercenaries of Cleombrotus. The mercenaries swarmed around them, broke their poorly formed defensive lines and drove them back to the Boeotian camp.

Once their men were ready, both armies set up their battle order. The Spartan lines were formed twelve men deep, with Cleombrotus, the Hippeis, and the four Spartan *morai* taking pride of place on the right hand side, whilst the mercenaries and allies formed the left. The Spartan cavalry started out in front of the line, with the allied cavalry sat on the left flank.[30] The Boeotians had placed the Thebans on the left wing, opposite Cleombrotus' position, with their allies forming the remainder of the formation to the right. The Thebans formed up fifty men deep, with the Sacred Band at the front led by Pelopidas, and the cavalry starting out on both flanks.[31] The Theban tactics were simple, crush the head of the snake – take out the king and his royal guard, send the Spartans into a panic and the rest of their army would flee in chaos.[32]

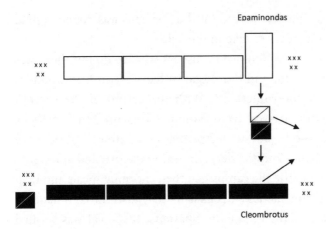

Map 9.1: Battle of Leuctra, phase 1.

The Boeotians sent out their own, more experienced, cavalry to challenge the Spartans and to mask their own movements as they began their march forward, with the right wing under orders not to engage with the enemy. This created an oblique attack, which aimed to isolate the Spartan king's position by drawing the left flank forwards from his position.

From behind his cavalry screen, Cleombrotus saw the enemy begin their advance and, spotting what they intended to do, began to march his army forwards to meet them.[33] As his men began to move, the Spartan cavalry were finally met by the Boeotian and were quickly routed. The cavalry fled the field south, some of them ending up crashing into the Spartan *morai* behind them.[34] The hoplite lines were in disarray, they were trying to get the crazed horses out of their way, gaps were opening throughout their phalanx and their minds were distracted from the Thebans who were still marching towards them.

The Thebans increased their pace and, with a final order from Pelopidas, the Sacred Band led the charge into the chaos that was the Spartan formation. The Spartans were able to take the initial shock of the charge. Drawing upon their extensive training and discipline they regrouped their formation and turned the tide against the Thebans.

The fighting centred on the position of Cleombrotus, who fell early to a mortal wound. The Spartan dominance was plain to see, as the dying king was easily extracted from the front lines and taken from the field. But the fighting grew fiercer and fiercer, and more Spartans began to fall.

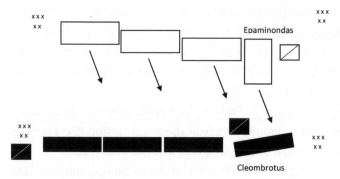

Map 9.2: Battle of Leuctra, phase 2.

As the Spartan commander Deinon died, followed by Sphodrias, and his son Cleonymus, panic was beginning to rest in the hearts of the Spartans. The speed and skill of the attacks against them were too ferocious to handle. The Hippeis were the first to succumb to the pressure, being at the heart of the combat, quickly followed by the rest of the *mora* stationed to their right. As the remainder of the Spartans saw their right flank retreat they too began to give way, maintaining their line as best they could as they headed back to camp.

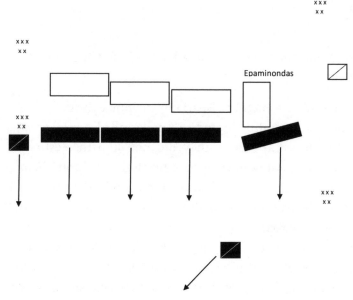

Map 9.3: Battle of Leuctra, phase 3.

Many of their number stumbled and fell in the ditch which preceded the camp, unceremoniously killed in their trap by the unrelenting Thebans. It was not until they entered the camp itself that they were left in peace. For the Thebans had won the day and returned to the field to give their offerings of thanks and to erect their trophy.

In camp, many Spartans were furious at their poor showing on the field. They demanded that their commanders lead them out to stop the Thebans erecting their trophy, and that they should collect the dead bodies of their comrades by force rather than under a truce. But the remaining commanders could see the true devastation of what had happened. Nearly a thousand Spartans had fallen that day, 400 of which were full Spartiates. Their allies had lost the will to fight, and some were even showing signs of pleasure at the defeat. After a short council it was decided that they were in no position to fight another battle. They sent a messenger asking for a truce to reclaim the bodies of the dead.[35]

The Thebans had survived the battle relatively unscathed, losing around 300 men. After they were sure that the Spartans were subdued in their camp they erected their trophy. On the arrival of the Spartan herald, the *boeotarchs* accepted the proposed truce and sent back the bodies, bringing an end to the Battle of Leuctra.

The Aftermath (Xenophon, *Hellenica*, VI.4.16–5.50; Plutarch, *Life of Agesilaus*, 29–30)

A messenger was sent from Leuctra to Sparta to announce the defeat. His arrival came during the festival dedicated to Apollo called *Gymnopaedia*. But when the *ephors* heard the news they did not stop the festivities immediately, allowing a choral performance to finish in the theatre before they revealed the names of the dead to their families. Whilst the families of the dead walked with their heads held high and a smile upon the face, the families of the survivors looked more downcast, if they showed their faces at all, so great was the shame of surviving such a defeat. King Agesilaus advised that the laws be allowed to sleep for one day, thus exonerating those who had shown cowardice in battle (the *tresantes*) from suffering the customary penalties.[36]

Whilst the Spartan defeat was resounding, its impact on their fighting strength was not great. The *ephors* sent out the remaining two *morai* under the command of Agesilaus' son, Archidamus, who was inundated with allied forces that joined him on his journey to Boeotia to meet up with the surviving 3,500-plus Spartans still camped after their defeat. But they were soon convinced by the Theban ally Jason of Pherae that Sparta needed to recover from its defeat, rather than attempt to right this wrong so quickly. They soon left their position and met Archidamus, while he was based at Aigosthena, before continuing their journeys together back to Corinth, where the allied forces were disbanded and the Spartans were led home.

For the Thebans, Leuctra was the catalyst for their ascendancy. Believing themselves to be the superior military power, they began to raid into the Peloponnese and in 370/369 BC the Theban army invaded Spartan lands. Not unlike the Spartans before them, the Thebans fell afoul of their inability to capitalize on their position. They did not take the city of Sparta herself, nor did they successfully entice the Athenians to become their allies, leaving a window of opportunity to come, which would ensure the Theban ascendancy was short lived.

Chapter 10

The Second Battle of Mantinea (362 BC)

The Background (Xenophon, *Hellenica*, VI.5.4 – VII.5.14; Diodorus, XV.62.1–83.5; Plutarch, *Life of Agesilaus*, 29.1–34.8)

Following their defeat at Leuctra, Spartan fortunes went from bad to worse. The illusion of their military invulnerability had finally been shattered, and the notion of their homeland being unassailable was quickly challenged.

In 370 BC Epaminondas led a strong Theban army into the Peloponnese at the behest of the newly formed Arcadian Federation.[1] The cities of Mantinea and Tegea had broken free from Spartan influence and had grouped together many of the smaller communities in the region to try and solidify a power base from which to resist the inevitable Spartan reaction, symbolized by the founding of a joint centre for the Federation called Megalopolis.[2] Agesilaus was chosen to lead a Spartan army into Arcadia, but the campaign was not productive. Getting as far as Mantinea, Agesilaus never felt secure in his search for battle and so left as quickly as he had arrived. For their part, the Mantineans did not pursue the Spartans, as they preferred to join up with the remainder of the Arcadian allies and await the arrival of Thebes.

When Epaminondas arrived he considered the Theban presence superfluous. He had brought his army to face an assailing Spartan force which had since disbanded, making the presence of such a large and expensive army unnecessary. The Arcadians tried to convince him to stay and lead an invasion of Sparta, something Epaminondas had no intention of attempting.[3] But the allies' persistence paid off. Sparta was in a weak position, not only in the Peloponnese but in Laconia itself as many *perioeci* and *helots* were abandoning the Spartan cause. Epaminondas would be able to march on Sparta relatively unopposed.

The invading force was split into contingents, each marching by a different route into Spartan lands.[4] The groups reunited outside of Sparta, looking across the bridge which forded the Eurotas River to the northeast of the city. The allies could see that the Spartans were ready for their attack, hoplites had formed a guard at the temple of Athena Alea and were prepared to meet them. Epaminondas decided to continue his march south, keeping the river to his right, as he pillaged the countryside and set fire to the houses he plundered.[5]

For the people of Sparta, the sight of the flames and smoke rising in the near distance was too much to bear.[6] The city was un-walled and undermanned so, in their desperation, the Spartan authorities offered a promise of freedom to any *helot* willing to take up arms in defence of the city. To their shock, 6,000 *helots* answered the call, raising concerns about arming so many men with a natural grudge against their overlords.[7] These concerns were swiftly allayed by the arrival of their allies from Phleious, Corinth, Epidaurus, Pellene and other cities.

The Thebans finally crossed the River Eurotas near to Amyclae, but the cold winter weather made for a dangerous time. The Theban allies set up camp around Amyclae and began to plunder the surrounding area for four days. Epaminondas was trying to coax out the Spartan army to win the greatest victory the Greek world had seen for over a century, but Agesilaus and the army under his charge did not move out to engage him.

A small group of Spartan cavalry was sent to disrupt the plundering, alongside a group of 300 young hoplites, with some success, but their numbers were never enough to challenge the Theban army. However, the cold winter weather, allied with the Fabian-style restraint of Agesilaus, forced Epaminondas to move his men on.[8] They continued to follow the Eurotas to the south coast, burning any undefended villages as they went, before laying siege to the Spartan dockyards at Gytheion.

Sparta turned to Athens for support and were sent a force under the command of Iphicrates to assist them, but it arrived too late to be of any use and turned back before it had even entered Laconia. Epaminondas, on the other hand, continued his unobstructed march back north and into the homeland of the *helots*, Messenia. The *boeotarch* wished to entrap the Spartans within their Laconian homeland, and so he repopulated Messene, the old capital of Messenia, giving Sparta a new threat to their security alongside Megalopolis.[9] He achieved all of this in just eighty-five days.

In 369 BC the lines were firmly drawn, with Sparta and Athens leading an alliance against that of the Thebans and Arcadians. As fighting focused around the north Peloponnese, the Arcadians began to have their own individual successes against the Argives, Corinthians, Athenians and even the Spartans, all without the help of Thebes, giving rise to a new found belief in their own capabilities.[10]

By 368 BC representatives from Mantinea began to push for the Arcadian Federation to form their own independent military command, which alienated their Theban allies. Delphi played host to a failed peace negotiation between the Thebans and Spartans, at the behest of the Persian king Artaxerxes.[11] The two sides could not agree, due to their joint desires to control what they believed to be rightfully theirs; for the Spartans that included Messenia and for the Thebans that included all of Boeotia.[12]

The arrival of a Syracusan force to assist the Spartans and Athenians caused some disagreement as to their deployment.[13] Athens wanted them sent to Thessaly, to oppose the supposed Theban aggression in the region. But Sparta wished them to join their own forces in Laconia and take part in a new campaign into Arcadia.[14] After a consultation between all of the allies, the decision was made in Sparta's favour and they joined the forces of Archidamus.

Archidamus marched his army against the small city of Caryae, taking it by force and slaughtering all those whom they took alive.[15] The army then moved into Parrasia, southern Arcadia, and ravaged the local countryside, burning the crops as they went. When Archidamus heard of a joint force from Arcadia and Argos heading towards him in aid of the Parrasians, he retreated his men into the hills and set up camp. While they waited, the Syracusan contingent's allotted time had expired and their leader, Cissides, approached Archidamus, informing him that they were due to depart for Sicily.

The Syracusans left immediately, heading south on the road to Sparta. As Cissides led his men through a narrow gorge along the road he was cut off by an army from Messenia, forcing the commander to send a message back to Archidamus calling for help. The Spartans quickly broke camp and headed to Cissides' position, but they were themselves cut off by the Arcadian-Argive force that drove him to the hills in the first place. Archidamus had to act quickly, setting his army into formation on flat ground next to the road. By the time that battle was met, the Spartan forces were baying for blood and victory was comfortably attained. The enemy were routed before contact was even made, and the Spartan cavalry cut down those that fled. The body count is not reported but, for Sparta at least, this was to be known as the Tearless Battle, for not one Spartan life was lost.

By 367 BC, Theban political pressure in Persia argued for the king to intercede in the war, which they did with characteristic bolshiness. Under the influence of the Theban agent in Susa, none other than the commander Pelopidas, Artaxerxes made two stipulations for the general peace that guaranteed that war would continue: Messenia had to remain independent of Sparta, and Athens was to immobilize her fleet.

When this treaty returned to mainland Greece, in 366 BC, it was not well received. The Athenians put their emissary to death for failing in his duties. In Arcadia their own messenger had refused the gifts of the king after feeling slighted during the proceedings, and he did little to encourage the Arcadians to support the treaty. The Corinthians were the first to officially refuse the treaty when it was directly proposed by Theban representatives, with many other cities following their lead.[16]

With no negotiated settlement in sight, Epaminondas looked to push Theban control more firmly into the Peloponnese. The Arcadian alliance was faltering with each passing year, so the *boeotarch* planned to take control of Achaea and create a new foothold in the area. With help from Argos, Epaminondas marched unopposed into Achaea and pushed his authority over the dominant cities without bloodshed. Taking pledges of alliance from the Achaeans, Epaminondas left the democratic factions in power and returned home.

The new allegiance caused discomfort in Arcadia and Achaea, thus forcing Thebes to send out their own governors to maintain control of the Achaean region. On arrival they dismissed all of the aristocratic parties from their cities; however, the aristocrats all banded together and began to retake each of the cities one by one. To make matters worse, once they had resumed their authority, the Achaean cities no longer maintained a neutral stance, but chose to align themselves with Sparta. The Thebans had hoped to reinforce their control in the Peloponnese, securing their influence over Arcadia, but in actuality they had now surrounded Arcadia with enemies to the north and south.

For Athens, the toll of the war was causing discontent. When the offer came from the Arcadians to establish an alliance they soon agreed, even though they sat on opposite sides of the Theban–Spartan conflict. Athens then moved to help secure Corinth against Theban aggression, but on the arrival of their guards the Athenians were sent home by the leaders of Corinth because they intended to negotiate a peace with Thebes.

Corinth implored the Spartans to join them in the peace negotiations with Thebes. Sparta declined the request but permitted any of their allies to join Corinth in the pursuit of peace. So the year 365 BC saw Thebes agree to a peace treaty with Corinth, Phleious and possibly others, but war with Sparta officially continued.

The following year saw Elis attack the Arcadian Federation member-city of Lasion, which drove the Arcadians to march against the Eleian position. With a categorical victory, the Arcadians drove on to Elis itself, where they were finally turned back after a hard fought battle in the Eleian marketplace.

Elis turned to Sparta for help against the next impending Arcadian invasion, who agreed and sent a contingent of troops. The Spartan army marched on the Arcadian city of Cromnos, but were swiftly besieged themselves. Sparta panicked and sent out another army under the command of Archidamus who was defeated at the hands of the new Arcadian *corps d'elite*, the Eparitoi.[17]

Tensions rose to new heights in the year of the Olympic festival of 364 BC. Cromnus had fallen to the Arcadians, and their plans for invading Elis once more were put on hold to assist the city of Pisa in running the Games. The holy truce for the month of the festival should have allowed Arcadia to forget their enemies for a short time, but Elis knew that they could not withstand the Arcadian forces forever and needed to send a message. The Eleians marched on the holy site of Olympia, with the military support of their allies from Achaea.

The Arcadians were shocked, no-one had expected this act of sacrilegious aggression. The games had already begun by the time the army's march had been observed; the horse race had been completed and the wrestling bouts that constituted the first event of the pentathlon had also finished.

The Eleian forces were matched by 2,000 Arcadian hoplites and 400 of their Athenian allies' cavalry and battle commenced. The fighting was stubborn on both sides, but the Eleians were finally turned away from the sacred precinct and they returned to their camp outside of Olympia.[18] The night was filled with the noise of Arcadian workmen ripping down the spectator stands for the games and turning them into palisades. By late morning, the men of Elis arrived to attack the precinct, only to find a formidable sight in these strong defences. They chose, instead, to retreat back home, content that they had proven their valour and bravery.

With Elis quiet for now, the Arcadian Federation shifted their focus inwards on a new problem that likewise derived from Olympia. Mantinea passed a resolution to no longer use sacred funds held at Olympia as a means of paying for the elite Arcadian force, the Eparitoi.[19] The use of funds given to the gods for military use was a sacrilege and offended the gods, but the Arcadian Federation saw Mantinea's actions as an attempt to harm the Federation itself and charged them on that count. When Mantinea refused to send a representative to the trial they were condemned, and the Eparitoi were sent to seize those men held responsible.

With the Mantinean gates shut to them, the situation was volatile for the fledgling Federation. Other member *poleis* began to agree with the Mantinean stance, and put pressure on the Federation to change their source of funding for the Eparitoi. The Assembly had no choice but to concede and, whilst the funding system was changed, the problem arose that the men who would submit their accounts that year, which would show the use of sacred funds, were likely to face the death penalty. These magistrates attempted to agitate the Thebans into intervening, claiming that the Arcadians were near to allying themselves with Sparta. Whilst the Theban advance was called off by other members of the Federation, the possibility of further military action caused the Arcadians to rethink the need for the war as it stood. By the start of 363 BC, the Arcadians returned the sacred precinct of Olympia back to the guardianship of Elis and an armistice was concluded.

The oath for the peace was administered in Tegea in 363 BC. The city was host to not only the Federation's representatives, but also a Theban governor with an entourage of 300 Boeotian hoplites. Whilst the majority of the Arcadian delegates feasted and celebrated the truce, the Theban governor brought together the magistrates who had tried to induce Theban action in the previous year, as well as members of the Eparitoi who shared their views on the peace, and shut the gates of the city. The pro–Boeotian force tried to arrest many of the magistrates who orchestrated the peace. Whilst they were able to capture a few, their lack of numbers, combined with the lack of support they received from the citizens of Tegea, meant that many more magistrates were able to escape, especially those from Mantinea who were of particular interest to the group.[20]

Mantinea applied political pressure on the Theban governor to release all of the Arcadian captives, which he relented to, but this was not enough. Envoys were sent to Thebes to denounce him and have him put to death, but Thebes did not agree. Theban–Arcadian relations had been strained for a long time, and the message was clear, the Arcadians were at fault for concluding a peace without consulting Thebes first.

While the Arcadian Federation sent envoys to Athens and Sparta for their support, Epaminondas marched a strong force of Thebans and allies straight to Nemea. This army made camp in the town and waited, hoping to cut off the Athenians as they entered the Peloponnese. But the Athenians chose instead to sail to Laconia and march to Mantinea from the south, where a large coalition army was forming to resist Epaminondas. When the coalition felt strong enough, they called for the final piece of their army to arrive, the army of Sparta led by their king, Agesilaus.

Epaminondas had moved his men south and encamped in Tegea. It was from here that he saw his opportunity. Sparta had been left empty and helpless; he needed to do little more than march on it to make the Spartans submit to his will.

When Agesilaus received a message from a Cretan runner, describing Epaminondas' intention, he left his cavalry, mercenaries and three regiments to join up with the coalition in Mantinea whilst the remainder of his men were marched quickly back home to resist the Theban onslaught.[21] The Thebans arrived first but were repelled by a sprightly resistance put up by a small garrison which had been left in the city. When Epaminondas heard of Agesilaus' imminent arrival, who in turn was being followed quickly by the full Mantinean army in support, he withdrew to Tegea, just a short distance south of Mantinea, where he prepared for a decisive battle.[22]

The Battlefield

The battle was fought at a narrow point in the plain that sits between Tegea and Mantinea. Epaminondas' camp sat at the base of the Maenalion mountain range to the southwest of Mantinea, facing northeast to the coalition's position. The road which ran through the landscape was skirted by a grove named Ocean, to the north.[23]

The battlefield had no features discernible from the sources, but its narrow shape would have reduced the probability of either side successfully outflanking the other.

The Armies

The army of Epaminondas is said to have led a combined force that numbered over 30,000 foot soldiers, and no less than 3,000 cavalry. This army was the coming together of Tegeans, the majority of the Arcadian Federation, many of the Achaeans, the Argives, the Boeotians, the Messenians, the Thessalians, and many more besides, including mercenaries. The cavalry formation had, dispersed amongst its number, *hamippoi*, light-armed troops trained to run alongside the horses, holding on to the tails of the horse and hem of the rider's cloak.

The army of the coalition is said to have numbered 20,000 foot soldiers and 2,000 cavalry. Of these, 6,000 were Athenian and the Spartans had a force of around 1,000 hoplites. The rest of the army was made up from the Mantineans, the Eleians, some Achaeans, the Euboeans, other unnamed *poleis*, and mercenaries.

Light armed troops must have been present for both sides, but none are mentioned apart from the *hamippoi*.[24]

The Battle (Xenophon, *Hellenica*, VII.5.4–27; Diodorus XV.84.1–89.2)

In Tegea, Epaminondas decided to rest his hoplites for the coming battle, but sent his cavalry to move swiftly into the surrounding lands of Mantinea. It was July, which meant it was time for the harvest. The Theban cavalry had a single goal, disrupt the harvest, massacre or capture the livestock and the thousands of people reaping the crops outside the safety of the city walls.

The Mantineans were aware of the imminent assault and sent word to the small town of Cleonae, where an Athenian cavalry force was resting before its final stage to the rendezvous of Mantinea. The message called for assistance to protect the cattle, slaves, elderly and the young children who were all caught outside of the walls. The Athenians agreed, departed as quickly as they could, and fell upon the enemy cavalry who were wreaking havoc across the agricultural plains. The fighting was brutal with brave men falling on both sides. The experience and prowess of their Thessalian and Theban counterparts was neutralized by the vigour and courage of the Athenian offensive. The enemy were finally driven from the plains, but returned later to retrieve their dead from the victorious horsemen of Athens.

As it was harvest time in Mantinea, it was harvest time in Thebes also and Epaminondas had very little time left before his farmer-hoplites would need to return home and begin their own reaping. He had to act now, or else forget the entire campaign. But leaving now would mean abandoning his allies to a newly united coalition, and it would also be a personal loss of face for the commander. He had failed to take Sparta with a vastly superior force, and his invasion had united many powerful and disparate *poleis* against him. It had to be battle, for victory would wash him of his sins, and defeat would bring him a glorious and heroic death in the eyes of the Theban people.

The camp in Tegea was busy in preparation, with helmets being eagerly whitened, swords and spearheads being sharpened, and the Arcadian hoplites painting the Theban club on their shields. Epaminondas marched them from their camp and deployed them in their battle order, creating the illusion that he was preparing for imminent battle. But, once his men were arranged as he wished, he led them away from the enemy's direction and headed to the base of the Maenalion Mountains to the northwest. On their arrival, Epaminondas reviewed his phalanx before ordering them to ground their weapons and shields, all to create the impression that he was about to set up camp and delay for another day.[25]

The movements of the Theban army caused a false sense of security in the coalition army, they no longer expected battle to commence and soon lost their fighting spirit. But Epaminondas was not finished. Once his men were all stationary in their marching columns he ordered them back into line, growing around his position on the left wing and spreading out to the right.[26]

When the coalition's men finally realized the enemy's intention they began to panic. Many ran, without orders, to their posts, others began to line up or bridle their horses, whilst others began to put on their armour, all without instruction. They were afraid, they were caught by surprise and they looked like men who knew they were about to suffer pain rather than inflict it on others.[27]

Beside the deep formation of the Thebans, which met as a wedge in the front and which Epaminondas led on the left wing, lay the Arcadians, with the Argives entrusted to the farthest right wing. The remaining allies filled the centre, with either wing flanked by cavalry and light-armed troops. An additional force was placed on the hills that sat on his right wing, to act as a deterrent to the Athenians if they won their fighting with relative ease. The hastily formed line opposite them placed the Mantineans on the right, opposite the Thebans, with the Spartan force next to them. Next were the Eleians, beside whom were the Achaeans, followed by the remaining allies, and finally the Athenians who held the left wing. Similarly to their enemy, the coalition army was flanked by their cavalry and light-armed troops.

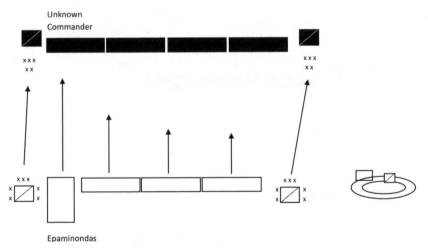

Map 10.1: Second Battle of Mantinea, phase 1.

Epaminondas orchestrated a combined arms attack, sending his cavalry in wedge formations against their enemy counterparts, whilst he led his wing from the front, driving his wedge-shaped ram of Thebans headlong into the Mantineans ahead of them. The rest of his army followed in an oblique advance, that is with the right wing trailing well behind, similar to Leuctra.

The impact on the Mantinean line was brutal, as the pointed assault pierced through the safety of the phalanx and shattered its cohesion. After an initial struggle, the Mantineans could not withstand the concentrated pressure anymore and were driven back, with the Spartans following to maintain the line. The Thebans saw that their victory was imminent and so moved to press home their advantage. Epaminondas led them on, cutting down the vanguard as he moved on in his thirst for more blood. The Spartans saw what was happening and made a last-gasp effort to reach the Theban commander. Their missiles rained down on his position, striking his shield, then his body, before Anticrates the Spartan was able to get close enough to Epaminondas and strike the commander cleanly in the chest with his sword.[28] The death of Epaminondas stalled the advance of the Theban line. Whilst the Mantineans and Spartans continued their retreat, the Thebans remained where he fell.

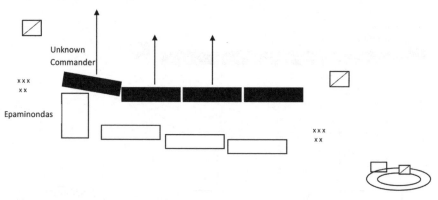

Map 10.2: Second Battle of Mantinea, phase 2.

The Theban cavalry had won their own engagements, with the presence of the *hamippoi* proving too much for the coalition cavalry to handle.[29] While the left flanking cavalry knew of Epaminondas' fall, and so did not pursue their fleeing adversaries, the right wing had yet to find out.

The Athenians had held their position on the left, waiting for the slow march of the Argives to finally reach them, and seemed unaware that their own right wing was in retreat. When the Boeotian cavalry won their fight and began their chase of the fleeing coalition horses, they left behind their contingent of *hamippoi*. These light-armed troops were reckless in their euphoria of victory and charged the lines of the Athenians, expecting them to be demoralized and to break easily, but no such thing occurred. The majority of the *hamippoi* were killed with ease, as the remainder retreated to a safe distance.

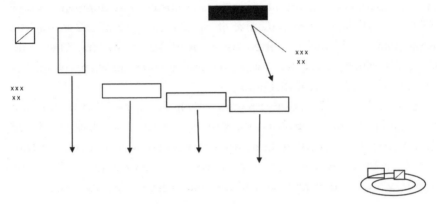

Map 10.3: Second Battle of Mantinea, phase 3.

With the conflict over, confusion filled the battlefield. Thebes had shattered the enemy wing, driving them from the field, but Athens had held its position and had defeated those sent against them. Epaminondas was dead, but the Thebans had control of most of the dead bodies on the field. Nobody knew who had won.

Both sides erected trophies in victory, and both gave back the bodies of the dead which they held as if victorious; in turn both sides received the bodies of their fallen as if defeated. The losses are unknown on either side, but one of the fallen from the Athenian cavalry is particularly, and poignantly known to us: his name was Gryllus, he died fighting in the earlier skirmishes around Mantinea, and he was the son of our main author Xenophon.

The Aftermath

With Epaminondas dead, and the Greek states uncertain as to who, if anyone, actually won the battle, a peace was called which brought an end to the conflict. The peace was signed by all except Sparta, who refused on the grounds that Messene was included as an autonomous *polis*, something they could not accept.

For Greek historians, this battle was the natural end of an era. With the death of Epaminondas, the absence of any strong and dominant power in Greece, and the continual demise of Sparta, the year of 362 BC was the closing point of histories written by many different writers. Our main source, Xenophon, clearly felt it was a natural cut-off as he abruptly finishes his vast work, *Hellenica*, at this point.[30]

Greece had created a power vacuum which would be filled by the first strong power to impose itself on the situation. The outbreak of the Third Sacred War (c.356 BC) invited the growing strength of Macedon into the fray, led as it was by a man schooled in the Theban military tradition.[31] This was Philip II, who would bring to an end the golden age of classical Greece.

Part III

Siege Warfare

Sieges are the one area of ancient warfare where the military and civic domains merge. While many of the traditional explanations of Greek warfare describe it as almost a sport, or a game – as if the Greeks were not afraid of, and built a society that revelled in, the very idea of it – sieges are the one area where this idea falls apart. Sieges did not conform to the idealism of Greek combat, past or present, and maybe this goes some small way into explaining how hard it is to find a book dedicated solely to the topic. Sieges were where the very nasty side of warfare, and the humans enacting it, came out to play. Unarmed men were killed on sight, simply because they were of military age. Greek women and children were ripped from their homes and sold into slavery. In the case of Melos, a small town which had dared to not join Athens as an ally, the populace were effectively dispersed, erased and replaced by an Athenian contingent of colonists.

It is the prevailing belief among scholars that the Greeks were not efficient siege experts. Cities were defended by full-length walls which were often enough to hide behind and wait for the offensive army to disperse. This did not usually take long, due to the farming commitments of the citizen-militia that formed the core of Greek armies. The most common tactic was for a besieger to try to starve the besieged into submission; success lay in persistence rather than tactical ingenuity. The Spartans, especially, used to ravage the surrounding countryside in an attempt to force the besieged to come out and defend their crops. For many of the *poleis* the cost of maintaining a siege was too high so many sieges ended in a somewhat embarrassing march home, having achieved nothing.

Whilst much of this is true, this section will try and restore some credibility into the Greek method of siege warfare. Although it does not compare in scale and technical ingenuity to that practised by the Assyrians before them or the Macedonians after them, classical Greek sieges were an important element of warfare as a whole. Tactically, the Greeks were reluctant to try and storm a fortification regularly, which gave rise to a very different and subversive set of siege skills.

Greek siege-craft was focused on subterfuge, infiltration, betrayal and deception. Lying at the core of these issues was the most important factor in every siege that is described here: morale. If the city could not maintain the morale of the people, it became highly exposed to bribery and internal treachery. As can be seen in the sieges of Plataea and Syracuse, the emphasis on this tactic resorted to an almost chess-like strategy game of action and counteraction, all in the name of morale, without the fortifications being the prime focus of assault.

One great difficulty in reconstructing these sieges lies in the siege equipment available, or more specifically our lack of knowledge about the equipment. The Greek texts use a word, *mechanai*, which can be translated literally as 'machines', but we do not ever get told, specifically, what this included. Pictorial evidence does not help because most of our depictions of sieges show little else but ladders – a useful tool, but hardly a siege machine. The only other machine we can be certain of is the battering ram, which makes its first appearance at the siege of Plataea. We are also told about the ingenious attempt of fire manipulation, such as at the walls of Plataea or in the grounds of the Drilae fortification, and a prototype flamethrower that was used at Delium and at Torone in the same year (See chapters 2 & 3 respectively).

At the turn of the 4th century BC, the shape of siege warfare began to change, thanks solely to the patronage of the tyrant of Syracuse, Dionysius I (c. 430–367). Dionysius made it his goal to push the military clout of Syracuse and, in doing so, revolutionized its navy, its military and its siege tactics. He brought together a large array of engineers and created a competitive air to their work, which in turn produced some of the grandest re-imaginings of Near Eastern siege-craft seen in the Hellenic world. It is believed that the proto-catapult was designed in Syracuse as an extension of an earlier (undated) invention which resembled a crossbow (*gastraphetos*, 'belly-bow'), the purpose of which was to match, or even exceed, the bow range of the defenders who had an elevated position from which to fire. And yet these innovations do not appear to have been replicated in mainland Greece during the period under review.

Toward the end of the classical period, a military training manual was written by an otherwise unknown author referred to as Aeneas Tacticus (Aeneas the tactician). In his work, Aeneas sets out how to best defend a fortified position, most commonly a town or city. The vast majority of the advice given amounts to ways of avoiding revolt or betrayal; he has an entire chapter dedicated to internal plots, in which he just lists example after example of internal betrayals during sieges of the classical period. So, regardless of the great innovations happening in Sicily, on the Greek mainland it was still the primary concern in a siege to protect against internal strife and its external exploitation.

The Greek siege was a matter of brains, rather than the usual brawn. What it lacked in tactical finesse and technological knowhow, it made up for in ingenuity and psychological manipulation. Whilst not always fully calculated, the siege aspect of Greek warfare showed just how flexible the traditional rules of war were allowed to be. Unlike the famous pitched battles, a Greek siege was not a fight for honour, but a fight for survival – creating some of the most savage and brutal of military scenes to be described by even the most taciturn of writers.

The Siege of Plataea (429–27 BC) is the longest account we have of what can be considered an extreme version of a 'normal' Greek siege. The city was surrounded by the Spartans, and a period of time was spent trying to take the walls by force before different plans were concocted to ensure the city's capitulation. We see the siege from both sides, with each attacking measure given the defensive countermeasure, showing a degree of intuitiveness to siege warfare that allowed for speedy resolutions to serious defensive problems.

The sieges of Pylos and Sphacteria (425 BC) are a fascinating insight into the multi-faceted tactics available to besiegers and besieged. The sieges incorporated a planned defensive position at Pylos under attack, an impromptu defensive position of Sphacteria under siege, a parallel naval battle for control of the wider area around the sieges, the repulsion of a forced naval landing on the beaches of Pylos, the siege of an island and the tactical deployment involved in launching it. That is not to mention the use of light-armed troops by Demosthenes to defeat the Spartan force on the island, nor the wider impact of a Spartan force actually surrendering to the enemy.

The siege of Syracuse (415–413 BC) is the largest siege undertaken by a classical Greek force from the mainland. It emphasises the importance of where the besiegers were positioned, and the relative helplessness of even a strong city like Syracuse when it was faced with a determined besieging army. During the siege we see the offensive measures and countermeasures that were enacted, in equal measure. We also witness the importance of strong leadership in the defending city, especially after the arrival of the Spartan commander Gylippus. Finally we see the importance of wider diplomacy, as both sides are forced to look externally for help.

The Siege of the Drilae (400 BC) is an oft-ignored event in Greek military history, yet it reveals to us so much about the nature and practice of sieges during the period. Xenophon gives us a view of how a Greek attack on a fortified position may have happened – including the dissemination of orders, the change in intelligence as the assault progressed, the limitations of the various types of troops in this form of assault, and the inherent dangers in seemingly innocuous defences such as earth mounds and a simple ditch. Xenophon also shows us some of the thoughts and dilemmas that ran through a commander's head whilst conducting a siege attack. It should also be acknowledged that this was Xenophon's first military action in which he was in sole command of an army, and that this is a rare example of a failed short-term siege which has been given a full recounting.

Chapter 11

The Siege of Plataea (429–427 BC)

The Background (Thucydides, II.2–6, Diodorus XXII. 41.2–42.3)

Whilst most of the other cities in Boeotia were 'united' in a confederacy under the leadership of Thebes, Plataea had been able to maintain its own unique, independent status without the overt control of more powerful cities.[1] To those in power at Thebes, this was a great slight to their authority. Not only was there a city that they could not control within their own sphere of influence, that same city that was a loyal outpost of Athens, meaning that the radical democracy in Athens had a presence in the oligarchic lands of Theban Boeotia.[2]

By 431 BC, two events occurred that set Theban minds to the task of unifying all of Boeotia. The Battle of Potidaea and subsequent siege of the city by Athens alerted Thebes to the very realistic possibility of pan-Hellenic war breaking out, something they needed to be prepared for. Due to their rivalry with Athens, it became important to secure their borders and the necessary passages for army movements and communications. Due to the positioning of the city, if war was to break out, Plataea stood squarely in the Thebans' way.[3]

The second event in 431 BC was as much an excuse as it was an opportunity, for no Greek city was ever fully united in its policies; Plataea had citizens who wanted to see Boeotia unified under Theban leadership.[4] This group, led by Naucleides, invited the Thebans into the city of Plataea and formulated a plot to allow them entrance without an alarm being raised. Thebes could not, and did not, pass up this opportunity to act before war had been declared. Once a declaration was made, then the element of surprise would have been lost.

The conspirators made their arrangements through Eurymachus, who was a very influential man in Thebes, and arranged to open one of the city gates which would be unguarded, ironically due to the state of peace that

Plataea found itself in. Thebes sent a force of just over 300 picked men, under the command of two Boeotian government representatives Pythangelus and Diemporus, who entered Plataea under a cloak of darkness.

Naucleides had hoped, maybe even assumed, that the Thebans would follow his suggestion and kill all his political opponents whilst they slept. So when the Thebans had set up in the *agora*, the Plataean conspirators asked them to set upon their enemies' houses. The Thebans refused.

Thebes needed an air of legitimacy in its actions; if it took Plataea by force then it could just as easily be made to give it up after any and all conflict had ended. If, however, Plataea could be shown to have *willingly* joined the Boeotian League then it was an act of political empowerment, not military domination. The Theban leaders began to proclaim aloud their offer to Plataea, for them to retake their place in the Boeotian federation of city states.

Plataea entered a state of panic. Theban troops had entered the inner sanctum of the city undetected. There was no time to organise a resistance. This panic, combined with the darkness preventing any accurate assessment of the size of the Theban force, encouraged the Plataean leaders to agree terms with the Thebans and not seek violence. After all, the Thebans had not shown them any aggression. During this negotiation of terms, the Plataean citizens became aware of just how small the Theban force was and decided to resist by force, contrary to their leaders.[5]

Exploiting the natural distractions of the negotiations and the darkness, the people of Plataea began to mine though the mud-clay walls which adjoined long rows of houses, allowing them to congregate in groups and begin to plan their resistance. Utilizing anything to hand, they began to prepare barricades and arm themselves for battle, all without stepping outside into the streets.

With daybreak soon to be looming, the Plataean resistance bided their time, waiting for the most opportune moment. It needed to be before first light; the Thebans were, after all, a crack force fully armed and ready for combat. If they were allowed the added bonus of full vision, then the Plataeans would have been little more than small waves crashing against a solid rock of discipline and courage. Conversely, in the dark, the Thebans did not know the layout of the streets; unlike the Plataeans, they had no local knowledge to guide them. It was just a matter of maximizing the Plataeans' own strengths whilst exploiting these Theban weaknesses.

When the attack finally began, the Plataeans poured out of their houses and onto the Thebans as quickly as they could. It would have been a terrifying sight for the Thebans, who thought that there would be no resistance. Instead they saw masses of people pouring out of dark houses and descending upon them in the blink of an eye. To the Thebans' credit, they formed a defensive line and were able to repel wave upon wave of assaults, but this was not conventional warfare. As the men charged at them, their screams being heard over the thundering rainfall, the women had climbed to the rooftops with their slaves and even their children, pelting the Thebans from all angles with stones and tiles, anything to hand. The Thebans could not hold out anymore, they broke ranks and fled.[6]

The Thebans were undone, their ignorance of Plataea was fully exploited as they aimlessly ran for safety, not knowing how to escape the city. Some made their way to the only exit they knew, the gate through which they had entered, but the Plataeans had already locked it. Finding the bolt to lock the gate missing, no doubt taken by the original conspirators, one Plataean had thrust the spike of his javelin into the lock; a gesture that may well have signalled to the Thebans the blood-soaked vengeance that was about to befall them.

Plataea became a bloodbath. Thebans were running for their lives with no escape possible. The Plataeans were whipped up into the sort of frenzy that could only come from fighting in the shadows of their own homes. Some Thebans scaled the walls and jumped to the outside, but very few survived this. Another group took an axe from a female assailant and cut through one of the gate locks, but again only a few were able to make their escape.

The main bulk of the Theban troops fled for the sanctuary of the city gates, in the hope of being able to find an exit. But they were confused by the darkness and, with only a quarter moon to light their way, found they had not entered a city gate but just a large building next to the city walls. With their enemy cornered and trapped inside, the Plataeans allowed themselves the luxury of time and deliberation. What should they do with the Thebans? Burn the building down was a popular answer, but they waited for the other Thebans to be rounded up and brought together. With only 180 of their number left, the Thebans declared unconditional surrender and lay their lives into the hands of the Plataeans.[7]

The news of the failure reached the Theban reinforcements who were due to meet up in Plataea at daybreak. They rushed as fast as they could over the 8-mile distance between Thebes and Plataea, but the rain had done its work and the Asopus River had flooded, impeding them greatly. By the time the reinforcements arrived the damage had already been done. They found only bloody corpses and the knowledge of the Theban prisoners being held.[8]

After messengers were sent back and forth between the two cities, a truce was agreed upon. The Theban reinforcements retreated back from Plataea, in compliance, but the Plataeans decided not to release the prisoners as had been agreed under oath, and instead massacred them all to a man.[9] In a cruel twist of fate, and foreboding, Plataea sent an envoy to Athens before the execution to inform them of what had been happening and the Athenians sent an envoy back with the instructions to *not* kill the prisoners – he was too late. The Athenians were not stupid, they were well aware what this act would mean. So they sent a supply of various provisions and took back with them most of the Plataean women, the children and less able-bodied men.[10] With a force of only 480 men, and 110 women to feed them, Plataea was preparing for a siege.

The Siege (Thucydides, II.71–8, III.20–24; Diodorus XXII.47, 56)

The hallowed ground of Plataea must have been an evocative sight for any Greek army to behold. Entering from the south, they would have marched past the supposed tomb of the Persian General Mardonius, the one-time scourge of Greece and enemy of freedom. Within 50 *stades* of the city walls they would have still been able to see the trophy that the allied Greek forces erected to declare their victory in 479 BC. Once within sight of the city walls they would have seen the three burial pits, containing the brave heroes who had given their lives to defend all of Greece against the Persian yoke.

To march on Plataea from the north would have meant walking through the battlefield itself, crossing the rivers and seeing the island that were all a part of folklore. To launch an attack on Plataea was to launch an attack on the memory of all that was achieved there. It was to betray the loyalty and the bravery that the city had shown in the face of Greece's greatest adversity.

As wide spread conflict began in Greece, Plataea was relatively ignored whilst Sparta and Athens accumulated their allied forces and began to flex their military muscles. It was not until the summer after the fall of Potidaea, in 429 BC, that Sparta finally decided to reproach the Plataeans for their actions against Thebes.[11] The Spartan King Archidamus II took a force into Plataean lands and, after setting up his camp, his men began to raid and raze the surrounding farmland.

Plataea beseeched him to reconsider his actions, calling upon their own role in the saving of Greece and the independence they were promised by the former Spartan commander, Pausanias.[12] Archidamus was moved by their words and offered the Plataeans an amnesty, protection and a promise that their freedoms would be reinstated after the war – as long as they remained neutral.[13] The Plataeans took advice from Athens, who promised to support any resistance against Sparta, and refused the offer. Archidamus most probably expected this and, in a move that appears more political than genuine, he prayed to the gods for permission to break the oath of his ancestors and attack Plataea herself.

The Spartan army went to work, cutting down the fruit orchards outside of Plataea and enclosing the city within a palisade.[14] With the city surrounded, Archidamus began his next structure: a siege-mound that would butt up against one section of the city wall, close enough that once it had reached the right height his troops could simply step from the mound onto the wall itself.[15] This was an audacious move. Archidamus hoped that the sheer size of the Peloponnesian force would deter the Plataeans from further opposition – he was wrong.

The Spartans took timber from Mount Cithaeron, on the northern side of which Plataea sat upon a spur, and hemmed in both sides of the mound as it grew. Using a lattice-work structure they were able to maintain the integrity of the mound, preventing it from spreading under its own weight, and they began to add wood and stones to the earth mound to help finish it. The mound took seventy days and nights to construct, under constant manning and supervision at all times by Spartan officers. To achieve such a large feat of engineering, they utilized a rota system to allow rest and sustenance to be taken in shifts.

The Plataeans watched as the mound grew and, anticipating the impending problem, began their own construction of a wall to go on top of their city walls: it became a contest to see whose was biggest. The Plataean extension used wood to build a primary structure and attached it to the relevant wall section. Then, using the bricks from neighbouring houses, they built a wall within the wooden structure, using the wood as a brace to maintain the strength of the new structure.

As always when using wood in defensive structures, the threat of fire was taken very seriously by the Plataeans, so they covered the new woodwork with animal skins and hides soaked in water. These protected the wood from burning missiles and also sheltered the workers who were still constructing the wall.

As the two structures were reaching higher and higher, the Plataeans opened up a second front with what can only be described as ingenious sabotage. They created a hole in their city wall where it made contact with Peloponnesian mound and began to extract the earth from the mound, bringing it into the city. This gave the dual impact of undoing the integrity of the mound at the same time as bringing more building resources into Plataea.

Once the Peloponnesians caught wind of this they filled the breach in their mound by throwing in a mixture of clay and reed wattles, giving the mound a greater consistency and, simultaneously, stopping it from just being carried away like the soil had. But the Plataeans were not to be undone. So, in a second act of sabotage, they dug a mine from inside the city that ended under the mound.[16] Calculated to perfection, the Plataeans were able to continue their tactic of removing the soil from the mound. So, as the besiegers added more soil to the top, the mound never grew, the new material instead filling the gaps that were being created underneath. The Plataeans had literally undermined its integrity.

But these countermeasures could not have worked indefinitely and, as time was passing with no inkling of Athenian support in the horizon, the Plataeans decided to further reinforce the city. They built a new wall that created a crescent shape behind the actual city wall that the mound was resting against. The aim was to produce a second defensive position that the Peloponnesians would have to scale in the same way as they had the main wall, but with the added bonus of the Plataeans having firing positions that would then flank the besiegers.

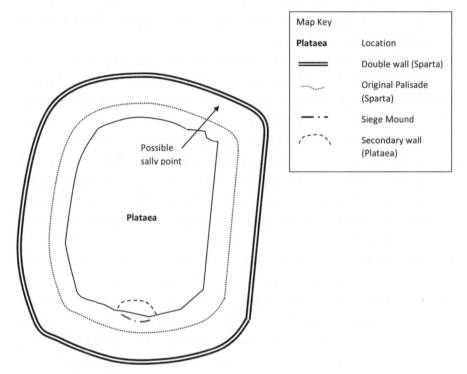

Map 11.1: Siege of Plataea, overview.

The Peloponnesians were growing frustrated by the lack of progress and decided to not only try to build a bigger mound, but they would also try to knock down the great outer wall the Plataeans had made. For the first recorded time in the histories, a Greek army brought up battering rams.[17]

From the top of the mound, the rams had a devastating effect on the temporary wall and very quickly began to take large chunks out of it. The Plataeans were understandably panicked but, as more rams were being utilized at other points along the wall, they began to execute some clever countermeasures. Some of the rams were lassoed by the defenders, lifted and dropped from the air to break them. Another method was to hang a large beam by strong chains from two poles projecting from the parapet, then draw up one end at an angle and release it to swing like a pendulum, so that it flew down and snapped the ram's nose, rendering it useless.

With all of their strategies being expertly counteracted, the Peloponnesians decided to try one more idea before digging in for a long siege – one last chance to end this before it sucked up all of their resources. They intended to put Plataea under a trial of fire.

First, they threw brushwood down into the small gap between the mound and the city wall. This filled quickly, so they began to throw the bundles of wood over the top and into the city. They then set the wood in the ditch alight using a mixture of pitch and sulphur, creating a flame so great that Thucydides believed no man had created anything like it before.[18]

The plan was to create a burning inferno and for it to spread over the walls and light the tinder that had been thrown over, creating a city-sized furnace and crematorium. Added to the danger of the flame, the mixture of sulphur and pitch produced a poisonous gas that would cause horrific injuries and excruciating death to any unlucky enough to breathe it in.[19] Luckily for the Plataeans, the fire never spread into the city due to a lack of wind, and the intervention of heavy rain soon put the inferno out as well.

With this final failure the Peloponnesians decided to leave a small force to maintain the siege and for the rest to be dismissed, most likely returning to service elsewhere in Greece. The remaining force built a wall, further away from the city, that was to completely enclose Plataea. The wall itself consisted of two actual walls placed about 16 feet apart, one facing Plataea to defend against a sortie, the other was to defend against any possible Athenian attack. The space in between was filled with living quarters for the soldiers, but it was built as a single block to create the appearance of it all being a single wall. Both walls were split up by large towers for every ten battlements. The towers were the same breadth as the two walls combined and the only way through them was through the centre. When the weather turned bad during the winter, the battlements were abandoned and the guard duty was kept inside the towers which were roofed in.

In addition to this, the Peloponnesians dug two ditches. By making two ditches they created extra lines of defence, one inside and one outside of the walls, and they also used the extracted mud to make bricks for the wall.[20]

Once complete, even more of the Peloponnesians were sent away and they left just enough to man half of the wall, with the Boeotians being expected to man the other half. So by the summer of 429 BC the siege of Plataea had settled into a full-on blockade.

By the winter of 428/7 BC the Plataeans were beginning to lose faith in an Athenian rescue and, with food supplies running low, they planned to escape by climbing the Peloponnesian wall. To do this they needed to make ladders that would definitely be the right size, this they achieved by counting the bricks in the wall and sizing their ladders accordingly.[21] By the time of action, only about 220 Plataeans decided to go through with the plan.

The Plataeans chose to sally by night, and a stormy night at that. With no moon to light their intentions, they had surprise squarely on their side. Due to the weather, the battlements were unguarded. As they crossed the first ditch and met the wall, they were still undetected by the guards in the towers. The howl of the wind covered most of their noise, but they took the added precaution of approaching in a dispersed formation, through fear of giving away their movements through the accidental clatter of weapons.

Armed lightly and each wearing only one shoe (the bare foot giving a better grip on a wet surface), they erected the ladders up the wall and onto the battlements. Once the ladders were in place, twelve of their number led by Ammias ascended with only a knife and breastplate each. They headed in two groups to the towers either side of them, killing the guards and securing their positions to wreak havoc on their enemy. Another group came up behind them who were armed with spears and shields. As more and more men made the climb, their actions were finally given away by one Plataean who accidently knocked a tile from the battlement.

With the alarm raised, the besiegers rushed out. Disorientated by the darkness and the storm, they did not know what faced them. To add further confusion, the Plataeans from inside the city decided to stage another sortie against a different section of the wall in an attempt to divert the besiegers' full attention from their comrades.

The Peloponnesians had a troop of 300 permanently assigned to deal with this kind of emergency, so whilst the others became lost in their disorientation these men rushed outside the walls and toward the original site of alarm. The besiegers used fire signals to communicate the alarms and messages, but the Plataean plans were too well constructed. In further assistance to their kin, those inside the city lit their own fire signals, making the attackers' unintelligible and ultimately useless.

With the two towers, and therefore the intermediate battlement, secure more and more of the Plataeans scaled the wall and tore down parts of the battlement, allowing the rest to pass over with greater ease. Once over, they took up stations along the edge of the interior ditch, shooting any defenders they saw coming to answer the alarm.[22] By the time the 300 had arrived on the battlements, all of the Plataeans had made it to the ditch and from that position unleashed their arrows and javelins on the troops.

With one last obstacle to negotiate, the Plataeans crossed the icy water-filled ditches and, as the rain turned to snow, they made their escape. But their cunning did not end here. Knowing that the besiegers would pursue them, they headed north toward Thebes, for who would have guessed they would head towards their enemy's land? The gamble paid off because the Peloponnesians headed toward Athens in pursuit, eventually giving up and returning to the siege. The escapees headed north for over half a mile before moving east toward Erythrae and then turning southeast along another road into Athens. For such a daring raid, the Plataeans lost very few men; 212 made it all the way to Athens, which shows just how well conceived and executed it was.

By the Summer of 427 BC, Plataea could hold out no more. Their food supplies had all but gone and the will to fight had gone with it. Athens had failed to deliver on its promise of support and the assaults on the city had taken their toll. When the assaults were renewed, the Plataean resistance was feeble. The besiegers were under the control of a Spartan commander who saw the defenders' resolve was weakening. But, rather than take the city by storm, which would mean it could easily be taken away again in times of peace, he was under orders to offer the Plataeans a chance to join the Peloponnesian cause voluntarily. He asked them to surrender and accept the Spartans as their judges, who in turn would punish the guilty in accordance with law. The Plataeans were not in a position to barter; better a Spartan judge than a Theban one, or none at all. So they surrendered, bringing an end to the two-year siege.

The Aftermath

Once the Spartan judges arrived in the city, they did not bring any charges against the Plataeans but instead asked one question: whether they had done the Spartans and their allies any service in the present war? The Plataeans had to recover from this surprising question, because of course the answer was no. After some time to confer, they returned with an answer which highlighted the past glories of Plataea, their role as carers for the graves of Spartans that had died in 479 BC and the fact that Sparta drove Plataea to become an ally of Athens. But, perhaps most interestingly, the Plataeans were afraid of the influence of Thebes and so called on Sparta to not allow their own reputation to suffer by their manipulation. Ultimately, Plataea beseeched Sparta to stop the Thebans from enacting their wrath.

Following their speech, the Theban representatives requested to speak. They argued that the Plataean alliance with Athens made them just as culpable for the Athenian expansion and that, most importantly, Thebes was the real victim after Plataea had slaughtered some of its citizens in cold blood. The Spartans heard all of the arguments and then persisted with their original question. Thus, one by one, the Plataeans were forced to answer that they had not aided Sparta nor Sparta's allies, thus knowingly commiting themselves to a death sentence. Over 200 were executed, plus 25 Athenians who had remained in the siege, and all of the women were enslaved. The city was razed to the ground and the land was leased out to Theban occupiers. So ended the independent *polis* of Plataea.

Chapter 12

The Sieges of Pylos and Sphacteria (425 BC)

The Background (Thucydides III.94–IV.6)

By 425 BC Athens had abandoned the restrained military approach of their former leader Pericles. They had established a small presence in Sicily, coming to the assistance of Leontini against Syracuse and their allies. They had taken Potidaea in northern Greece, and secured areas of their alliances by seeing out attempted revolts in Mytilene and Corcyra. While still reeling from the effects of the plague, however, they continued refusing to engage with the Peloponnesians during the now-annual raids on Attica.

In 426 BC, an Athenian fleet was causing havoc to the west of Greece when they were convinced by the Messenians to attack the Aetolians, who were a threat to their new home city of Naupactus. The entire campaign was an unmitigated disaster for Athens; losing 120 of their best hoplites they were forced into a retreat back home. Their leader, Demosthenes, stayed in Naupactus out of fear of reprimand but, after greater success in Naupactus and then in the field at Amphilochia, he felt able to return to Athens a year later with a reputation based upon success rather than disaster.[1]

In the spring of 425 BC, the Peloponnesians began their raids into Attica and Athens began to plan its strategy. The intention was to secure their foothold in Sicily, especially as the city of Messana had revolted against them and invited Syracuse to occupy the city. Athens sent out forty ships under the command of Sophocles and Eurymedon. They were to go to Sicily via Corcyra where they were to help with a small issue of raiding exiles.[2] Demosthenes saw an opportunity and successfully applied for permission to use the fleet along the coast of the Peloponnese, if he so wished.[3]

Travelling around the peninsula, the fleet had reached the southwest coast of the Peloponnese when they received troubling news; the raiding exiles in Corcyra had received the support of a Spartan fleet. The two Athenian fleet commanders wanted to rush up to the island and help, but Demosthenes had his eyes fixed on a much closer goal. He suggested landing on the near-by Messenian coast, at Pylos. His intention was to create a fixed position within the Peloponnese from which to terrorize the Spartans in the same way that they were terrorizing Attica – frequent raids. Demosthenes had chosen his position well; Pylos was in Messenia which was the land from which the Spartans drew their slave peoples, the *helots*. If there was any place that could incite a slave revolt, and allow Athens a strong foothold, it was Pylos. But the commanders disagreed with Demosthenes, and wanted to continue north.

Fortune smiled on Demosthenes as a change in weather came to his aid. A storm forced the ships to take shelter in the natural harbour, disembarking at the northern end.[4] He did not waste this good fortune and, observing the abundance of wood and stone in the vicinity, Demosthenes encouraged the force to fortify their position. He was openly mocked by the two commanders; this was a desolate area with no inhabitants for miles and considered by them to be a waste of time and money. But Demosthenes disagreed, this was exactly what he had hoped to find and, once fortified, he could bring in a garrison of Messenians to be relied upon to cause untold damage to Sparta.[5] He failed to convince the commanders. He could not even talk the troops around to his way of thinking, so he stopped trying and waited out the bad weather like everyone else.

As time passed and the storm continued, the Greek soldiers began to get restless. Restlessness quickly turned to boredom, so they decided to disobey orders and fortify their camp.[6] Using the most minimal of equipment – they had no iron tools – they went about strengthening their position in earnest. The area was a naturally strong defensive position, so the army only took six days to achieve the majority of their work, which was to reinforce the landward element of the defences on the eastern side. Once completed, and the storm having now passed, the fleet commanders left Demosthenes with 5 ships and their crews, numbering 1,000 men, to garrison the fortress while they continued their journey up to Corcyra.[7]

Sparta, for their part, did not react with much urgency at the news coming from Pylos. They were celebrating a religious festival at the time, but they assumed that once their presence was felt in the area the Athenians would run away. The majority of the Spartan army was in Attica, engaging in its usual raids, and the soldiers in Sparta itself had no intention of moving until they knew that this force was on its way back.[8] When the news did reach the army in Attica, the Spartan King Agis marched his army with haste back to Sparta being most vexed about just how close to home the new Athenian fortification was.

Map 12.1: Sieges of Pylos and Sphacteria, overview.

The Siege of Pylos (Thucydides, IV.7–23; Diodorus XXII.61–63.3)

With Agis on his way, Sparta finally released a strong force to head towards Pylos, while simultaneously recalling their fleet of 60 ships in Corcyra to assist them; they also called upon their allies to send troops down.[9] Before the Spartan fleet arrived at Pylos, Demosthenes had himself sent word of the present danger to an Athenian fleet, harbouring at the nearby island of Zacynthus, and requested their help. This fleet was en route by the time the Spartans had disembarked and begun to plan their assault on the Athenian stronghold.

The Spartan plan was simple enough, they were going to use a two-pronged attack by land and sea, and attempt to storm the fort and overwhelm what they believed to be a hastily constructed wall and a miniscule garrison. If they had failed to achieve this by the time the Athenian fleet had arrived, they intended to block the entrances to the harbour using their own fleet, thus preventing the Athenians from having any naval support.[10] But this did not solve all of their problems. It was always possible that the Athenian fleet could land on the island of Sphacteria, which lay just off the coast opposite Pylos, and fortify yet another position. To pre-empt this, Sparta sent a small detachment to defend the island, thus preventing Athens from landing anywhere in the vicinity of Pylos.[11]

Demosthenes did not wait for the Spartan assault to begin. He was a man of action and quickly increased his numbers by giving shields to the ship's rowers and recruiting forty Messenian hoplites that, by chance, happened to be in the vicinity. He set his men defensive positions within the fortress, anticipating where the Spartans would most likely attack. He then handpicked sixty hoplites and a group of archers to join him outside the walls, on the beach side, where he believed the Spartan naval force would try to land.

In light of the struggle that awaited them, Demosthenes gave a speech in which he highlighted the advantages that the Athenians held over the Spartans: they were on uneven ground which made it harder for the people landing, the Spartans' numerical superiority was worthless as they would have to land in small groups anyway, and to try landing whilst faced with a strong hoplite formation was exceedingly difficult. As long as the Athenians held their position, they held the advantage.

The Spartan assault began and, just as Demosthenes had predicted, the Spartans attacked by both land and sea in the exact positions he had stationed his men. The Athenians fought bravely, holding their position on the beach as the small Spartan detachments attempted to force a landing. Initially, the Spartans fought with a gusto expected of a proud society that had interlopers in their territory, led from the front by their Spartiate commanders. But as their assaults kept being beaten back, and no ship had successfully disembarked, morale began to fall. Seeing the growing reticence in his men, one of the Spartan trireme captains drove his ship into the beach at full speed in a moment of either inspired leadership or emotional madness. This was none other than Brasidas, the Spartan commander who later became famous for taking Amphipolis in an inspired military campaign through Thrace (see Chapter 3).

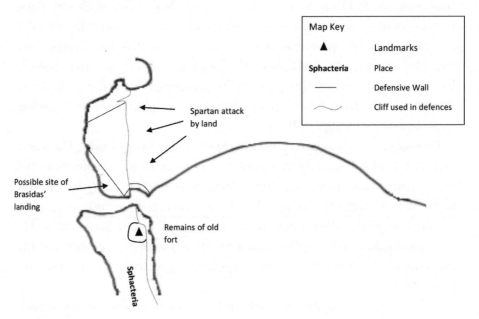

Map 12.2: Siege of Pylos.

But Brasidas was not finished. Once aground, he was the first onto the gangway and into the fray against the Athenian opposition. After receiving innumerable wounds he was eventually forced back, having created a pile of Athenian bodies, to his ship, where he finally fell from his feet and into the bow of the ship. As his strength left him, his arm finally released its vice-like grip on his shield, which slipped from his fingers and into the sea.[12]

The dual assaults continued for another day, with no sign of an Athenian weakness being revealed. The Spartans realized that this was not some ragtag band of disorganized civilians, and that their assaults by land were grossly under-equipped, so they sent a small contingent of their fleet around the south of the Messenian peninsula to Asine in search of timber for siege equipment.[13]

It was now that the Athenian fleet finally arrived; having been reinforced by more ships from Naupactus and by their Chian allies, they brought fifty ships ready for battle. As they arrived they were able to see just how dire a situation Demosthenes was facing. The mainland coast was covered with the movement of hoplites, and the island of Sphacteria was just as active. The only chance of helping Demosthenes was to lift the naval blockade of the harbour. They needed to induce the Spartans to set sail and face the Athenians at sea. The problem was that the Spartans were well aware of their deficiencies and the Athenians were a renowned naval force; there was little chance of the Spartans breaking away from their strong position in the harbour. Yet the Spartans had made one major error in the execution of their plans; they had not successfully blocked the entrances to the harbour. The Athenian fleet saw this weakness and exploited it head on.

Rowing hard into the harbour, the Athenian fleet put the Spartans to flight, taking five ships captive and destroying yet more. Not done, they then turned their prows to the ships that were still mobilizing on the shore. After a devastating ramming they tied them to their own ships and took yet more captives. The Spartan hoplites on land were overcome with shock and fury at the sight of such a disaster. They ignored all elements of logic and rationality and, fully armed, charged into the sea, attempting to pull the ships back onto land. The mêlée would have been horrific, with the added element of uncertain footing in the sandy harbour, the blood-frothed sea lashing against the heavy armour weighing everyone down. Amazingly, the Spartans were able to reclaim a few ships, pulling them back onto the beach, but the damage had already been done. Control of the harbour had been lost to the Athenians, and the Spartan force on Sphacteria was now cut off from the mainland. Having erected their trophy, the Athenians were cruising around the harbour and gloating in their victory. The Spartans on the mainland could do little for their compatriots on the island, they just had to stay where they were in front of Pylos and wait for developments.

When news reached Sparta the reaction was immediate, something very uncommon for the Spartans. They sent officials to Pylos to assess the situation in full and then to make the necessary arrangements. Once they arrived and saw the full extent of the disaster that had occurred, they sent envoys to Athens to negotiate the release of the Spartan men on the island.

The strength of negotiations lay with Athens, who did remarkably well out of it: the Spartans would give the Athenians at Pylos all of the ships that had fought in the sea battle and would make no attack on the fortifications.[14] For their part, the Athenians were to allow the Spartans on the mainland to send provisions to those on the island, but it had to be done openly, under the watchful eyes of the Athenians, to prevent any secret reinforcing or evacuation. The Athenians were given further permission to guard the island by sea, as they were already doing, but could not land on it nor attack the force that was there.

The Spartan situation was a dire one. Athens had a foothold in Spartan lands and were holding over 100 fully fledged Spartiates hostage. They offered Athens a peace treaty, in an attempt to secure the fragility of their home front, but amazingly Athens refused. The Athenians smelled the weakness of the Spartans and wanted more. They demanded that the Spartans restore many of the cities that had been liberated from Athenian control, but Sparta could not agree to this and suffer a loss of face with their allies. They asked for time to confer but the Athenians, headed by Cleon, got angry and demanded a response there and then – the answer had to be no.[15]

Once the envoys returned to Pylos, so did the conflict. The Spartans asked for their ships back but the Athenians refused, claiming that the Spartans had broken the armistice early with an unauthorized attack on Pylos. Sparta denied the claim and so war broke out once again. Pylos went back under siege and the Athenian fleet, reinforced with another twenty ships (now numbering seventy in total) reinstated the blockade of the island.

The Siege of Sphacteria (Thucydides, IV.26–38; Diodorus, XII. 63.4–5)

The situation in Pylos was bad indeed; the Athenians were low on drinking water. Even though the fortress had a natural spring inside it, it was too small for the number of men and many were forced to dig into the beaches and drink any water they could find. They also suffered with cramped conditions, the fort was very narrow and, for want of room, many Athenians had to eat their meals on the beach or in the harboured ships. What made matters worse for the besieged Athenians was that the Spartans on Sphacteria should have been suffering even more, but they did not seem to be. The island had an even poorer supply of water and it was assumed the Spartan garrison would not last more than a few days – and yet there they were, stoutly holding out without any sign of discomfort.

What the Athenians did not know was that the Spartans on the mainland had promised legal freedom to any *helot* who would risk sailing supplies over to the island, and high prizes of reward to freemen to do the same. It was mostly *helots* that took up the challenge, who used the cover of darkness to sail to the island from the western side in high winds and were able to avoid being discovered by the Athenian fleet. The *helots* ignored the value of their boats and, more often than not, chose to ram them into the shore as they landed in the hope of getting to the garrison that much quicker. But not everyone escaped capture, for those who did not want to take this very dangerous option chose instead to attempt their journey by daylight and, inevitably, got caught. Those without boats even attempted to swim across, dragging the supplies in skins behind them; but the Athenians soon got wise to this and assigned lookouts.

Back in Athens, the mood of confidence was quickly changing to one of concern. The men in Pylos were suffering and there was no way of resupplying them; winter was soon coming which would most likely end any hope the Athenians had in their siege; the blockade of an island without any harbour was both costly and inefficient and would have to be ended, which meant the Spartans could get their men back and remove one of Athens' great bargaining chips. But, most concerning of all, the Spartans had not sent any more envoys – just how strong a position were Sparta in to not have to open any new negotiations?

The people of Athens quickly turned on Cleon, whom they blamed for not taking the peace treaty offered by Sparta originally. Cleon had to respond, so he proposed that a force be sent to take Sphacteria once and for all. He suggested his rival, the general Nicias, to lead the expedition, but what transpired was for Cleon to be shamed into taking command himself.[16] Cleon announced that he would not take any citizens from the city, instead choosing the force of Lemnians and Imbrians that were present in Athens.[17] To this he added a small force of *peltasts* that had arrived from Aenus and 400 archers from another area outside of Athens. He intended to utilize the Athenian force already in Pylos and, to that end, announced that Demosthenes would act as his colleague.

Back in Pylos, Demosthenes had not been static. He had intended to conduct his own amphibious raid on the island, and began his preparations in haste. His greatest concern was that the island had, until now, been uninhabited so the woodland was thick and without paths. This favoured the defenders, who could easily destroy a much larger force using their concealment to aid a guerrilla style of warfare. There were further concerns: the heavy woodland meant that he could not reliably establish intelligence regarding the Spartan position, plus it was likely that the Spartans would by now know the terrain and exploit the Athenians' ignorance. It was a similar situation in Aetolia that had led Demosthenes to disaster a year ago, so he was understandably cautious.[18]

Luck was on Demosthenes' side again. One of his men had landed on the island, for want of room to eat his dinner, and accidently begun a small fire. The wind soon carried this little flame and, by the time it was noticed, most of the woodland had caught ablaze. When the flames had finished their work, Demosthenes finally had a clear view of the Spartan force, and fortunately at that because he had underestimated its size.

As he began preparations to make the assault, Cleon finally arrived with his reinforcements. Having met up with Demosthenes, Cleon sent a herald to the Spartans outside of Pylos, telling them to order the island to surrender itself. The Spartans obviously refused and the Athenians set out that night, landing on the island at dawn.

Cleon's landing force was 800 strong and they beached on both the eastern and western side of the island in as few boats as possible, to elude detection.[19] Once aground, the Athenians ran to meet the first Spartan post toward the middle of the island. Catching the 30-strong garrison by surprise, they put many of the small Spartan force to the sword. As day broke, the rest of the Athenian forces landed: almost all of the ships' crews, lightly armed; 800 archers; 800 *peltasts*; and innumerable Messenian reinforcements as well as the rest of the Pylos force (not including a garrison left in the fortress), giving a fighting force of well over 2,500 men.

Yet even with this vast numerical superiority – remembering that the Spartans only had around 420 hoplites on the island – Demosthenes' tactics did not include any form of close combat battle. Instead, he split his forces into companies of around 200 men and got them to occupy the highest ground. He intended to bombard the Spartans in their defensive positions without giving them a tangible opponent to sally against. Using a system of cross-fire, he would immobilize the Spartans, as they would become even more vulnerable if they pursued one of the many missile forces.

Map 12.3: Siege of Sphacteria, phase 1.

The Spartan commander, Epitades, saw the first outpost overwhelmed by the Athenian army and decided to go out and engage with the Athenian hoplites, ignoring the impending encirclement of his own men by the enemy's light infantry. Walking straight into Demosthenes' plans, Epitades' men could not ignore the cross-fire and, with each small contingent breaking off to chase down the assailants, the Spartan morale dropped with each failed venture.

With their men becoming demoralized and physically tired from chasing shadows, the Spartans began to slow down and fight with much less enthusiasm. The Athenians were quite the contrary. With morale at an all-time high they saw the infamous Spartan hoplites weakening under the weight of their armour. Now the reality of their numerical advantage hit home. The legendary status of Spartan warriors had been shown wanting. Fear and apprehension was converted to disdain in the hearts of the Athenians and they poured from the hills and woodland upon the helpless Spartans, hurling everything and anything they could upon them.

With their war cries they filled the Spartans' ears, as they ran they blinded them with the dust and ash from the newly burnt forest, and upon Epitades' men rained their assault and barrage. This was not hoplite warfare, the warfare of which Sparta were unquestioned masters, this was different and it was destructive. The Spartan spirit would not break, but neither that nor their helmets were enough to stop the missiles; their bodies could not sustain the wounds, but they still had no real force to confront in the conventional style.[20] As bodies began to fall and the wounded resembled pin cushions rather than warriors, the remaining Spartan force closed their ranks into a tight formation and began an ordered retreat to the last outpost on the northern coast.

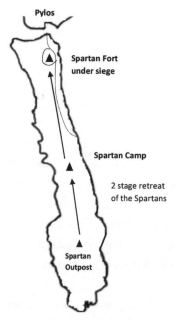

Map 12.4: Siege of Sphacteria, phase 2.

Seeing the legendary Spartan scarlet in retreat emboldened the victorious light infantry. With their screams growing louder and louder they chased down and killed any Spartans they could get their hands on. By the time Epitades and his men made it to the last defensive position, they had just enough time to station the soldiers for the ensuing assault. The Spartans had picked their position well, they held the higher ground and the Athenians could not encircle the fort, they had to rely solely on frontal assaults. The siege raged on for most of that day, with neither side faltering in the face of thirst or the heat of the summer sun.

With this stalemate, the battle could have raged for days. The Spartans had nullified all of the Athenian advantages and were in a good position for a hoplite force to hold out, especially one with Spartan discipline. But they had neglected to protect the cliff face to their north, considering it a perfect natural defence.[21] Cleon and Demosthenes were asked by the commander of the Messenians, Comon, to give him a force of light-armed troops and archers with which he hoped to find a way to get behind the fort and exploit this Spartan oversight.[22]

With an agility that was not possible for heavily armed hoplites, the small force made it around the fort and they took to the higher ground overlooking the Spartans. The Spartans had no response, they had been outmanoeuvred and were left at the mercy of their enemy. Demosthenes and Cleon had successfully surrounded the fort, it was now just a matter of what to do – destroy the Spartan force to a man, or offer them the chance to surrender? They chose the latter, for there could be no greater prize than to take full Spartiate prisoners back to Athens.

They made their offer to the Spartans, who were well aware of the precarious position they were now in. They had already lost their leader, Epitades, in the fighting and his second-in-command was dying from his wounds; they had also lost 130 of their comrades. They asked to be allowed to contact the Spartan force on the mainland with the proposal. The Athenians allowed it but sent one of their own heralds rather than allow even one Spartan to be released. Messages passed back and forth to the mainland until finally the last message from the mainland was definitive: 'Decide for yourselves so long as you do nothing dishonourable'.

The Spartans on the island consulted for a short time before deciding on the unimaginable, a move that sent shockwaves through the Greek world – the Spartans surrendered.

The Aftermath

With that, the 70-day siege came to an end. The Athenians raised their trophy and took 292 Spartans, 120 of whom were full Spartiates, back to the city to be used as a bartering tool for the rest of the war. For Greece, the myth of Spartan invincibility was severely shaken. Not only were they defeated, but the manner of the surrender revealed the limitations of the greatest army in the land. As the prisoners were marched through the streets of Athens one man berated them, saying that their fallen comrades were the bravest and most noble of them. But the prisoners had not lost their laconic tongue, one responded with equal derision that a spindle would be worth a great deal if it could pick out the bravest and most noble men. Referring to javelins and arrows as spindles implied they were the tools of women.

Whilst the Spartans and Athenians withdrew from Pylos, the Messenians from Naupactus sent a force to the area to start raiding Laconia. This caused a level of destruction that forced the Spartans to repeatedly pursue peace treaties with Athens, so that they could deal with this incursion. Sparta was on the brink of a *helot* revolt and Athens would get no better opportunity to exploit this internal weakness. The war raged on.

Chapter 13

The Siege of Syracuse (415–413 BC)

The Background (Thucydides, III.86–88, 115–IV.1, VI.6–71; Diodorus, XII.82.3–XIII.6; Plutarch, *Life of Nicias*, 12–16)

An Athenian presence on Sicily had been established in 427 BC, when the city of Leontini beseeched Athens to aid them against the aggression of Syracuse, whose forces had besieged the city. Athens agreed to help for three reasons: firstly, Leontini had an ancient alliance with Athens, based upon their common Ionian descent, which compelled them to aid each other; secondly, Athens had half an eye on taking control of all of Sicily and needed more reconnaissance before committing to a campaign of that size; finally, there was the benefit of allowing the Athenians to blockade the vast corn supplies being sent from the island to Athens' enemies in the Peloponnese.[1]

Athens sent out a fleet and based it in the pro-Athenian city of Rhegium, at the tip of the 'boot' of Italy. From here they began a series of raids into Sicily and committed themselves to engaging in a fruitless conflict that lasted three years, until a temporary peace treaty was signed and the Athenian force sailed home in 424 BC. So enraged were the people of Athens by this failure to dominate Sicily, as it was unfairly assumed that they could, the commanders of the fleet were both fined under the charge of taking bribes to leave.

Athenian attention did not return to Sicily for another nine years, seven of which were taken up by the fragile 'Peace of Nicias' treaty that did not really bring peace to Greece, but certainly restrained the two main participants of Sparta and Athens in their actions. However, the Sicilian issue reared its ugly head in the winter of 416/5 BC when envoys from one of Athens' Sicilian allies, Egesta, called once again on Athenian aid and assistance in the wake of Syracusan domination.

Egesta had engaged in a confrontation with neighbouring Selinus over boundary issues. Selinus went to Syracuse for help and, in turn, forced Egesta to look externally for help: originally they went to Syracuse, then Carthage, until it had to turn to its old ally, Athens.[2] The concern for Athens was that, if Syracuse was able to eradicate the Athenian support on Sicily, then, in all likelihood, the pro-Peloponnesian elements on the island would summon together an army to send in aid of the Spartan cause. The Athenians were apprehensive, they were not convinced by the idea of embarking on – or more importantly *financing* – such a large enterprise. To take on Syracuse was to embark on a war as considerable as the one they had been fighting against the Peloponnesians; and although the peace treaty was formally in place, who knew how long that would last?

Egesta gave promises of financing the expedition themselves, but Athens was suspicious of such claims and agreed to send out envoys to assess the situation in Sicily, as well as confirm the amount of treasure that the Egestans had available. When they returned, they brought with them assurances of the financial support available, as well as a down payment of sixty talents to cover a month's pay for sixty ships that the Egestans wanted sent as soon as possible. Unfortunately for Athens, the Egestans had lied and deceived the envoys. They did not have the money to support any great expedition, the money and wealth they displayed had been borrowed from the citizens and neighbouring allies, all in an attempt to convince the Athenians to intercede in their cause.[3]

Athens voted to send sixty ships to aid the Egestans, the fleet also being tasked with restoring the Leontines to their city.[4] Finally, their job was to put Sicilian affairs into an order that favoured Athens; meaning that diplomacy was as large a part of this expedition as conflict was. This venture had popular support, but it also had its disparagers, not least of which was one of the commanders for the expedition, Nicias. His concern lay in the fragility of the peace treaty in Greece and the opportunity this venture would give to Athenian enemies nearer to home. He also pointed out that the distance from Athens to Sicily was so great it was unfathomable how they intended to keep it subdued permanently, assuming that they actually succeeded in taking control of the island. But popular opinion remained against him and another of the elected commanders, Alcibiades, further enflamed their desire for action.

To this affront, Nicias proposed a new argument – the venture was very dangerous, and Syracuse was very powerful, for Athens to succeed it would need to send a much bigger force. Nicias' aim was to discourage the voters by increasing the Athenian commitment of men as well as money. Unfortunately for him, the Athenians agreed and voted to give the commanders the power to recruit over 5,000 hoplites, a further 40 triremes to add to the original 60, as well as archers, slingers and mercenaries.[5]

The sight of the completed fleet was one to behold. It was so magnificent a spectacle that huge throngs of the citizen body went to the Piraeus to wave off their friends and family on their voyage. Only as their goodbyes were being said did it finally hit home just how dangerous and precarious an expedition this was. It was not an unprecedented size of armada, but the amount of pomp and ceremony that surrounded their voyage, combined with the size of the entire venture made this undoubtedly the most impressive force sent out by any *polis* to date.[6] After the necessary libations, prayers and songs, the fleet began its long voyage west, stopping at Corcyra first to meet up with the allied forces that were joining the expedition.

In Syracuse, word came early of the Athenian fleet's intent but it was not taken seriously by many. The political instability within the city came to the fore as speakers like Hermocrates, who warned of the impending danger, were accused of fear mongering for their own political gain. After all, Athens was far too small to try something as foolish as to attack Syracuse.

The Athenian fleet moved out of Corcyra and settled at Rhegium, before deciding on their next plan of action. It was here that they received two very concerning bits of news. First, Rhegium refused to join in the Athenian cause, deciding they would rather remain neutral. Secondly, the Athenians finally discovered the deception of the Egestans, who, as it transpired, could only supply a further thirty talents to fund the expedition. Now the Athenians had to re-design their plans; they had relied upon the financial and physical support of their allies around Sicily but, without it, what could Athens really achieve?

Nicias suggested that they engage with Selinus, as was first suggested, and use this as a show of strength before returning home. Alcibiades was against the disgrace of going home early, suggesting that they stay put in Rhegium and secure the allegiances of all of the other Sicilian cities before continuing in their original aims of attacking Selinus and Syracuse. The third commander, Lamachus, suggested taking swift action and attacking Syracuse while it was still ill-prepared. By utilizing the elements of shock and surprise he expected the Athenians to be victorious, thus preventing Syracuse from being able to accumulate Sicilian allies, who would be more likely to wait and see which *polis* was the more powerful before committing to one side or the other.

By way of a vote, the decision was made to try Alcibiades' plan and send out envoys to the various cities. But, when they came back with negative responses, the Athenians decided to sail to Sicily and try to use the threat of force to help these cities change their mind. They began to raid through Syracusan lands, they even had some luck in convincing cities to allow them inside their walls. But this rampaging was cut short by an envoy from Athens with a summons for Alcibiades; he was to stand trial for blasphemy, something he had no intention of doing and, subsequently, he fled into exile.[7] With his departure, the two remaining commanders split their force but achieved very little on the Sicilian coast.

Syracuse had been receiving reports from all over Sicily regarding the Athenians' actions, and the people were fed up with the indignity of not opposing it. They began by sending out small forces to wherever they knew the Athenians were, these actions were to present a presence rather than a serious confrontation. But the Athenian commanders noticed the pattern and exploited it for their gain. Tricking Syracuse into sending a larger force to the city of Catana, the Athenians sailed around the coast and landed outside of Syracuse herself, taking up a strong position from which to prepare for battle. By the time the Syracusans had realized what had happened, they could do little more that return in haste and prepare for combat.

The Battle of Anapus River (415/4 BC) was hard fought, with both sides seemingly evenly matched until Syracuse's inexperience was revealed and, with the help of a storm, the Athenians broke their lines and won the day. After this, Athens planned its campaign for the spring, while Syracuse prepared itself for a siege; extending their walls, and fortifying key positions and areas they expected Athens to confront.

The Siege (Thucydides, VI.88–VII.87; Diodorus, XIII.7–34; Plutarch, *Life of Nicias*, 17–29)

Both sides went in pursuit of more allies.[8] Athens had drawn first blood and pursued the Sicilian cities with a new optimism that they could garner support, something they succeeded in, especially with the native Sicel people. Syracuse looked to the Peloponnese but, although they had enthusiastic support from their old *metropolis*, Corinth, the Spartans were less enthused. It was not until the Athenian exile, Alcibiades, persuaded them that it was in their interest to curb Athenian control of Sicily that they, finally, agreed to send over a small force under the command of Gylippus.[9]

We are not told how big the Spartan contingent sent was, but we do know that Gylippus only requested two ships, so it was certainly not any real army to speak of. In reality Sparta was sending one of their commanders to assist and advise in the defence of Syracuse, which, taking into account the size of Syracuse and its population, was probably something they needed more than numbers, even if those numbers would have been made up of Spartans.

In the summer of 414 BC, the first concern for Syracuse was the prominent position of Epipolae, a vast highland overlooking the city to the immediate north of the walls. If the Athenians took control of it then they held a distinct advantage in being able to see every happening within the city. The Syracusan college of generals decided to form a core troop of 600 hoplites under the command of Diomilus, with the job of holding the position against the Athenians. Rather unfortunately, while they were assigning Diomilus and his men their role to the south of the city, the Athenians had already landed in Leon and made a forced march to Eureyelus on the north-western point of Epipolae.

In a panic, Diomilus ran his men over the three miles to try to confront the Athenians before they were able to establish their position, but they were disorganized and were easily defeated, losing around 300 hoplites and Diomilus' own life.[10] After returning the dead, Athens descended onto Syracuse in the hope that they would send out an army to face them, with no success. So Athens returned to the high ground and established a fort at Labdalum, to hold their money and equipment whilst they were besieging the city.

Athens soon received reinforcements from their new Sicel allies and, along with those sent from Naxos and other cities, their ranks swelled with a surge of cavalry who, combined with the original Athenian cavalry force, now numbered 650 horses. This was perfect for their next venture, because they intended to start their siege works and circumvallate the city, which would have made their working parties vulnerable to enemy cavalry.

The Athenians marched quickly to the southern side of Epipolae to Syca and built a circular fort, which would form the central point of the blockading wall. The generals in Syracuse were concerned with the efficiency and speed with which the fort went up, and the wall was most likely going to be put up just as fast, so they hastily sent out an army to disrupt the construction. By the time the Syracusans reached the Athenians, the enemy were already in battle order, the high ground was working its magic and the inexperience of Syracuse was exposed once again, so the generals recalled them rather than witness another massacre. The cavalry was left to try and continue the disruptions, but they were soon seen off by the superior Athenian cavalry and a single unit of hoplites. Building resumed as the Athenians sent the wall on a northern circuit around the city first, which would end at Trogilus on the eastern coast.[11]

Syracuse knew it could not confront the Athenians in battle, choosing instead to build their own counter-walls that would disrupt the Athenian siege works. They started building out towards where the Athenians would logically build their southern circuit of the wall, with the intention of bisecting it. Athens allowed the counter-wall to be built without resistance. They did not want to split their force or slow down the construction of their own wall, but they succeeded in their own act of sabotage by destroying the underground pipes that brought fresh water into Syracuse.

Syracuse left a small force to man the counter-wall, while the rest of their forces retreated to the city. But, because the Athenians had not attacked the garrison, they became complacent. Biding their time, Athens handpicked a crack force of 300 men who attacked and pursued the garrison, who took refuge in the outworks of a statue of Apollo Temenites, followed behind by the rest of the army.[12] Although the Syracusans beat them back, the aim of the Athenians was not to take the meagre lives of the garrison, but to tear down the counter-wall, which they then did while stealing the poles from the palisade to add to their own building materials.

The Athenians restarted their construction work, sending a wall out of the circle fort to encircle the south of the city. Syracuse resurrected their tactics for delay; they began another counter-wall further south than the first, but they also dug a large ditch with it to prevent the Athenians from continuing their wall down to the Great Harbour. The Athenians saw this begin and, after finishing their first section to the cliff edge of Epipolae, they descended upon the Syracusans before they had even completed the original palisade.

A swift battle ensued before the Syracusans were forced into retreat, but in the confusion of combat Athens suffered losses, including one of their generals, Lamachus.[13] Seeing the change in fortune, many who had fled to Syracuse came out of the city to further oppose the Athenians on the plain. These were in addition to a force who went up to the circle fort, in an attempt to take control of it whilst it was so weakly defended. They succeeded in destroying 1,000 feet of the Athenian outer works but, thanks to the ingenuity of Nicias, the circle fort was saved.

Nicias had remained at the fort because he was taken with illness, but with no garrison to defend the works he had to take drastic action. He ordered his servants to set fire to the siege engines, and the timber that lay outside of the fort, to delay any assault on his position. It worked, the Syracusan force retreated before the flames and, seeing that the Athenians had finally driven off their enemy in the plain and that the Athenian fleet was beginning to enter the Great Harbour, they returned to the city.

All hope was lost. Athens had taken the Great Harbour, they had received further reinforcements from their allies, and Syracuse could not stop the growth of the encircling wall. Factionalism broke out in the city and the generals were removed from their posts, while they began to discuss the options of surrender. With Syracuse on its knees, Nicias' army began to close in around the city, ready to choke it until they relented.[14]

With the ring of walls almost closed, a single ship arrived carrying the Corinthian Gongylus, who brought word for the Syracusans: Gylippus the Spartan had arrived and would be with them very soon.[15] With a surge of hope injected into the people of Syracuse, they sent out a force to meet him.

Gylippus, for his part, had been marching through Sicily, obtaining allies and growing his army. With it he marched up Epipolae, via Euryelus, and, after meeting with the army of Syracuse, he marched directly towards the Athenian lines.

It was a stalemate, neither side would instigate combat. Gylippus was well aware of how disorganized the Syracusan element of his army was, so he could not risk the exposure of an offensive action. For their part, the Athenians were safe behind their walls but they were also in a slight state of chaos over the sudden arrival of this Peloponnesian force. Gylippus was the first to act. Waiting a day, he set his army into a battle formation in front of the Athenians and sent one contingent off to attack the poorly guarded fort at Labdalum. With no chance of relief from the main Athenian army, the fort was put to the sword.

After this success, Syracuse began yet another counter-wall which intended to intercept the unfinished wall from the circle fort to Trogilus. Gylippus ordered an ill-fated attempt to attack an Athenian force close to the fortifications, nullifying his superior cavalry from influencing the battle.[16] It was a mistake he quickly learned from, and when Nicias sent out his forces to face the Syracusans a few days later, Gylippus took his army further away from the walls before forming its lines. During the ensuing battle, the Syracusan cavalry attacked and routed the Athenian left wing, while the rest of their army soon fell back from the Syracusan pressure to the centre. As the Syracusans rested and continued their wall it must have occurred to them that they had just beaten the Athenians in open battle, the tide was most definitely turning.

With the counter-wall complete, Athens was left impotent and lacking in motivation. While Syracuse grew from strength to strength, calling more and more allies to their cause of removing the invaders, Nicias called on Athens to send more support or else he would have to bring his army home. He also requested to be allowed to relinquish his command, as he was still struggling with illness. Athens agreed to reinforcements of 1,200 hoplites on 65 ships, to be headed by Demosthenes, the hero of Olpae and Pylos, but refused Nicias' resignation and sent two more commanders to assist him.[17] The Peloponnesian powers, likewise, sent reinforcements to Sicily: Sparta sent 600 non-Spartiate hoplites, the Boeotians sent 300, Corinth sent 500, and Sicyon sent a further 200 hoplites.

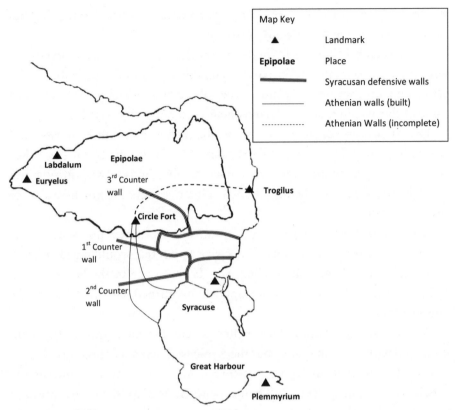

Map 13.1: Siege of Syracuse.

Gylippus was buoyed by the military and diplomatic successes of late and encouraged Syracuse to develop this further. By 413 BC, he convinced them to build and train a large fleet, to confront the Athenians at sea as well as on land. With the support of Hermocrates he persuaded them and, with his new fleet, Gylippus set his eyes on the fortified position of Plemmyrium, which Athens had established in the Great Harbour to protect their naval supply lines.

With great speed and efficiency, Gylippus' men took the fortified position, nullifying the, understandable, disappointment of the subsequent defeat of his fleet in the Great Harbour. The Athenians were in a panic, their grip over the Great Harbour was slipping from them, and their morale was at an all-time low. Even with their reinforcements on the way, they would have to arrive very soon, or else it would not be a matter of Athens retreating but rather Athens being thrown out, or worse.

Nicias used his alliances in Sicily to slow down the rate of reinforcements entering Syracuse. In one instance a conglomeration of Sicel tribes laid a set of traps and ambushed a large force, killing 800 soldiers and envoys. But none of this would matter if Demosthenes did not arrive with his army.

The Syracusans did not wait, they launched a joint attack by land and sea with great success. Consistently taking the Athenians by surprise they were able to press home their advantage; finally the tide was turning and the Athenian threat was being subdued. That was, until Demosthenes' force finally arrived.

With a new flush of morale and optimism, the Athenians went on the offensive once more, in search of a decisive action that would make or break their expedition. Demosthenes began by laying waste to the lands around Syracuse and, after receiving no opposition, turned his attention to the counter-wall.

Without any hesitation, Demosthenes sent his men against the wall, equipped with battering rams, but the Syracusan defenders used fire thrown down from the walls to negate that threat. After his army was consistently repelled from scaling the walls, Demosthenes decided to change his approach and attack Epipolae itself at night.[18] His force, which was 20,000 strong and split roughly evenly between hoplites and light-armed troops, scaled up by the Euryelus fort and quickly overwhelmed the small garrison there.[19] The Athenians pressed on and swiftly saw off the Syracusan forces camped along the plateau who had heard the alarms. By the time Gylippus and his forces had arrived, the Athenians were organised and pressing on across Epipolae.

The Syracusan army was not prepared for this audacious night attack and soon capitulated to the disciplined Athenian line. As they ran, the Athenians could not help themselves; they pursued, like dogs on a hunt, breaking up their formidable lines in their lust for blood. It was the small Boeotian element of Syracuse's army that noticed the break in the Athenian formation and took the educated gamble that, if they could form themselves into a strong formation, they would hold the tactical advantage.

Their gamble paid off and, by confronting the disordered waves of Athenian hoplites, they turned them to rout. What transpired next, tactically, has not been recorded, the battle broke down into complete chaos. Men were terrified in the darkness, the moon presented the only light available on the battlefield. The Athenians could not trust who were their allies and who were the enemy, so ended up killing anyone they came across. The Syracusans quickly learned the Athenian watchword, allowing any groups broken off or separated from the army to make their way back through enemy lines safely – the Athenians had no such luck. The constant cheering and yelling from Gylippus' men made it impossible for orders to travel the battlefield. Many of the Athenians were new to the island and did not know the terrain very well, and the narrow descent from Epipolae meant that many fell to their deaths after stumbling in the dark.

By morning, most of the surviving Athenians had made it away safely, and the Syracusans raised two trophies; one at the point of Athenian ascent onto Epipolae and the other where the Boeotians made their stand. After this surging victory for Syracuse, Gylippus knew that he needed to be quick in order to capitalize on it. He began a new diplomatic campaign bringing in more allies, more support to help him in his final push to remove Athens from the island. With this last Athenian offensive resisted, the siege was finally over.

The Aftermath

Down in the Athenian camp, to the southeast of Syracuse, all talk was of going home. The army was weak, the men were tired and disgruntled, it was the high season for disease in a campaigning army, and Demosthenes proposed that they return to Athens to help them in a growing crisis that superseded their role in Sicily.[20] Nicias talked them out of the move, arguing that Syracuse would also be struggling and that the greater honour was to die in battle than to be executed back in Athens for so public a failure and retreat.

They decided to stay exactly where they were for now, but when Gylippus arrived back with more allies and movements were made to restart the conflict with a direct assault on the Athenians. Nicias finally relented and agreed to move to a more favourable position. The gods, it seems, disagreed, with a lunar eclipse being interpreted as an omen. This began a chain of events that ended in an unforeseeable disaster for Athens. As the eclipse ended, Nicias declared that the Athenians would stay where they were for a further twenty-seven days, as demanded by the soothsayers.[21]

Gylippus, for his part, demanded his men partake in more training on and off the sea and, when he felt they were ready, he moved into the harbour to take on the Athenian fleet. He succeeded and, with this naval victory, Syracuse had finally impaired the Athenian position and ultimately destroyed their morale. Syracuse had, for the first time since 415 BC, taken back control of the Great Harbour. Their thoughts no longer lay with survival, but with how to crush the Athenians and not allow any of them to escape.

Gylippus blocked off the harbour with small boats, to prevent any attempt by the Athenians to flee; so the only way out was for the Athenians to man their remaining fleet and try one last-gasp effort to fight their way out. They called upon as many of their men as they could, thinning their defensive lines to just those on the harbour, and fought one of the greatest naval battles ever seen in the classical Greek world. After hard fighting and much blood spilt, Syracuse finally took the day.

The shock was palpable. In their emotionally numb state, the Athenians had even forgotten to request the return of the bodies of their fallen comrades.[22] The Athenians had been decisively beaten on the sea. No amount of cajoling or inspiring from the generals was going to convince the soldiers to man even more ships and attempt a second battle. Their cause was lost. Their only hope was to march overland, re-evaluate their options and try to find another way home.

Hermocrates was concerned that the Athenians would try to slip away at night, so he sent them false information that the roads were all guarded and that they were better off waiting a day to recover first. The Athenians heeded the warning and took the day to pack up their equipment; all the while, Syracuse was sending out troops to strategic locations along the roads that could be used to march inland.

The next day, a sorrowful and remorseful Athenian army marched out of camp and headed inland. Although 40,000 strong, they did not resemble a fighting force anymore, but a gaggle of men in fear of capture and disgrace. As they marched, the Syracusans never let them settle, forcing them to fight every step of the way. The Athenians first headed north but, under relentless pressure from cavalry and missiles, they never had a moment's rest.

With setback after setback, the Athenians decided to make a run for it, heading south and as far away from Syracuse as possible. Before too long the army became disjointed and ended up in two separate groups, one led by Nicias, the other by Demosthenes.

As they were both swiftly surrounded, they negotiated terms. Demosthenes asked that none of his men be killed, and promised that they all would go quietly; the Syracusans agreed and 6,000 Athenians surrendered. Nicias, on the other hand, offered to pay for the freedom of the Athenian army which Syracuse refused – why should they let this Athenian force go when they were in such a strong position? – and Gylippus attacked Nicias' army with missiles.

As morning broke, with his men running low on food and starved of water, Nicias aimed to make it to the Assinarus River. On arrival, however, he found a Syracusan force waiting for him. Deranged and delirious, the base need for water overrode all common sense and training, and the Athenians just broke from their ranks and ran into the river to drink. As they drank they were subject to showers of arrows coming from the banks and, when a small band of Peloponnesians arrived, the river became hued with the blood of a massacre. The survivors still stood in the soiled water, drinking the blood-frothed liquor like their lives depended on it.

Three days into the retreat, Nicias finally surrendered to Gylippus and the Athenians were all taken back to Syracuse for trial. Nicias and Demosthenes were executed, much to the dissatisfaction of Gylippus who wanted the honour of taking them back to Sparta as trophies of their success.[23] The remaining 8,000 Athenians were kept in the quarries for months before either dying or living long enough to be sold into slavery.

Chapter 14

The Siege of the Drilae (400 BC)

The Background (Xenophon, *Anabasis*, II.1–V.1.16)

In 401 BC, the rebellious Persian prince, Cyrus the Younger, was defeated at the Battle of Cunaxa (see Chapter 17 for the battle itself). The contingent of Greek mercenaries that provided a strong infantry core to Cyrus' army refused to lay down their weapons and accept defeat. They asked to be allowed to leave the Persian Empire fully armed, without fear of assault from any Persian armies. The Greeks were not granted their full request, but they were allowed to begin their exodus with constant Persian supervision whilst a truce was being negotiated.

After much to-ing and fro-ing, the Persians managed to manipulate the fears of the Greek commander, Clearchus the Spartan, convincing him that his own army contained troublemakers that were trying to coordinate with the Persians to remove Clearchus from power. Clearchus had many interesting personal traits, but the most dominant was his paranoia, so it did not take long for him to be convinced that there was a plot aimed against him.[1] He agreed to another meeting with the Persians, which would include all of the Greek commanders. Walking like lambs to the slaughter, the trap was sprung and the commanders were all taken as prisoners and subsequently executed over the next 2 years.[2]

The Persian plan was to cause panic in the Greek ranks, and it worked. The night they received the news of what had befallen their commanders, many of the men could not sleep. Those that could, slept wherever they found themselves, rather than in camp with their weapons. They were stranded in close proximity to the Persian King's headquarters, they were surrounded by the enemy on all sides, they had no guide to show them how to get home, and home itself was over 1,100 miles away.[3]

When morning came, the Greeks called a meeting to vote on what to do next. They elected new commanders, with another Spartan, Chirisophus, taking overall charge. Our main written source for the expedition, Xenophon, was given charge of the rear, alongside another inexperienced commander named Timasion. The immediate concern, and a concern that would haunt the Greeks through their entire ordeal, was a lack of supplies, so they began to move out in search of some.

A Persian force of 200 horsemen and 400 slingers and archers, under the command of Mithridates, began to harass the Greeks at every turn. The speed and mobility of this small force was unmatched by anything the Greeks could muster; they were just a force of slow-moving hoplites and a few lightly armed men. With unabated success, the Persians saw their chance to remove this Greek embarrassment from their lands and Mithridates returned with 1,000 horsemen and 400 slingers and archers. But the Greeks had not stayed idle. They realized their exposed weakness of immobility and went some way to rectifying it by allocating horses within the supply train to 50 capable horsemen. They also allocated the Rhodian contingent of their army to lay down their hoplite weaponry and assume the duties of slingers, a skill the men of Rhodes were renowned for.[4] These, combined with the small force of *peltasts* that was already in place, gave the Greek force a mobile arm. Its sole purpose was to chase the Persians off and inflict losses on them, as easily as they did on the Greeks. The plan worked and Mithridates' army was forced into a retreat, losing many men in the process.[5]

The Greeks continued their march, following the River Tigris north, with Mithridates a constant thorn in their side. As the Persian pressure kept mounting and army morale was beginning to wane, a decision needed to be made regarding the route of the exodus. To the south was the city of Babylon and the bulk of the Persian empire; to the east were Susa and Ecbatana, which were the Spring and Summer residences of the Persian King; to the west was the Greek region of Ionia, but the necessary river crossing was blocked by the Persians. This only left them the option of going north into the mountains of the Carduchians. If they survived this cold and unforgiving terrain they would end up in Armenia and by the Black Sea, which would give them a simple journey back to Greece.[6]

The Carduchians fled before the marching Greeks, up into the mountains. The Greeks did not want to encourage their animosity, so they only took food from the empty villages they passed, but even this was not enough to prevent the odd small-scale assault from Carduchian bands of warriors. By the time the Greeks had reached the mountains proper, the Carduchian resistance was full-scale, and the fighting retreat that had begun in the heart of Persia now continued through the freezing mountains of southern Armenia. They fought for every hill, for every path they wanted to take and for every river they needed to cross until, finally, they left the Carduchians in the gruelling mountains and entered the Armenian plains.

By this time, the Greek army's reputation was preceding its own advance. Western Armenia was run by a favourite of the Persian King, a man called Tiribazus, who requested a conference with the Greek commanders. Here it was negotiated that he would not initiate any violence against them, as long as they, in turn, did not burn any of the houses of his people, although they could take any provisions they needed from the villages. The Greeks quickly agreed to such a fortuitous truce and proceeded north once more.

Heavy snow slowed their march and the truce with Tiribazus was quickly realized to be a stalling tactic of the Persian ruler, so that he could amass an army of mercenaries with which to ambush the Greeks. Fortunately the plan was exposed by a Persian prisoner, but any hope the Greeks had of a simple march through Armenia was very quickly quelled by this betrayal.[7] With no relief from the cold and snow, and constantly on the march as they tried to distance themselves from Tiribazus' army, the Greeks lost thirty men to the weather and many more were showing signs of bulimia, snow blindness, extreme frostbite and even depression.[8]

Descending upon any village they could find in order to rest from the cold, and fill their bellies with food and wine, the Greeks kept marching through Armenia. Once they reached the River Phasis, which formed the border into the lands of the Chalybes, it was not long before resistance was met once more, in the form of an alliance between the Chalybes, the Taochians and Phasians. After defeating this force, they entered the land of the Taochians, in which they quickly ran low on supplies, due to the Taochians having removed all of their provisions and placed them into their heavily protected strongholds. On finding one of these strongholds poorly garrisoned, the Greeks attacked it in search of food. The fighting was fierce and the taking of the stronghold came at a larger and unexpected cost to the Greeks: Xenophon describes with horror the scene of Taochian women throwing their children off the cliff that housed the stronghold, and jumping after them to their deaths.[9]

After resupplying, the Greeks headed west and back into Chalybian territory, fighting for every step of the way. The Greeks finally left Chalybia, after crossing the River Harpasus, with a great appreciation for the fighting prowess and valiant nature of the Chalybes. Their fortunes began to change in the lands of the Scythenians (the south-eastern corner of the Black Sea), where they were able to replenish their supplies and they were even sent a guide by a local ruler. Admittedly, this guide had the sole intention of directing the Greeks through the territory of his ruler's enemies, with the hope that the Greek army would ravage their lands – but still, the Greeks were always happy to gain a guide.

By the fifth day of their guided tour, the Greeks reached the mountain of Theches when they saw the Black Sea for the very first time. 'Thalatta, Thalatta!' went the cry, 'the sea, the sea!' The sight stopped the army in its tracks and they fell into each other's arms, cheering and crying with joy. This was the first moment that the men believed they could make it home, that the worst could be over, and that the family they had been thinking of for so long were within their grasp once again.[10]

Leaving the Scythenians behind them, the Greeks marched through the rather hospitable lands of the Macronians, into the more hostile domain of the Colchians, along the Black Sea itself. Fortunately for Chirisophus and his men, the Colchians did not have the mettle to face the strong hoplite force and never gave any threatening resistance. Once they had reached the Black Sea, the Greeks encamped in some Colchian villages not far from the Greek city of Trapezus. From here Chirisophus' men launched raids on Colchis, with supplies coming in from the Trapezuntians. The Greeks were happy: they were well fed and, after holding an athletic competition, they were well entertained as well.

After the rituals and frivolities came to an end, the time came to decide on the next course of action. The most popular idea was to acquire some ships and sail back to Greece, rather than continue marching overland. Chirisophus was sent to meet with a Spartan naval commander in the region, Anaxibius, with whom he was well acquainted, to try and get the necessary number of boats. While those who were left, under the ostensible command of Xenophon, would try to acquire more ships as well as necessary supplies, and some much-desired booty.

The Siege (Xenophon, *Anabasis*, V.2.1–28)

Organized raiding parties were sent out to forage and plunder the Colchian countryside for what they could, but very few returned with any success. On one occasion, two companies went out under the command of Cleaenetus to attack a well-defended position, but the parties suffered a great many casualties, including Cleaenetus himself. These excursions were dangerous and fruitless; before too long it became impossible to go out, forage and plunder, and return back to camp all in the same day.

Xenophon decided to change tack and uprooted half of his army to penetrate into different lands in search of supplies, while the remaining half held the camp against a possible Cholchian reprisal. With guides from Trapezus directing them, Xenophon and his army marched south into the territory of the Drilae.[11]

The land was rugged and mountainous, and the Drilae themselves were considered the most war-like of all the peoples on the Black Sea. They were pastoralists, yet uncompromising in their methods. When the Greeks advanced into their lands, the Drilae began setting fire to their own villages as they retreated to their strongholds in the mountains. As the Greeks were forced deeper and deeper into their territory they found little for their troubles other than the occasional ox or pig, nothing of great substance. Most of the Drilae had retreated into a central stronghold, referred to by Xenophon as their mother city, and it was here that the Greeks would make the push for their supplies.

From the Greeks' marching route, the stronghold was situated beyond a very deep gully that appeared to surround it. The fortress was built on top of a mound, which was formed from the soil excavated from a large moat which circumnavigated it. Atop this mound was a wooden palisade with defensive towers interspersed at short intervals. Inside of the walls was a small town filled with wooden houses and a strongly defended acropolis.

The Greek army was led by their force of *peltasts*, who ran over 800 metres ahead of the main hoplite force. The *peltasts* were the first to see the stronghold and, after spotting the vast array of livestock available inside the palisades, they raced further ahead, crossing the gully and launching an attack. They were joined by a large group of 'spearmen', combining forces so that the first assault numbered 2,000 lightly armed men.[12] Their attack was grossly unsuccessful; they had underestimated the Drilae and were quickly paying the price.

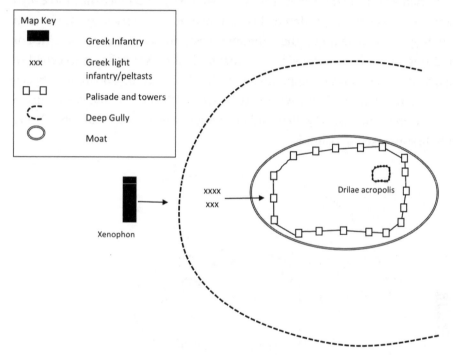

Map 14.1: Siege of the Drilae, phase 1.

As they went to retreat they realized that they could not do so without descending into single file, which would not only slow them but also leave them horribly exposed to the Drilae, who would sally from the palisades and attack them. Unable to move, they sent a messenger to Xenophon asking for help.

Xenophon crossed the gully with his company commanders, leaving the hoplites on the other side while he determined what to do. The question was whether it was best to cut their losses and try to evacuate the isolated assailants as safely as possible, or whether the stronghold could be taken with the hoplite reinforcements? The commanders decided that it was possible to take the stronghold, so that was what they intended to do. This was a foolhardy decision for such a well defended position, but Xenophon trusted his diviners, who had also foreseen in their omens a victory that day, and so he concurred with the other commanders.

Xenophon recalled the *peltasts* from the stronghold, whilst his company commanders brought the hoplites across the gully. Once his force had amassed, Xenophon ordered his commanders to organize their own companies in a manner they thought best, to make the most efficient fighting force. In a masterstroke of manipulation, Xenophon succeeded in exploiting the natural competitiveness that had become apparent between his commanders. Each one wanted to be seen as the bravest and so organized their men in the best way they could to achieve the bravest of all acts – being the first to take the palisade.

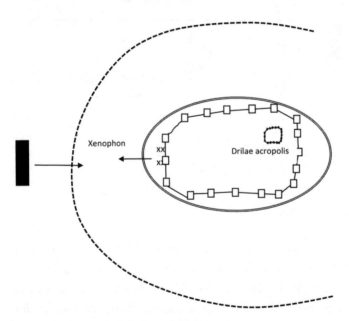

Map 14.2: Siege of the Drilae, phase 2.

Xenophon readied his missile troops, giving strict orders for the *peltasts* to have their javelins looped, the archers to have their arrows notched and the slingers to have their bags full of shot, but none could fire without his signal.[13] Once everyone was ready they stood in a large crescent, due to the terrain, so that they could all see each other. They began to chant the *paean*, the trumpets blew and, with a harrowing war-cry to Enyalius, they charged up the mound to begin the attack.[14]

As they began to run, Xenophon gave his signal and the missiles began to fly – arrows, spears, stones and lead shots, even fire had been brought in an attempt to take the palisade quickly. The sheer weight of the missiles was enough to clear the walls and towers of defenders.

Seeing the palisade clear, two men laid down their armour and shields, helped each other climb the wall and took control of the defences. The *peltasts* and light-armed troops, presuming that the palisade had been taken, and that the Drilae would be panicking and trying to escape through other exits, ran blindly through the main gates to begin to plunder. Xenophon kept most of the hoplites outside of the gates, noticing as he did that the enemy had begun to appear on ridges outside of the walls, which they could easily defend. His greatest concern was that the Drilae warriors may attempt to negotiate the rough terrain and attack any Greeks they found isolated and exposed.

Greeks screams and cries for help soon diverted his attention, they were coming from inside the stronghold. Men began to run out of the gate, clutching at any loot they had managed to grab and, before too long, their number included many who were wounded. In the panic and the overpowering din that occurs with so many voices at once, Xenophon's questions went unanswered until finally someone informed him that the Drilae were not evacuating the town, but had regrouped in their strongly defended acropolis. From this position of security they were sending out sorties, which in turn were having great success in their attacks on the Greeks in the town.

Xenophon had to think quickly. He ordered his herald, Tolmides, to tell any of the men outside the walls that if they wanted any loot they should enter into the stronghold. This quickly reversed the tide of human traffic leaving the gates and added the necessary impetus to force the Drilae back into their acropolis. Many of the hoplites were used to guard the palisades and towers, as well as the one road which went from the main gate up to the acropolis; while the lighter armed men began to grab anything they could get their hands on.

The Greeks were in a difficult position. Having taken the walls, and forced the Drilae back, they were safe from any sortie, but once they decided to try to leave the stronghold they would be very vulnerable to attack from the acropolis. Xenophon wanted to take control of the acropolis, stripping the Drilae of their last defensive position, but could not think of a way to do so.[15] It was more important that he could conceive of a way of minimizing the losses as his men departed.

First, he got each company to tear down the nearest section of palisade to them, then got his commanders to dismiss anyone who was injured or heavy-laden with booty. He also had them send away most of the hoplites, except for those the commanders felt they could rely on most. These men would act as a rearguard to cover the withdrawal. This was not going to be an easy fighting retreat, and Xenophon knew he needed his very best men to maintain discipline if it was going to work.

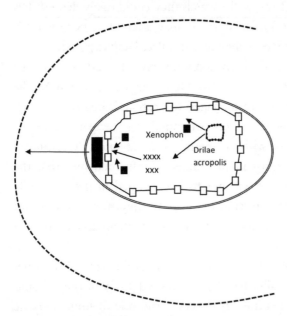

Map 14.3: Siege of the Drilae, phase 3.

As dusk began to fall, the encroachment of darkness caused even greater concern for the remaining Greeks. The retreat began and, as anticipated, the Drilae spewed forth from the acropolis in a rage befitting besieged men.

Armed with wicker shields, spears and helmets, the men of the Drilae engaged in hand-to-hand combat, while others mounted the house roofs to shoot down on the Greeks from a safe vantage point. Stationed on both sides of the main road to the acropolis, the Drilae caught the Greeks in a crossfire, throwing anything they could get their hands on. The Greeks were in serious trouble, to retreat was now just as dangerous as to stay where they were.

The only saving grace for Xenophon was that his remaining force were his most reliable and disciplined men. They held out for as long as they could, long enough for the situation to change, and change it did.

Either by design or by accident, a house on the right hand side of the road was set ablaze, causing havoc amongst the nearby Drilae. The dry timber used for most of the buildings quickly caught light and flames spread indiscriminately. Xenophon acted quickly, ordering the houses on the left hand side to be set alight as well. This forced the defenders to abandon these positions, giving the Greeks respite from the constant onslaught.

With just the force in front of them left to deal with, Xenophon ordered those out of range of the missiles, still raining down, to build up a fire to block themselves from the Drilae advance. Once this was ablaze, they set light to more houses next to the palisades, in a last ditch attempt to redirect Drilae attention from the Greeks and onto the survival of their own town. It worked, and finally Xenophon was able to evacuate the remainder of his men from the fortress. The stronghold was completely consumed by the flames, and burned to the ground; palisades, towers and all. The only remaining vestibule of this formidable stronghold was the unassailable, and evidently indestructible, acropolis.

The Aftermath

When the Greek army returned to their camp, they quickly realized that Chirisophus was not going to arrive anytime soon; they also knew that they did not have enough ships to take the army home. Consigned to their fate they put the injured men, along with the women and children, onto the few ships they had commandeered, and marched east to the Greek colony of Sinope.

At Sinope the Greeks shared out the money made from the sale of their prisoners and, for the first time since the Battle of Cunaxa, they counted how many men survived from the original 'Ten Thousand' – they had 8,600 men left.

The adventure of the Greeks was not yet over. They headed west, finally crossing the Hellespont to Byzantium; from there they became a mercenary force, first employed by the Thracian leader Seuthes II and then later under the employ of the Spartan commander in the region, Thibron.

Part IV

Greco-Persian Conflicts

onflict between Greek cities and the Persians began from the infancy of the Persian Empire. Cyrus the Great pushed his influence into Lydia in the 540s BC, where he was briefly opposed by the ruler Croesus, before embarking on a brutal campaign through Ionia in revenge for their support of a failed rebellion against the Persian ruler.

Relations between the outlying Greeks and the powerful Persian Empire varied over a short period of time, but ultimately the mainland held little interest to the Persian kings. When the Athenians finally appealed to Persia for help against the aggressions from other powerful *poleis* in 507 BC, the Greek mainland finally came into the Persian King Darius I's sphere of interest.

By the 490s BC and the failed attempt at revolt in Ionia, Greco-Persian relations soured once again when Darius looked to push his influence into Greece, culminating in the Battle of Marathon. The mission was not an invasion, but following his army's return, Darius began to plan an invasion imminently, though he died before it was completed. The mantle was taken up by his successor Xerxes I, who launched a fierce campaign through mainland Greece (480–479 BC). The king left Greece following his naval defeat at Salamis, but it was not until the coalition of Greek states won the Battle of Plataea that the Persian army was finally ejected from Greece.

Greco-Persian relations soured still further, with Athens especially pushing against Persia's periphery. By the Peloponnesian War, however, Greek attentions on Persia subsided, as they focused more centrally on the war in hand. Persia went from being a nemesis to being a powerful ally, and their financial contributions had a major impact on the outcome of the conflict.

By the end of the Peloponnesian War (404 BC), Persia had crowned a new king, Artaxerxes II, but his brother Cyrus the Younger had his own designs for the throne. In 401 BC, Cyrus amassed an army to invade the heartland of his brother's empire, with a large contingent of Greek mercenaries. Following his defeat at Cunaxa (401 BC), Cyrus' Greek mercenaries embarked on a gruelling march home (see Chapter 14).

Greek interests returned to the Persian Empire at the turn of the fourth century BC, when the Spartans sent over an army into Ionia to liberate the Greek *poleis* under Persian rule. With the arrival of the Spartan king Agesilaus (396 BC), an expansive campaign was underway to undermine Persian rule throughout the western coast of Asia Minor (see Chapter 5). Agesilaus' successes were cut short by unrest in mainland Greece that drew him back in 394 BC, unrest which had been specifically funded by Artaxerxes.

For the Persians, warfare against the Greeks posed a variety of unique problems, but the hoplite was not one of them. The heavy infantry bias to a Greek army was not necessarily a new experience for the Persians, having defeated both the Assyrians and Egyptians who each had strong infantry arms to their forces. That experience showed in the relative ease in which the Persians defeated Greek armies in Ionia, following two separate rebellions. One of the problems for the Persians when fighting the Greeks arose from the geopolitical climate of Greece, which was an eclectic land and sea frontier. This meant that a land campaign always needed a parallel naval campaign to assist it. Likewise, any inroads made were hard to consolidate because the Greeks sat so peripherally to the heart of the Persian Empire. This problem had been overcome in nomadic Scythia by the close proximity of Central Asia to major Persian centres such as Bactria, which allowed for more administrative influence. With Greece, however, the peoples were not disparate nomad groups but closely quartered, independent, city-states who each required subduing, negotiating with and controlling in turn.

On a purely military level, Greece itself is very mountainous. This did not necessarily hinder Persian tactics, which relied heavily on its infantry-archer mixed units, but allowed the Greeks to nullify the numerical advantage of the Persians.

The Persians must have had to adapt their own fighting style against the Greeks, compared to the tactics they will have used in the vast plains of Scythia or the lands around the Nile, but unfortunately we do not hold any detailed military accounts of Persian campaigns and battles outside of their relation to Greek history. One tactical element that they did not change, and was proven useless against the Greeks, was the overreliance on archers, who had very little impact on any of the Greco–Persian conflicts considered here.

For the Greeks, the Persians posed a set of problems quite outside of the realms of Greek warfare. The Persian army was highly mobile, with a strong cavalry arm that the Greeks greatly feared. Yet it is interesting that the Persians, in actuality, rarely relied upon their cavalry for a definitive impact in battle.

The core of the Persian army was highly structured and well disciplined: sections of ten men, companies of 100, divisions of 1,000, each with their own specified officers. This was a level of organization that was unheard of in Greece, even in Sparta. This structure gave rise to a much greater threat to any army that faced them, the massed archers of Persia. Each file of core Irano-Persian troops would consist of one man at the front holding a large wicker shield, which would be planted on the floor and reach above his head, and behind him would have been nine archers who would shoot in relative safety. The front rank of shield bearers would form a solid wall and the effect of mass shooting over the top could have been devastating. However, Persian archers were made impotent by a combination of the strong arms of the Greeks and, more importantly, the Greeks' tactical decision to charge the enemy. This moved them swiftly through archery range, with minimal loss of life, and into a mêlée, where the second Persian strength came into play. The Persian archers were also armed as infantry, meaning that they never lost their numerical advantage during a battle.

Greek tactics during the Persian Invasions (490 and 480–79 BC) were driven by their defensive position in their own lands. We see bold actions in both the Battle of Marathon and Plataea which verged on insanity, including a long run across no man's land and attacking the Persian shield wall with a broken formation. The tactical ingenuity of the Peloponnesian War and later period was not present here, perhaps an indication that Greek warfare had not yet matured into its classical form. But equally it underlies the desperation of the Greek position, where adrenaline and impassioned zeal were worth more in battle than tactical ploys. It seems audacity, and a little bit of luck, played a more important role than intelligence and foresight.

By the time of the Battle of Cunaxa, the military landscapes had changed for both Greece and Persia. The Greek force at Cunaxa were experienced, battle-hardened fighters from the Peloponnesian War, who possessed a (albeit still limited) tactical ability and basic regimental discipline unimaginable to their illustrious predecessors. However, this tactical capability reveals itself to have been predictable to an experienced commander. We know this to be true within the Greek military landscape, but at Cunaxa it can be seen that the Persians had a similar capability to manipulate Greek military tendencies – i.e. the Greek charge and pursuit of the infantry in front of them, exacerbated by the lack of discipline to stop a pursuit and regroup to rejoin the main battle.

For the Persians, they had almost a century more experience in fighting against Greek soldiers, as well as managing the innumerable nations within their own Empire. However, we cannot be certain whether there was a change in the Persian military or whether the Persians were always adept at evolving their tactics depending on the geography of the region and the enemy they were facing. For instance, at Cunaxa we see the first use of scythed chariots, but the landscape of Mesopotamia is better suited to their utilization than Greece is. This means that their appearance does not necessarily reveal a new military practice, but would serve equally as evidence for a tactical adaptation by the Persians, based upon the necessity that arises from differing circumstances.

A further argument for adaptation comes from the weakened left wing of the Persian army at Cunaxa, which was itself flanked by a strong cavalry force. The Persians placed an inexperienced force on the far left, opposite the Greeks, with the much more experienced force of Egyptians next to them. The Persian left wing broke and fled without a fight, and the Greeks pursued, as was their way. But the Persian cavalry that sat on the flank simply ignored the Greek force as they ran past, and headed straight for the baggage train of Cyrus' army. Whether or not the Persian rout was planned is open for debate, but the cavalry's action seems coordinated with this behaviour, as if it was already predicted. The Persian commander(s) knew that the Greeks would take the right wing, they knew the Greeks would lead the attack from there, and they knew that they would struggle to resist a prolonged pursuit against a fleeing enemy. In other words, the Persian commanders were able to pre-empt what the Greeks were going to do and plan their tactics around that. In the same way that the Greeks had nullified the power of the Persian archers at Marathon with their run, so too had the Persians nullified the strong Greek infantry arm of Cyrus' army with little effort.

Each of these three Greco-Persian battles are too unique to form any common consensus of Persian warfare, nor is it really possible to create a single model of Greek warfare when facing them. What we see at Marathon, on a small flat plain between two, nearly-equal, infantry based forces, is not the same as the vast armies on the battlefield of Plataea which is broken up by numerous geographic landmarks. Whereas Cunaxa seems to mix elements from both battles, a vast flat plain that is filled with large armies, it does not equate in military climates to the previous two, and the Greek army is part of a larger Persian-mercenary force anyway.

What becomes clear from these three instances is that the two military traditions were not static, neither in contemporary battles nor over the period of eight decades. What we see is not the continuity of tactics but the constant ability from both sides to adapt to the surroundings of battle, and to the makeup of the enemy they faced.

Chapter 15

The Battle of Marathon (490 BC)

The Background (Herodotus, III–VI)

When Darius I took his place on the Persian throne in 522 BC, he held power over a vast and turbulent empire. His succession had not been a smooth one. The previous king, Cambyses, had already been succeeded by his own brother Bardiya, but within six months Darius had defeated him and taken the royal title for himself.[1] Darius' coup was just the beginning of an intensive three-year period, which he spent subduing rebellions and insurrections throughout his empire; from Armenia in the west, to Arachosia (near the modern Afghan-Pakistan border) in the east. During one campaign in Babylonia (October and December 522), Darius had to simultaneously respond to uprisings in Persia, Elam, Media, Assyria, Egypt, Parthia, Margiana, Sattagydia, and Scythia.[2]

By 519 BC Darius' position as the Great King was all but secure, so he looked to expand the borders of the empire he had inherited from Cambyses. To the east, Darius pushed beyond Afghanistan and into the Indus River valley (in modern Pakistan, and northern India), and created a new province called Hidush. To the southwest he moved beyond the now-stable region of Egypt and into Libya.

In 514/13 BC, Darius ventured northwest, beyond his lands in Asia Minor and into southeastern Europe. His army was heading for the vast plains of Scythia which lay across from the Danube and north of the Black Sea. Darius led a vast army across the Bosporus and marched through Thrace, while his adjacent fleet was sailing into the Black Sea and up the Danube to build a bridge for his army to later cross.

The Scythians implemented an ingenious strategy for dealing with the invaders.[3] After they directed their families and flocks north, out of harm's way, they sent an advance force to make contact with the Persians. Darius' army was discovered three days in from the Danube, and the Scythian advance force began a scorched earth policy, all the while maintaining a slim one-day lead ahead of the Persian camp. This close proximity maintained the Persians' interest in hunting down these horsemen, allowing the small Scythian force to lead the Persians further and further inland.

Once the Persians reached the desolate regions north of the Black Sea, Darius began to construct a network of forts. But the small Scythian force was not going to let him settle. One day, the Persians woke to find the Scythians had simply vanished, so Darius ordered his men to head back west, assuming that this was the direction the enemy had fled.

The race continued back through Scythia where the Persians finally caught sight of two small Scythian contingents, but Darius could not force a battle to occur. As the king's frustrations grew, the Scythians changed tactic and began to harass the Persian cavalry whilst they foraged, but avoided an all-out attack in case the Persian infantry were too near. Meanwhile, the Scythians also sent a small contingent of their army to the Danube to encourage the Persian garrison in charge of the bridge to destroy it, so as to strand Darius' army. The garrison was made up of Ionian Greeks from the westernmost point of the Persian Empire, and they agreed to do as they were asked until the Scythians left, when they continued to loyally guard the crossing.

Back in Darius' camp, things were getting a lot worse. Provisions were running low, his men were under constant harassment, and he had just received an enigmatic gift sent from the Scythian king Idanthyrsus: a bird, a mouse, a frog and five arrows. Whilst Darius perceived this to be a version of the earth and water demands that signified submission to the Persian king, his adviser Gobryas took a different interpretation. For Gobryas the message was a threat: unless the Persians turned into birds and flew into the sky, or mice and ran underground, or frogs and moved into the lakes, they would be shot by these arrows.

The Scythians followed up on their threat and prepared for battle. But for the intervention of a small hare, a bloody battle may have commenced. When Darius saw part of the Scythian army leave their positions to hunt the small game he took it as a sign of contempt for his army, born from some knowledge of Scythian superiority, and decided to evacuate his men by night and head back to the Danube crossing.

The Scythians arrived at the bridge first and again put pressure on the Ionians to destroy it. The Ionians agreed and had to begin the process before the Scythians would leave, but once this happened the Greeks immediately stopped their dismantling. When Darius arrived at the crossing he was able to be transported across the river, with the help of the Ionians, and continue his march through Thrace and back into Asia Minor. He left one of his commanders, Megabazus, to subjugate southern Thrace, the Hellespont and, by 510 BC, Macedonia.

As the final decade of the sixth century arrived, Darius held a secure rule over the largest empire in the known world. He was able to draw an extraordinary amount of tax from the provinces, and he had an unparalleled army whose numbers could be called upon from dozens of different military cultures, bringing with them different tactical expertise and a wide array of arms that gave him a variety hitherto unseen in the historical record. The end of the century was not treating every one so well.

In 510 BC the city of Athens was in the grips of a sour tyranny.[4] The tyrant Hippias had grown paranoid, following the assassination of his brother in 514 BC, and implemented a harsh regime over the *polis*. Athenian exiles implored the Spartans to intervene and, subsequently, bribed the Delphic oracle to support their mission, so that every Spartan consultation with the oracle led to the instruction 'liberate Athens'. Sparta did not need much incentive to assert their influence in Athens and one of their kings, Cleomenes I, was sent to overthrow Hippias.

An initial landing on the plain of Phaleron, southwest of Athens, was unable to resist the superior fighting force of the Thessalian cavalry, allies of Hippias, who slaughtered many in the Spartan army and drove the rest back to their ships. Cleomenes assembled a larger expedition and marched overland, defeating the Thessalian force that awaited him. He continued his trajectory into the city of Athens, where he hemmed the tyrant's forces inside an old Mycenaean fortress atop the Acropolis. After the capture of the children of the tyrant's supporters, the siege was brought to a swift end. Hippias fled into exile on the Asian side of the Hellespont.

With the tyrant gone, the exiles of Athens returned and a new struggle for power raged. By 508 BC, Cleisthenes emerged victorious, with the support of the common people, and implemented the new form of democracy for which he became famous.[5] His main rival for authority was a popular aristocrat named Isagoras, but this new democracy did little to deter Isagoras' desire for power.[6] In the face of defeat, Isagoras looked to Sparta for help, hoping they could repeat with Cleisthenes the exile they had enforced upon Hippias. Cleomenes jumped once more at the chance of influencing the governance of Athens. Using an ancestral pollution that besmirched the line of Cleisthenes, Cleomenes sent word to Athens that Cleisthenes should be cast from the city and that Athens was in need of cleansing.[7]

While Cleisthenes did leave on his own accord in 507 BC, Cleomenes still entered Athens with a small army and began to undo the democratic reforms. He banished over 700 households from the city walls and put the power in the hands of 300 supporters of Isagoras. When the Council refused to obey the changes being implemented, Cleomenes and Isagoras' supporters took control of the Acropolis. At the sight of their Acropolis in the hands of the Spartan king, the people of Athens rose up and placed him under siege. By the third day a truce was called and the Spartans were allowed to depart, but the supporters of Isagoras were detained and killed.

The people of Athens recalled Cleisthenes and the 700 households who were in exile, but Athens was still in a very precarious position. It had created a dangerous enemy in Cleomenes and the Spartans, and could not trust large elements of its own aristocracy who could so easily betray them. Athens needed to look outside for help and, in the face of the Spartan military might, only the strongest of allies would do. The Athenians sent an embassy across the Aegean to Sardis, to the palace of Artaphernes, a *satrap* for the Great King Darius.

The Athenians had a simple request: the support of the Great King, as they prepared to defend themselves from Spartan aggression. Artaphernes' response was simpler still: offer earth and water as a sign of submission and the king would protect them as he would any of his vassals. The envoys agreed to the terms and left Sardis with the promise of Persian help.[8]

For two years, Athens repelled the armies of Sparta's allies, but they never received the promised help from Persia. They were able to defeat the joint armies of the Boeotians and Chalcidians, and later an invading force from Thebes. The situation was not going as Sparta had hoped, for Athens was proving a stronger adversary than had been previously anticipated. The

Spartans decided to try and undo their earlier errors and reinstall Hippias as tyrant of Athens, but their allies refused to allow such an overt and radical interference in the governance of another *polis*.

With the stalling of Sparta's plans, Hippias returned to Asia and continued his journey into the lands of Artaphernes, to garner the support of the influential *satrap*. Artaphernes ordered the Athenians to accept Hippias back as tyrant, something he felt capable of doing thanks to their offering of submission just two years earlier.[9] The Athenians refused the demand and severely damaged their relations with Artaphernes and, by proxy, Darius.

In 500/499 BC Athens received one of the Persian-supported tyrants in Ionia, Aristagoras of Miletus. The tyrant had angered Artaphernes after a planned military action in Naxos led to an embarrassing failure for the Persians, one that they blamed on Aristagoras. With the distinct feeling that his time in power was coming to an end, Aristagoras decided to revolt.[10] Having convinced several of the Ionian *poleis* to join him, the tyrant was in mainland Greece mustering more support. He had failed in his quest at Sparta and now turned to the other power base in Greece, the mother city of Miletus, Athens. Aristagoras used every trick available, including the telling of lies about the poor military equipment of the Persian armies, until the Athenians voted to support the revolt and send twenty ships to assist the Ionians.[11]

The Ionian revolt began with a glorious success for the joint force of Ionians, Athenians and a contingent of Eretrian allies who had likewise joined to support the uprising. The army entered Lydia and took control of its capital, Sardis, driving Artaphernes and his garrison to the top of the acropolis to defend themselves. The Greeks set fire to the city, driving the Lydian citizens into the arms of the Persian garrison as they escaped the flames. The defenders fled to the *agora* and began a resilient defence out in the open. When the Greeks saw how their actions had unified their enemy they were reluctant to engage directly in battle, and when news came that Persian reinforcements would arrive imminently the Ionians left in the direction of Ephesus, back to their ships. The Persian relief force met the Greeks outside of Ephesus and defeated them in a fierce battle that ended in the slaughter of many Greeks.

This defeat saw the Athenians and Eretrians abandon the Ionian cause, less than one year after joining it. Regardless, 497 BC saw the revolt spread further afield, with cities on the Hellespont and in Caria joining the Milesians. Most importantly, in the eyes of Darius, the strategically important cities of Cyprus also joined the revolt. The island became the main focal point for the Persian reclamation and, after fierce Cypriot resistance, Darius' army was able to reassert its control by 496 BC.[12]

Further Persian victories on the mainland of Asia Minor turned the tide of the revolt decisively in their favour. In 494 BC, the Persians concentrated their attack on Miletus itself. Combining their various forces in Asia Minor together, they marched on the city, while their large naval force followed by sea. The Ionians decided to leave the Milesians to defend their walls while the rest would take to their ships and defend the city there. The Persians were victorious in the subsequent naval battle, the Battle of Lade, and Miletus fell that same year.

The following year, 493 BC, saw the final embers of the revolt put out in the Hellespont. It also saw the tyrant of the Chersonese region, an Athenian named Miltiades, flee his charge and return to his mother city. The Persian reconquest was at times brutal, with cities being burned, beautiful boys castrated and beautiful girls taken for the king, but Artaphernes finally brought peace to the Ionian Greeks through arbitration and the re-establishment of order.

Darius selected his son-in-law, Mardonius, to command the armies in Asia Minor in 492 BC, while the rest of the commanders in the region were recalled. Mardonius spent a short time in Ionia, deposing many of the tyrannies that were established in the cities and introducing democracies to govern.[13] He then continued his march north, to the Hellespont, where he met with a large Persian army and fleet to continue the consolidation of Persian influence in the north Aegean. His army reached inner Macedonia and added Macedon to the formal *satrapy* of Thrace. Yet, after suffering heavy losses at sea and further losses on land, during an ambush from the one of the local Thracian tribes, Mardonius resolved Persian affairs in the region and returned to Asia.

Darius was beginning to prepare to extend control over the Greek Aegean islands and, in 491 BC, he sent out the demands for earth and water. This act stirred up a paranoid state within Greek diplomacy, and it did not take long before the citizens on the island of Aegina were accused by the Athenians of 'medizing', that is siding with the Persians.[14] Athens made the accusation to Sparta, in search of assistance, and the Spartans sent Cleomenes to march on Aegina and arrest those guilty of the crime. After an unsuccessful first attempt, he was able to return and punish those most prominent in the decision to submit to Persia by sending them to Athens as hostages.

The year of 491 BC did not end well for Cleomenes, however. He was discovered to have orchestrated the removal of his co-king, Demaratus, and was forced to flee to Arcadia, where he attempted to unite the *poleis* against Sparta. He was swiftly brought back to Sparta, where he is said to have gone mad and killed himself. When the Aeginetans heard of his death they demanded the return of the hostages held by Athens, in the beginning of 490 BC, which the Spartans agreed to, but the Athenians were less willing.

When the authorities on Aegina heard of the Athenian refusal they arranged the ambush and seizure, during a sacred procession, of an Athenian ship which held many important and influential Athenian citizens. The Athenians, in turn, encouraged internal strife on the island, offering support to an exile, Nicodromos, but his insurrection was mercilessly put down by the authorities. The Athenians finally arrived at the island with a fleet of seventy ships and won a decisive sea battle, followed up with a victory on land as well.

While the Greeks were distracted with internal politics, Darius spent this time planning and executing his next area of expansion. Mardonius had been relieved of his overall command, and two new commanders were named, Datis and Artaphernes, the eponymous son of the *satrap*. In 490 BC, the two commanders met with their large army in Cilicia where they boarded a fleet of 600 ships, including some custom designed to carry horses. The fleet embarked for Rhodes, where they failed in their siege of the city of Lindos, before continuing on to Ionia.[15] From the island of Samos this expedition was tasked with the goal of consolidating Persian control through the Cycladic Islands, starting with Naxos.

Naxos quickly succumbed to Persian authority, and Datis moved on to Apollo's holy island of Delos. After offering generous supplication to the god, Datis received needed supplies from Ionia and continued travelling through the islands, most of whom had already offered earth and water to Darius. Datis was looking to enlist more recruits for the secondary aim of his expedition, to exact punishment on Eretria and Athens for their role in the Ionian revolt.

The Persian fleet headed for Eretria, on the southern coast of central Euboea, and put it under siege for six days, before the gates were betrayed by two Greek citizens. The Persians were ruthless as they plundered the city, set fire to the sanctuaries, and enslaved the populace. Datis hesitated once the city was taken, so the Persian army maintained its camp in Euboea. Datis most likely wanted to return to Asia, having achieved his main objectives, but one of his entourage had different plans. The old tyrant Hippias was putting pressure on the commander to continue on to Attica and attack Athens. But Datis did not have the manpower to take the city and the popularity of Hippias was undiscerned, making a betrayal similar to Eretria less likely.[16]

Hippias finally convinced Datis that he knew of a perfect landing spot that would benefit the Persian horses, and nullify the Greeks' strength in narrow terrain. He led them to a bay northeast of Athens, a bay which had seen his father invade Athens with great success almost sixty years earlier. He led them to the bay which lay before the small village of Marathon.

The Battlefield

The battle was fought on the flat plain in the base of the bay of Marathon. To the west loomed the mountain range that encased the small village nestled within them, while to the east lay the bay and the Aegean sea beyond. The Persians were based in the north of the plain, next to the Macaria Spring, whilst the Greeks were encamped in the hills to the south, next to the sanctuary of Heracles. Behind the Persian battle lines was a marsh or an inlet from the sea.

The Armies

The Persians, led by Datis and Artaphernes, had a fighting force of 16–20,000 men, with less than 1,000 cavalry.[17] It was an infantry-based force with a large contingent of archers. The army was not a polyglot mix of ethnicities but predominantly Iranian and Scythian in make-up. This was not an invading army, it was a show of strength as part of a diplomatic assault – the threat that supported the demands for earth and water.[18]

The Greeks were led by a committee of 10 generals, including Miltiades, the old tyrant of the Chersonese, and one commander, Callimachus.[19] The Athenians were able to field 9–10,000 hoplites, and their only allies present were the Plataeans with another 600 hoplites. Whilst the Greeks had no cavalry present, they would have been supported by light infantry of an indeterminable number. Although the Athenians were not outnumbered by as large a factor as traditionally described, they were still facing anything upto twice as many men as they themselves had.[20]

The Battle (Herodotus, VI.103–124; Plutarch, *Life of Aristides*, 5)

While Datis' army had paused in Eretria he sent a messenger to Athens, offering them the chance to surrender, which was subsequently refused. Runners were immediately sent from Athens to all of the Greek states, looking for support, but only two returned in favour. Their erstwhile allies in Plataea said yes, as did the Spartans – in theory. The professional runner, Pheidippides, made the 150-mile journey in under 36 hours when he was informed that the Spartans would help Athens, but that they could not leave the city in force before the end of the Carnea festival, which had a further six days to go.

When the various reports returned to Athens another meeting was called to decide on what to do. Many argued for shutting the gates and defending the city walls; the campaign season would be coming to an end soon, meaning Athens only needed to hold out for a few months before the Persians left, due to the winter storms that could damage their fleet. But Miltiades put forward a motion that, as soon as they heard where the Persians had landed, the men of Athens would take their provisions and meet the invaders in the field, leaving the city in the hands of the gods. His motion was passed.

As the Persians arrived at Marathon and set up camp by the Macaria Spring, the knowledge of their arrival would have entered Athens in a very short period of time indeed. The men of Athens were called to muster and soon marched out of the city, taking the southern road into the plain, following the coast.[21] On arrival they set up camp in the high ground, near to the sanctuary of Heracles, in turn securing a reliable source of water, and were soon joined by the small army sent from Plataea.

The Athenian generals were in a quandary. Half of them believed that they were too few in number to fight the Persians, and that they should put off an engagement until the arrival of the Spartans. But the other half felt that a battle needed to happen and soon, with concerns no doubt arising about how long Athens could be left relatively unguarded. Miltiades went to the overall commander, Callimachus, to cast the deciding vote, and successfully persuaded him to vote for battle.

Following this vote, the Athenians still refrained from entering the field. They could not simply march into the plain as sacrificial tender to the Persian arrows and horses, they needed a plan of action. The Persians, for their part, were content with the delay, as they had little desire to fight such a large Greek force. Datis was relying on internal strife striking the Athenians, either in camp or back in the city, allowing his army free access to its target. Each day the Persians would set up in battle order and then, when no battle was offered, they would begin to maraud the countryside. This pattern repeated itself for a few days, and Miltiades studied it closely.[22]

The Persians would not begin to leave camp until daylight had come, with the infantry leading the way. Once their horses were fed, watered, bridled, saddled and ready for action, they were then taken through a narrow road between the spring and the mountain to its west, onto the plain, where they were the last to take up their position in the Persian formation. The act of marching past the spring took the cavalry almost an hour on their own, before they could arrange into the formation set out on the plain. Miltiades watched this again and again, waiting for his day to lead so that he could act.[23]

Miltiades prepared the Greeks early on the morning of his command, and struck up the order for the lines to form. Callimachus took his rightful place on the right wing, whilst the ten tribes of Athens were counted and fell into place, with the Plataeans taking the left wing. The deployed line began the march into the plain.

As Miltiades' army arrived, the Persian infantry had already begun to set up its lines, giving Miltiades the final piece of his tactical puzzle. Knowing that the Persian line was longer than his own, he had already arranged his army to accommodate this, thinning the centre of his army and extending his wings, whilst leaving them with a greater concentration of men as well. Seeing the Persian line as it arranged itself allowed the Greeks to match it to perfection, preventing any fear of being outflanked.

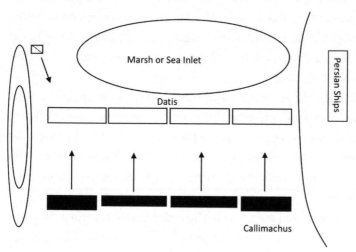

Map 15.1: Battle of Marathon, phase 1.

The Greeks stopped within a mile of the enemy and composed themselves. Sacrifices were given and the omens read favourably. It was now or never. The Persian lines were all but complete, but the horses were still nowhere to be seen: the command was given for the Greeks to advance.

Datis watched from the centre of the Persian lines in shock at the sight before him. The Greeks were not only coming to battle, they were coming at a run.[24] Where were the Greek archers to cover their advance? Where were the Greek cavalry to support their flanks and protect against enemy horse? What madmen would break into a loose formation and charge down a larger enemy force head-on? But this was the sight that faced him.[25]

As the Greek charge came closer and closer, Datis set out his orders. Miltiades may have feared his Persian horse, but Datis had a greater weapon in his army.[26] The Persian front lines set up their giant shield walls, while Datis' infamous archers nocked their arrows and waited. When the Greek charge brought them within one eighth of a mile of from the Persian line, the order was given and a cloud of arrows set loose.[27]

An ominous shadow glided over the Greek hopliter as they ran. Undeterred, their advance never faltered and most of the Persian arrows fell harmlessly to the floor where the Greeks once were. While a few hoplites were struck, the charge did not lose its impetus. As the Greeks met the Persian line, the tall wicker-shield wall was ripped down and a brutal mêlée erupted, as the Persian archers replaced bow with axe, sword and spear.

The fighting was evenly matched for long periods of time. The weakness of the Greek centre could not hold for long. Its job was to hold for as long as it could, giving each wing the greatest chance of winning their contests. As the chaos grew, one giant Persian soldier, with a beard that covered much of his own shield, drove forwards and slaughtered the hoplite in front of him. The brutality of the death caused the next Greek hoplite in his path, Epizelus, to immediately shut down psychologically and lose his ability to see, but the Persian passed him by like a phantom in the night.[28]

The elite Persian centre was pressing harder and harder into the Greek line, until it finally began to give way. Datis just needed to finish his job in the centre and then use his most elite fighters to flank the soon-to-be-isolated Greek wings, but the full report of the battle reached him as more of the Greeks began to flee in his path. The Persian wings had been defeated and Datis was in danger of being encircled.

The fighting on the wings had been likewise brutal, but the Greeks had been able to match the manpower of their Persian foes and forced them back. As the Persian lines began to break up they quickly turned to rout. This gave time for the exhausted Greeks to recover and regroup, resisting the urge to cut the enemy down as they ran.

Datis could not allow himself to get cut off from the ships. He ordered his men in the centre of the battlefield to turn back and head to the shore. As his men briskly moved into retreat, the gap between the two Greek wings had still failed to close, giving him a window of opportunity to fight his way out. When the Greeks saw Datis' advance, both wings moved to attack the flanks, but they lacked the coordination and discipline to cut him off entirely.

By the time the two Greek wings converged, they were chasing the backs of the Persian soldiers toward the ships on the shore. The fastest of the

Greeks were able to cut down some Persian stragglers, but it was not until the Persians attempted to board their boats that the Greeks reached them en masse and a new mêlée ensued. Many Persian bodies fell under the point of the Greek spear, others slipped in the wash and were mercilessly dispatched. But the Persians fought to the bitter end, with the spear-riddled body of Callimachus left as a morbid trophy to their desire to survive.[29]

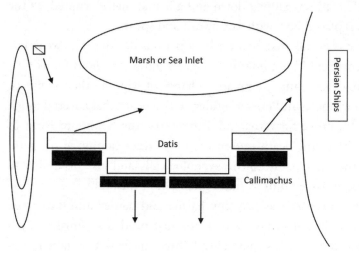

Map 15.2: Battle of Marathon, phase 2.

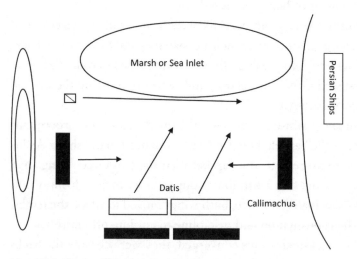

Map 15.3: Battle of Marathon, phase 3.

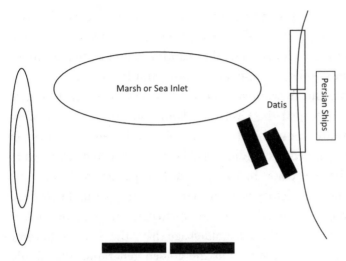

Map 15.4: Battle of Marathon, phase 4.

The Greeks tried to seize the boats before they were able to get out to sea, but one man at least lost his hand in the process, struck from his arm with the blow of an axe.[30] For their troubles, the Greeks could only claim seven ships, as they watched the great fleet depart their shores and reflected on the hard-fought battle they had just survived.

One of the 10 tribes, led by Aristides, was left on the field to guard the captives and booty that had been claimed, and to watch over the Greek fallen. This amounted to 192 dead Athenian hoplites, but an unknown number of Plataeans and light infantry. They also had the grim task of stripping 6,400 Persian bodies of their armaments and valuables.

The Aftermath

The Athenian army could not waste time revelling in their victory. The Persian ships had not left the bay and headed north, nor east, they had travelled decidedly south where they could traverse Cape Sounion and land right next to Athens itself, bypassing the Athenian army at Marathon.

The Persians had received a signal from the city inviting them to land, most likely at Phaleron. The Athenian army rushed home and arrived before the fleet. Their military presence was enough to dissuade the anchored

Persian ships from attempting a landing, so, instead, Datis ordered his fleet back to Eretria. He collected his 780 captives from the city, men women and children, and took them to Ionia where they continued on foot to Susa to see the Great King. Only 400 male captives survived, and 10 women.[31]

For the Persians, the mission had been a success. They had control over Naxos, they controlled the Cycladic islands, and they controlled an unobstructed sea route from Ionia directly to the Greek shore. The Persian Empire had been expanded, its holdings had been secured, and any plans to invade Greece in the future now had a safe and short passage to do so.

For the Athenians this victory was the start of their legend. Their dead were burned as heroes and a great mound constructed in their honour. It marked the beginning of the glorious golden age that Athens would become famous for, and cemented these men as the golden generation that would inspire future victories.

Chapter 16

The Battle of Plataea 479 BC

The Background (Herodotus, VII–IX.26)

With the death of the king, Darius, the Persian throne passed to his son Xerxes I (486 BC). At the age of 36 he held control over the largest empire known to the western world, and very quickly went about reasserting that authority.

Thanks to a lack of opposition regarding his ascension to kingship, Xerxes was able to utilise the vast forces and resources at his disposal to bring unity and cohesion back to the rather-fragile empire that he had been left by his father.[1] This started with the two most troublesome regions: Egypt and Babylonia.

The exact cause of the rebellion in Egypt is unknown. Causes such as heavy taxation, the deportation of craftsmen to Iran, and even the impact of Darius' defeat at Marathon have been cited as possibilities.[2] Whatever the cause, it had been rumbling within the empire since the reign of Darius. Darius had even intended to march on Egypt to subdue the uprising; this was the reason why Xerxes had been named as his heir in the first place. The discontent had spread from Egypt proper, and was igniting older issues within the nearby area of Palestine.[3]

In 485 BC, Xerxes marched at the head of his army to quell the Egyptian rebellion but, rather unfortunately, we do not know any more than that he succeeded and imposed very harsh conditions on the Egyptians. There is a small suggestion that the rebellion was over as early as the January of 484 BC.

After his campaign in Egypt, Xerxes began preparations to renew his father's interest in Greece. Darius had intended to conduct a full invasion of Greece, spending three years putting together an army capable of such a feat, only to be distracted by the events in Egypt ... and his own subsequent death.[4] Xerxes had used his father's preparations as a springboard to dealing with Egypt, thus he had to start preparations for Greece all over again.[5]

Yet the year 484 BC brought even more trouble for the new king, as the very heart of his empire was up in rebellion. Babylonia revolted over the same sorts of issues as Egypt: taxations, the deportation of expert craftsmen, the heavy expenses extorted for the upkeep of Persian forces and palaces. Although the revolt was very short lived, not more than two weeks really, the threat was a serious one. The rebels had managed to take over cities such as Borsippa, Dilbat, and even Babylon herself. The rebellion was suppressed and the perpetrators were dealt with, but the city of Babylon was given great leniency due to Xerxes' personal fondness for it.[6] This leniency was exploited two years later with a second revolt; but Xerxes did not make the same mistake again. He sent Megabyzus to systematically destroy the resistance, which he achieved after besieging the city. Megabyzus had the city walls destroyed and its priests executed. Major temples were damaged and their treasures taken. He even went so far as to have the statue of the god Marduk removed, which meant that no legitimate king of Babylon could ever be crowned again.[7]

Babylon had lost its autonomy, and was now just another province in Persia's mighty empire. More importantly, Xerxes had no more distractions and the army he had been building in Asia Minor was nearing completion; he could finally direct his attention to Greece.

Starting in Asia Minor (481 BC), Xerxes intended to take his vast army through the north of Greece, while a fleet sailed parallel to the march.[8] To achieve this he had to first cross the Hellespont, which he did by building two pontoon bridges, anchoring several hundred ships side by side, linked as they were by large cables. Planks of wood were laid between these cables, and then an earth causeway was built atop that. To finish it off, a fence either side was put up, to hide the sight of the water from the animals that were being made to cross. After a few setbacks due to bad weather, and Xerxes having the sea whipped for its insubordination, they finally crossed and marched on to Doriscus in Thrace (480 BC).

From Thrace, the Persians marched west into Macedonia (a region that was on friendly terms with Persia) and followed the coastline round into northern Greece – all the while recruiting more and more soldiers. As they headed toward Thessaly they should have met the first element of Greek resistance, an army of 10,000 men from mainly Sparta and Athens. The

Greeks intended to make a stand at the passes of Olympus but they feared being surrounded and annihilated, choosing to retreat south and leave Thessaly to join the Persians.[9]

So, on the Persians marched, without opposition, until they lay on the precipice of Greece proper. It was here that a Greek resistance finally materialized, at a small mountain pass known throughout history as Thermopylae; they also made a naval stand at Artemisium.[10]

With the capture of Thermopylae, all of central Greece was open for the Persians to control. They moved south through Doris, Phocis and Locris, then entered Boeotia without opposition, as the Boeotians decided to join the side of the Persians. This left Xerxes to descend upon Attica and Athens herself unabated. Athens evacuated its people to Troizen, Aegina and Salamis, leaving their mother-city to the whim and destruction of the Persians.

The Greeks' plan was to face the Persians at sea, utilizing the natural geography around the island of Salamis. The battle was a morale-shattering defeat for the Persians, usually so confident in their own superiority. With this humiliation, Xerxes chose to return to Persia and left Mardonius in charge of an army, with the strict intention of conquering the rest of Greece.

Mardonius was able to choose the troops that he considered the best available and he spent the winter of 480/479 BC in the pro-Persian region of Thessaly. He was later joined by a small force led by Artabazus, who had escorted Xerxes to the Hellespont and had recently failed in an attempt to besiege Potidaea.

By the spring of 479 BC, Mardonius was trying every available option to woo the Athenians onto his side but to no avail, so Mardonius advanced south and occupied Attica once more. The Athenians fled again to Salamis and implored the Spartans to repay their loyalty by sending an army to help them face the Persian threat. But, as they so often did, Sparta stalled and chose instead to try and fortify the Corinthian Isthmus, cutting the Peloponnese off from the rest of Greece.

Sparta was finally shamed into action by Chileus of Tegea, a respected voice inside Laconia – unusually so for a foreigner. So, out they sent 5,000 Spartans, with 7 *helots* each, some 35–40,000 men in all, under the command of a regent, Pausanias. On hearing this news, Mardonius gave up all hope of converting the Athenians and, instead, demolished much of Athens itself, before retreating into Boeotia.

The Spartan army met up with the Athenian army at Eleusis and marched north to Erythrae. A small skirmish was fought at Erythrae, where the Greek archers and cavalry gained a morale-boosting victory after they killed Masistus, one of the Persian commanders. This skirmish laid the way for a more decisive clash to take place, with both armies making their preparations for the battle that would take place at Plataea.

The Battlefield

Situated between the northern slopes of Mount Cithaeron and the northern banks of the Asopus River, the battlefield was potted with numerous geographic landmarks, many of which are now sadly unidentifiable. The Greeks set up camp on the slopes of the mountain, with the slighted city of Plataea nearby to the west. The Persians were encamped on the northern side of the Asopus (roughly 3 miles to the north).[11]

Outside of the city walls of Plataea sat the temple of Hera and, most likely, the 'island' described in Herodotus, which lay between two tributaries of the River Oeroe. To the east lay the town of Hysiae (behind which the Greek supply train waited). Outside of Hysiae's northern walls was the temple of Demeter, and the Gargaphia Spring was situated west of the temple. The town of Erythrae lay further east still.

Heading north from Plataea and Hysiae, before the River Asopus, lay two main ridges, the Asopus and the Pyros ridge, where the Greeks took up their positions. From these ridges lay flat land down to the river, continuing on to the other side. The Persians were arrayed for battle on the northern bank, but further behind their lines they had built a fortification due west of the town of Scolus. Behind that fort lay the rest of Boeotia and the city of Thebes in particular.

The Armies

Herodotus gives not only the nations/*poleis* present in each army and their corresponding figures, but also the relevant position they held within the formation. So on the one hand the information he gives is both extremely detailed and vitally important; on the other hand, however, the numbers he uses are astronomical and so the figures here will be based upon modern estimates.

The Greek army, commanded by the Spartan regent Pausanias, was made up of 24 different *poleis*, contributing in total about 70,000 hoplites and light-armed/archer troops (Herodotus says 110,000). Included in those lightly armed troops were the Spartan *helots*, who, we are told, were armed for battle and outnumbered the Spartiate hoplites by a ratio of 7:1.[12] If this is true, and Herodotus' other clarification that the non-Spartan hoplites were matched at a ratio of 1:1 by their light-armed troops, then this means the Greek army was made up of a majority of light-armed troops, with a core of around 20–25,000 hoplites, and no real cavalry to speak of. The left wing was held by Sparta, the right wing by Athens.

The Persian army, commanded by Mardonius, was made up of 18 different nations, bringing a combined force of c. 70–80,000 infantry and 10,000 cavalry (Herodotus said 350,000 including cavalry).[13] This polyglot army would have had a strong emphasis on archery and lightly armed troops, but it cannot be ignored that the Immortals (10,000), Greek allies (c. 10,000 hoplites, 10,000 light troops) and the Egyptians (unknown number) especially, were all highly regarded forms of heavy infantry that were more than capable of matching their Greek opponents hand to hand.

The Battle (Herodotus, Histories, IX.36–70)

The two armies consulted their diviners, both of which declared that success would only come in a defensive position. This created a stalemate for eight days, with more Greeks crossing the mountain passes and reinforcing the Hellenic army on the Asopus Ridge every day. Following the advice of a Theban named Timagenides, Mardonius decided to try cutting off the pass through the mountain that allowed these reinforcements.

Waiting until nightfall, Mardonius sent out a force of his cavalry to close the proverbial hole in the dyke, at a pass known as Three Heads. The move allowed him to draw first blood, capturing much of the Greek supply train and killing the people tending the wagons. Once they had had their fill of slaying man and beast, the Persian cavalry rounded up what was left and drove it back to Mardonius. Yet, even this could not initiate a full-blown battle, with both sides at a standoff either side of the river. Two more days passed, with little more than skirmishes and cavalry harassment to describe as direct action. By day eleven Mardonius was getting frustrated and exasperated by the lack of progress, so he called a meeting of his commanders to discuss their options.

Contrary to the advice given by Artabazus, and the Thebans before him, Mardonius decided to continue the search for battle rather than retreat behind the walls of Thebes. His great fear was that the Greek army would grow and outnumber his troops, a situation that the Persians had not yet experienced in Greece. A second, and not inconsiderable, factor was that his army was running very low on supplies; they would last for no more than three days, giving Mardonius a very short time frame with which to be proactive. His mind was made up; he was going to confront the Greeks the following day.[14]

Mardonius was buoyed on the first day of the battle. With both armies encamped, he sent over a message challenging the Spartans to a battle of champions, 10,000 men each, to decide the outcome of the day. The Spartans did not respond to this and Mardonius began to act. He sent another cavalry force to circle around the eastern wing of the Greeks to attack the Gargaphia Spring which lay behind their lines, successfully blocking it and rendering it unusable. The Greeks were in a panic, the Persians already controlled the water of the Asopus and now they had destroyed the nearest water supply. The commanders congregated around Pausanias to decide what to do. They had to move and secure water, but a moving army became an easy target for the Persian archers and cavalry. They would have to move during the night. The target was the 'island', just north of Plataea, which would allow them to take control of another water supply and, hopefully, reopen their supply train over the mountain.

The entire day was filled with Mardonius sending wave upon wave of cavalry assaults. They would come within firing distance and pepper the Greek line; being able to run away if any Greek resistance decided to try engaging with them. It is also unlikely that the comparatively few Greek archers were able to make any impact on the horse archers, all were left at the whim of the Persian arrows as they fell.

As night fell, Mardonius finally relented and recalled his cavalry to camp. The Greeks waited until the agreed hour, then they began to move south in the darkness. Once in motion, however, the effects of the day got the better of them and the further they got away from those Persian horses the better. They continued marching beyond the 'island' and did not stop until they reached the temple of Hera, just outside the walls of Plataea. Once there, most of the men laid down their arms in front of the sanctuary and set up camp.

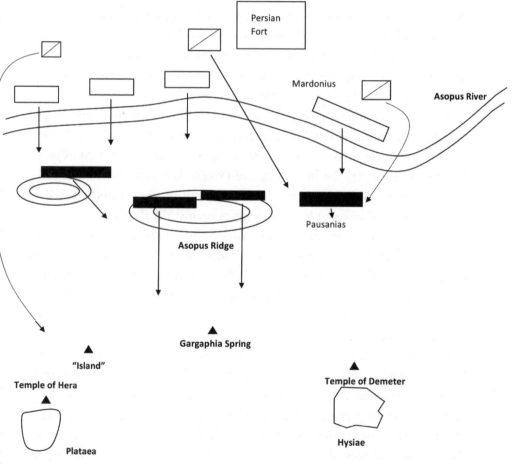

Map 16.1: Battle of Plataea, phase 1.

Pausanias was not having such luck with his wing. One of his Spartan captains, by the name of Amompharetus, was refusing to be seen as 'retreating' from his position – almost a cardinal sin in the post-Thermopylae eyes of Sparta. Pausanias was in a quandary: should he leave this insubordinate captain and his men behind, or maintain Spartan cohesion whilst trying to talk him out of his decision? Spartan sentiment got the better of him, so Pausanias kept all 10,000 together while he argued with Amompharetus.

The Athenians had also maintained their original position, they were waiting to follow the lead of the Spartans, whom they greatly distrusted, as had the Tegeans, who were camped with the Spartans. As day broke, Pausanias was at breaking point and finally declared that he would leave Amompharetus to be killed while he retreated with the rest of the Greeks. With a quick order, the Lacedaemonians and the Athenians both began their own retreat to Plataea. It did not take long for Amompharetus to panic at the prospect of being isolated and his men quickly followed; they finally re-joined their comrades at the temple of Demeter.[15]

This was all happening in daylight and Mardonius saw his opportunity. Sending his entire cavalry force, he had them attack the empty spaces left by the retreat and shoot upon any retreating Greeks they found. Mardonius became complacent, the bravest of the Greeks had just been found to be fleeing at the sight of his army, he was assured of victory and wanted to inflict a great punishment for their wrongs against the Persians.

A large contingent of the Persians crossed the Asopus at a great pace and, without orders, began charging out of battle order, towards the retreating Greeks before them – or so they thought.[16] In reality they were charging towards the Spartan and Tegean force led by Pausanias, whilst the Athenians had retreated across the plain toward the temple of Hera to meet the remaining Greek troops.

Pausanias turned his men to face the oncoming horsemen, set them into battle formation and sent a horseman to the Athenians, requesting their help. The Athenians were on the cusp of moving to help, when they were suddenly confronted with the formidable sights and sounds of a Greek phalanx marching towards them. The Hellenic allies of Persia had entered the fray and had their steely eyes set on the Athenians. As their mêlée began, Pausanias was left alone to fend off the Persian onslaught.

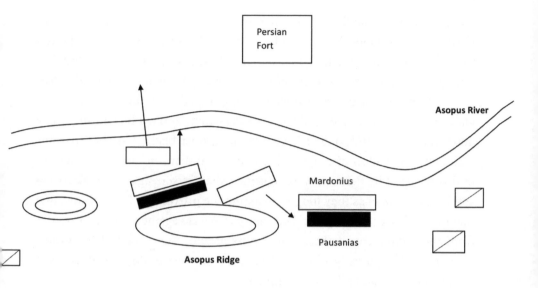

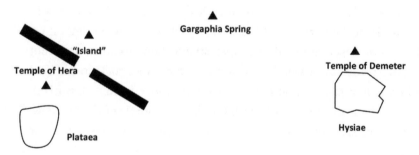

Map 16.2: Battle of Plataea, phase 2.

Mardonius had his horsemen attack first while his infantry took position behind them. With his heavy infantry, his Immortals, setting up a strong, wicker-shield wall beside the temple of Demeter, the ranks of archers could begin to fire behind this safe barrier.[17] Pausanias could not begin to engage without the correct omens, which were not forthcoming. So as they waited for the gods to join them on the battlefield, the Spartans and Tegeans began to fall under the heavy arrow fire.

The Tegeans could not wait for the religious rites, they were too few to afford these losses and morale would have been faltering. They marched out toward the shield wall, leaving the Spartans to their superstitions. Fortunately for them, the omens changed and the Spartans quickly followed suit. The Persians prepared for the showdown, dropping their bows and arming themselves with spears and swords, ready for hand–to–hand combat.

The fighting began up against the shield wall, but the Greeks finally knocked them over and closed with the Persian infantry. The fighting broke down into a raw and violent brawl, blade against blade, but the Spartans maintained a shadow of a battle line – allowing them to maintain cohesion in this furore. The Persians were fighting gallantly, seizing the Greek spears and breaking them as they fought, bringing the proximity of the killing zone that much closer to the fighter. But they had never regained their composure from the excitement of the original pursuit and often attacked the Greek lines in small groups, head on, allowing the phalanx to do what it did best hold its position and kill indiscriminately.

The Spartans maintained their composure and directed their forward momentum toward the heart of the Persian lines, where Mardonius was fighting alongside 1,000 of the best handpicked Immortals. This core was the beating heart of the Persian fight and the Spartans had finally met their match. The pure desperation of the Spartan position becomes apparent through a later tradition in which a Spartiate picked up a rock and hurled it at Mardonius in a last-gasp attempt to gain an upper hand – it worked. Mardonius fell to the ground, dead. With him fell the morale of the Persians. They routed at the sight of his corpse and fled back, across the river, to their fortification.

On the western side of the battlefield, many of the Greek allies of Persia fled from the Athenians, but their greatest rivals from Boeotia did not. The Thebans especially fought hard, loosing 300 of their best men in their attempts to break the Athenian lines, but to no avail as they too were finally routed.

As the full-scale rout was in motion, the Persian army was saved from a humiliating slaughter by the Boeotian cavalry, who did their best to cut off the Greek advances. The Greeks who had not so far fought, those stationed at the temple of Hera, caught wind of the victory and began to rush over to join in the expected massacre. All that they found was an expectant cavalry ready to pounce. This one action saw the Greeks lose 600 men, as the horsemen cut down the disorderly group.

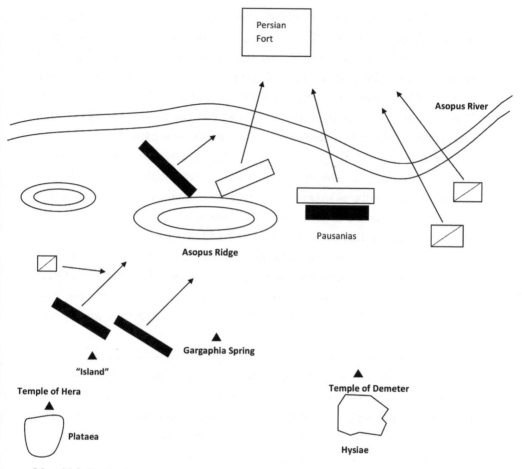

Map 16.3: Battle of Plataea, phase 3.

All the while, the majority of the Persian forces made it back successfully to defend their fortress against the impending assault of the Spartans and Tegeans. The Spartan assault of the walls turned this conflict ever fiercer, as the Persians became the defenders and fought with the tenacity that comes with that position. Many Spartans fell at the palisades as the Persians looked like they were going to hold out indefinitely until the Athenians finally arrived, giving an added impetus and knowhow to force their way in. After many gruelling hours of intense, close-quarter combat, the Athenians had finally managed to mount the walls and tear them down; opening the flood gates for the Greeks to stream in, the Tegeans first.

The Persian resistance crumbled; they were trapped in their thousands and could not escape. The Greeks were running on pure blood lust. These were the barbarians that challenged their freedoms, who had killed their comrades and who had tried to kill them – the revenge was brutal, even barbaric. Herodotus claims that the Greeks killed over ninety per cent of the Persians who had faced them that day. Most of those losses would have been met in the massacre that ensued after the assault on the fort.[18]

How reliable we find this report depends on how many of the Persians were in the fort, as the massacre itself is undeniable; in which case Herodotus' percentages may not be as ridiculous as they sound. If we accept that Artabazus held one seventh of the Persian force, roughly 10,000, and Herodotus' only reliable figure is that of the 3,000 survivors – because these would have been sold as slaves and thus recorded as booty – then that leaves roughly 57,000 combatants that need accounting for. They may not all have died, neither on the battlefield nor in the fort, because they may not have all run to the fort. But, without a Persian source to correct us, we can only assume they were all killed.

The Greeks' losses are more confusing, both historically and within modern scholarship. Some scholars cite Herodotus' figures after the battle to suggest that the Greeks only lost 159 men, but we know from the actions of the Boeotian cavalry that 600 were wiped out in one poor decision to run out of formation – so that makes 759 at the very least. Also on two separate occasions we are told that the fighting intensified and the Lacedaemonians were struggling, first against the Immortals around Mardonius and then at the siege – yet they only lost 91 men?[19] Furthermore, are we to believe that these figures also include the light-armed infantry who originally outnumbered the heavy infantry two to one?

Plutarch, a much later source, claims the Greeks lost 1,360 men, and Diodorus says they lost over 10,000. Unfortunately there is no way of discerning which figure is the closest to the truth, but the constant reiteration by Herodotus of the Spartans struggling and taking losses, makes for a strong argument to lean nearer Diodorus than Herodotus.

The Aftermath

A vast amount of loot was taken from the Persian camp. One tenth was given to the gods Zeus, Apollo at Delphi, and Poseidon, while what remained was divided amongst the men. With the battle over, and the Persians finally out of Greece, it was time for the different *poleis* to recuperate and celebrate their victories. But there was one more victory yet to be accomplished because, for all of the importance surrounding the Battle of Plataea, this was not the last battle of the Persian invasion. The final, full-scale battle was fought at Mycale, on the Ionian coast. This Greek victory brought the invasions to an end, but details are scarce in our sources. Legend has it that this battle was fought on the same day as Plataea.

Even so, Plataea was the battle that successfully ended the Persian incursions into Greece. Never again would the Persians look to Greece as a point of expansion, although they remained constantly entwined in each other's political affairs.

Chapter 17

The Battle of Cunaxa (401 BC)

The Background (Xenophon, *Anabasis*, I.1–8.1; Plutarch, *Life of Artaxerxes*, 1.1–7.4; Diodorus, XIV.11, 19–22.4; Ctesias, *Persica*, Fr. 16

In 404 BC, the Great King of Persia, Darius II, lay at death's door and sent messages to his four sons to be at his bedside. His death quickly followed their arrival and his eldest son, Arsicas, was crowned as his successor, Artaxerxes II. As the eldest son of the king, Artaxerxes' succession had been arranged years in advance, but it was not received well by his immediate, younger brother Cyrus.[1]

Cyrus was a powerful prince in his own right. He held a new *satrapy* which had been created for him by his father, which merged three existing *satrapies*: Lydia, Great Phrygia and Cappadocia. Alongside this gift of authority, he was named the supreme commander of Anatolia. From this position of power he had influenced proceedings in the Peloponnesian War, offering help to the Spartans by paying them to maintain a strong enough fleet to defeat the Athenians. His frustration at being overlooked as the new king was further compounded by his mother, Parysatis, who favoured him over all her other sons. She filled his head with delusions of grandeur, claiming that Cyrus was the rightful heir to the throne because he was the first son born to Darius while he was king.[2]

Cyrus' personal ambitions were already becoming a problem for the other *satraps* in Anatolia. In 405 BC Cyrus had killed two members of the royal family for not treating him in a similar fashion to a king, a crime he was called back to the court of Darius to answer for.[3] Within days of Artaxerxes' coronation, Cyrus found himself accused of conspiracy to murder his brother in the temple of Anahita. The accuser was none other than the old *satrap* of Lydia, Tissaphernes, who had lost his lands to the young prince and instead became a trusted advisor in his court.[4]

Tissaphernes brought forward Cyrus' old teacher, who claimed to have knowledge of the plot. The teacher was known to be upset that his old student was not the new king, and thus his testimony was believed at face value. Cyrus was immediately arrested and was only saved from execution by the intervention of Parysatis. It was Parysatis, not Artaxerxes, who sent Cyrus back to the western coast, far from the court in Babylonia, to protect him. But Cyrus was not safe from the influence of the Great King. On his arrival back in Anatolia he found the great city of Sardis had been taken from him by the garrison commander of the city, Orontas, under the orders of Artaxerxes.[5]

Cyrus was able to subdue the revolt of his city, but he lost control of the majority of his vast *satrapy*.[6] Most importantly, he lost the Ionian Greek *poleis* within his lands to Tissaphernes, who had also been reinstated as the *satrap* of Caria. Tissaphernes overthrew all of the pro–Cyrus regimes that had been installed by the Spartans toward the end of the Peloponnesian War, and directed the vast amounts of tribute from the cities to Artaxerxes, who was planning a campaign against Egypt.[7] For Cyrus, the loss of financial income, added to the loss of face he had experienced at the hands of his brother and his growing enmity for Tissaphernes, meant a conflict was imminent.

Artaxerxes felt little concern for his younger brother, knowing him well enough to expect him to focus his rage on the nearest antagonist, Tissaphernes. He was not wrong. Cyrus instigated a two-pronged attack of overt diplomacy and military threats inside his old territory. Meanwhile, Cyrus also instructed his mercenary commander friends to start hiring soldiers of the highest calibre they could find: in the vicinity of Ionia the mercenaries were mostly made up of seasoned Greek veterans.[8] At the same time, he sent word throughout his wider Greek network for others to do the same, all under the pretence of a war with Tissaphernes.

During 403/2 BC, many of the Greek *poleis* in Ionia flocked to Cyrus, but others continued to resist.[9] Cyrus' forces were growing quickly, but he did not wish to rouse the suspicions of his brother, so he never accumulated them in one place. He had various contingents laying siege to resistant cities in Ionia, another force fighting against the tribes of Mysia, whilst others were allowed a greater autonomy for the time being until he had need of them.[10] During this conflict, Cyrus maintained regular contact with his brother, and was even sending him the tribute raised from the Ionian cities, all to create the image of a dutiful subject.

By the winter of 402 BC Cyrus had control over most of Ionia, but one city still resisted him. The city of Miletus had intended to join his cause, but when Tissaphernes received word of this intention he immediately intervened, killing many of the Milesian ringleaders and exiling the rest. Cyrus sent an army, in conjunction with a fleet, to simultaneously put Miletus under siege by land and sea. With his forces so disparately engaged across Anatolia, nobody was aware of how large an army Cyrus had at his command. Now he just needed to wait for the right opportunity, and he did not have to wait long.

Artaxerxes had been planning an invasion of Egypt from as early as his inauguration. Since 410 BC the situation in Persian-held Egypt had become volatile, with concerns for revolt being overridden by concerns for Egyptian expansion into Phoenicia.[11] By 406 BC and the end of the Peloponnesian War, rebellious Egyptian dynasts looked to exploit the animosity between Athens and Persia by asserting their independence in Egypt with greater fervour.[12] Unfortunately, the dynasts had underestimated the devastation that had been inflicted on the Athenian fleet during their final defeat to Sparta, and they received no support. This gave Artaxerxes time to properly plan his subjugation of the rebels, which was three years in the making.

In 401 BC Artaxerxes had collated a strong force in Phoenicia under the command of Abrocomas, which would serve as the vanguard of his campaign into Egypt.[13] The success of the expedition was almost guaranteed, as Egyptian rebellions had a history of refusing to fight in the wake of such overwhelming odds. But the plans were halted by news from Anatolia.

Tissaphernes had been watching the actions of Cyrus, who had declared a new intent in 401 BC to subdue the Pisidians who were terrorizing his territory. Cyrus used this pretence to finally muster all of his forces together. He was joined in Sardis by more than 8,000 mercenaries before he began his march inland, with more troops ready to join him along the journey. To Tissaphernes, the force at Sardis was already too large to have the humble aim of subduing the Pisidians and so he quickly sent word to Artaxerxes, warning him of what he suspected: that Cyrus was going to challenge the Great King in battle.[14] The king sent a messenger to recall Abrocromas from

Phoenicia, while he prepared to meet Cyrus with the army he was already in the process of levying for the Egyptian campaign.[15]

Cyrus marched his army out from Sardis, heading southeast to Colossae, near the Pisidian border. Here he was joined by the Thessalian commander Meno and a band of mercenaries numbering another 1,500 men. Cyrus then marched east to Celaenae where he was joined by more mercenary troops, including 2,000 veterans led by Clearchus the Spartan. The army stayed in Celaenae for a full month, in which time they were properly organized into their companies, with each of their commanders being given their official roles within the hierarchy.

Cyrus marched his newly formed army east, slowly and with caution. Passing through Phrygia and Lycaonia, the pretext of this campaign could no longer be relied upon to protect Cyrus from his brother's attention. Rumblings of discontent within his own army were threatening to undermine his goals and, whilst payment of overdue wages gave him some respite, it would not hold the men's loyalty forever.[16]

Cyrus' route took him further east, to Dana, before he finally headed south into Cilicia. The Cilician ruler, Syennesis, had sent his wife, Epyaxa, to Cyrus with money and a show of support for the young prince, but Cyrus could not be certain of the old man's loyalties. As the army looked set to march through the narrow Cilician Gates, Cyrus had already sent Epyaxa home with a strong guard force led by Meno, via an alternative route. Meno's force was to escort Epyaxa to Tarsus, the capital of Cilicia, and pose a threat to any Cilician army that may have been sent to block the Cilician Gates. Any plans of Synnesis were duly abandoned when he realized that Meno's contingent was already in his lands, and, to add to this threat, there was news of the arrival of triremes owned by Sparta and Cyrus – the remaining elements of Cyrus army had finally arrived.

Meno's force had suffered losses on the march through the mountains into Cilicia. Their anger and frustration was duly unleashed on the city of Tarsus and, by the time Cyrus' army had joined them, most of the inhabitants had already abandoned their homes. Cyrus managed to placate the situation and re-establish an uneasy alliance with Synnesis, but his army had finally seen through his lies. Rumours were already spreading that this was an army destined for war against Artaxerxes. For twenty days, the men refused to march. Turning on their own commanders, they threw stones at Clearchus for trying to force the issue. To continue the march, Cyrus promised a pay rise for the mercenaries and created a new lie, telling the men that his target was the army of Abrocomas in Phoenicia.[17]

With his army finally marching again, Cyrus met up with the fleet, which had so threatened Synnesis, at Issus, swelling his Greek contingent to 10,400 men.[18] They continued to march through Cilicia and into Syria, before turning east and speeding their route to the River Euphrates, aiming to reach the crossing before Abrocomas could.[19] The army reached the city of Thapascus, on the western bank of the Euphrates, where Cyrus finally revealed his plans to his officers. When the plan was relayed to the men, they simply demanded more money and agreed to continue the march.[20]

Cyrus crossed the river and followed its route southeast, towards Babylon. They started this course well provisioned, picking up supplies along the way, but once they passed the town of Corsote they entered the desert and were forced to start feeding on their own starving pack animals. After a gruelling thirteen days in the scorching heat, Cyrus' army finally came upon the prosperous city of Charmande where they could buy new supplies. In this glut of replenishment, rivalries flared and Clearchus overstepped his authority by punishing a man under the command of Meno for a dispute with one of his own men. The following day, Clearchus was attacked by Meno's contingent, escaping narrowly with his life, and returned with his force of Thracians to fight out the issue. Only the timely intervention of Cyrus was able to calm the matter down, with Clearchus in particular in need of restraint.

Moving out from Charmande, Cyrus marched for three days through Babylonia, with only the threat of betrayal from Orontas marking an otherwise straightforward journey.[21] Cyrus was now within a day's march of the king's defensive trench, which extended inland from the Euphrates. Expecting the king to have amassed his forces at the trench, or at least to have a strong guarding force present, Cyrus spent the night arranging his army into formation, ready for the battle he expected the next morning.

Come early morning, Cyrus marched on the ditch only to find it empty and the small passageway next to the river undefended. To further boost his confidence, footprints and hoofprints could be seen on the ground beyond the ditch, implying that the defensive forces had fled. Cyrus assumed this meant Artaxerxes had abandoned plans to fight and allowed his own army to become lax and lazy on their march, with only a handful maintaining their marching order, while the majority of the mercenaries marched unarmed.

Two days had passed before a trusted scout came racing toward the army of Cyrus, bringing news that a vast army was heading toward them, led by the king himself. The men were in a panic, petrified that the Persian army would fall upon them at a second's notice. Cyrus took control of the situation. Jumping from his chariot, he armed himself and sent out the orders to do likewise. The sun was rising high in the late morning sky, battle was finally imminent and there was not long to arrange the battle formations.

The Battlefield

Just outside the small village of Cunaxa, less than 90km from Babylon, the battle was fought on a vast plain buffered by the Euphrates on Cyrus' right-hand side. The river may have been lined with levees which would have offered a sloping rise towards the water, but the soil, which was cultivated, would have been very soft. Although we do not know where the village of Cunaxa was in relation to the battle, we do know that it was overlooked by a hill with a large plateau.

The plain was a barren and desolate expanse, perfect for cavalry manoeuvres and infantry formations in equal measure: but especially ideal for the use of chariots.[22] The ground was hard, baked as it was by the late summer sun, and covered in a dust which formed choking clouds across the battlefield. In the heat of the afternoon temperatures could reach 38°C (100°F), and the sun would set by 6pm without any twilight.[23]

The Armies

Very little is certain about the constituent parts of either army. The only certain number we have is for the Greek and Thracian contingent of Cyrus' army, which consisted of 10,400 hoplites and 2,500 *peltasts* (including 200 Cretan archers). The vast majority of his army were near-eastern troops, of which we know the presence of 1,000 horsemen from Paphlagonia. Also, it seems likely that Cyrus had access to 20 scythed chariots, but they do not appear in the battle narrative.[24] The figures for the rest of Cyrus' forces given in the sources are astronomical, but modern estimates place the strength of his non-Greek troops at approximately 20–25,000, inclusive of cavalry.[25] This gave Cyrus an army of roughly 30–35,000, if not more.

Artaxerxes' forces are almost completely unknown. The sources only offer phenomenal numbers from 400–900,000 men, which cannot be believed.[26] Modern estimates place the king's army between 50–60,000 men, with a large force of scythed chariots.[27] The army had a mixture of lightly armed infantry, heavily armed Egyptian infantry, and large amounts of archers and cavalrymen. The king had his bodyguard of 6,000 cavalry and presumably his whole retinue, which would have included the 10,000-strong Immortals as well as the 1,000 handpicked elite which formed his infantry bodyguard.[28]

The Battle (Xenophon, *Anabasis*, I.8.1–10.19; Plutarch, *Life of Artaxerxes*, 8–14; Diodorus, XIV.22.5–24.7; Ctesias, *Persica*, Fr. 16, 20–22)

Cyrus' men were in a fluster. Grabbing their arms and armour, they rushed awkwardly to their positions, desperately trying to establish their lines. Clearchus took his position on the right wing next to the river edge with the majority of the Greek forces, flanked by the Greek *peltasts* and the 1,000 Paphlagonian cavalry for support. To Clearchus' left formed the Greeks under the command of Proxenus, with Meno and his Thessalians forming the left-most unit of the Greek corps. Cyrus placed himself in the centre, with his heavily-armed bodyguard of 600 cavalrymen. The left wing, which was to be taken up by Cyrus' second-in-command, Ariaeus, extended the line with infantry, with cavalry on the extreme flank. Ariaeus himself took immediate control of the cavalry.[29]

Cyrus' lines grew slowly through the hot midday sun, but even the sight of billowing dust in the distance did little to increase the speed of his men's movement. By the time the royal army spewed from the dirt cloud, Cyrus' lines were still not fully formed, with Ariaeus' flank still taking shape.[30]

Artaxerxes' army marched on in battle formation. On his left wing, next to the river, shone the white body armour of 500 cavalrymen under the direct command of Tissaphernes.[31] Beside him sat a corps of lighter-armed infantry pulled from the wider Persian empire, next to whom stood the experienced warriors of Egypt, heavily armed with shields that reached to the ground. The rest of the army extended out beyond Cyrus' lines, with Artaxerxes taking the central position which lined up opposite Ariaeus' infantry.[32] With all of the infantry organized into solid block formations, they formed a seemingly indomitable wall. The right flank was protected by cavalry whilst the formation was headed by a large number of scythed chariots.

Artaxerxes' army continued to advance, but the cacophony of noise, which Cyrus had forewarned his men to stand firm against, did not come. In an eerie silence, the king's army closed the distance. Cyrus could finally see the layout of his brother's forces and sent word to Clearchus: the Greeks under his command were to move against the king's position in the centre and break the Persian lines.[33] Clearchus refused. His hoplites were in a strong position by the river where they could not be outflanked, and to move his men would mean leaving a large hole on the right wing, which the enemy would easily exploit. Cyrus was not disheartened by the refusal, for the omens were in his favour and the sacrifices had been well received; the gods were on his side.

The Greeks waited anxiously, while the watchword was passed through their lines: 'Zeus the Saviour and Victory'.[34] When the enemy had come within 700 metres, the Greeks struck up the *paean* and began their advance. Their nerves overcame their experience and, as they advanced, some of the men began to speed up. Those that fell behind soon began to run, inducing those ahead to begin to run. Before long the Greek lines lost all semblance of order as they raced toward the enemy, with many starting to bang their shields with their spears to frighten the horses.[35] The Persian line stood and waited.

As the Greeks closed the gap they began to slow down and reform their lines. The deafening noise of their charge had startled the horses of the chariots, many of which bolted in every direction, toward the Greeks in front and the Persians behind them. As the chariots ploughed into Clearchus' lines, the Greeks anticipated their trajectory and opened up a gap, allowing them to pass.[36] Apart from one man who was stunned into immobility and struck by an unpiloted chariot, the Greeks remained unscathed and pressed on, through the flying arrows overhead, into the disrupted enemy lines.

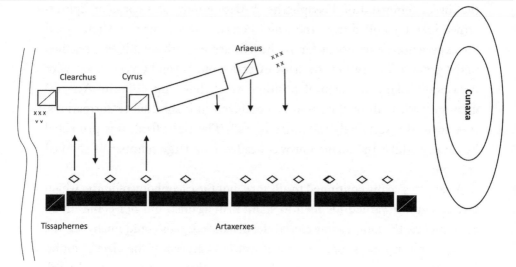

Map 17.1: Battle of Cunaxa, phase 1.

By the time the Greeks had entered missile range, the Persian light infantry began to flee before them. However, before Clearchus could take control of the situation, his men began to chase the Persian infantry off the field. To his right, Clearchus saw the cavalry of Tissaphernes charge along next to the river, routing the Paphlagonians without a fight. But the *peltasts* had taken the higher ground on the levees, where the ground was too soft and the slope perhaps too steep for the Persian horses to ride across, and inflicted losses as they rode past.[37] Tissaphernes had predicted the Greek pursuit and looked to exploit the gap behind them, before heading straight for the Greek camp.[38] Clearchus was helpless to stop him. He had lost control of his men to the lust of the chase. His only hope was to try and regroup them before they became isolated miles off the field.

Waiting in the centre, Cyrus saw the Greeks break the enemy flank and took heart, with many of his entourage doing him homage as if he was already king. But Cyrus did not join the pursuit and, instead, waited to see what his brother was going to do. Artaxerxes was unfazed by the activities on his left wing. In fact all was going to plan, and his right wing was still closing the gap between them and his brother's forces. With the strong Greek contingent now out of the way, and Tissaphernes' small cavalry force at the rear of

Cyrus' lines, Artaxerxes ordered his right wing to cut inside and move to outflank the unfinished lines of Ariaeus.

Cyrus decided to act fast.[39] Ignoring the unbroken lines of the Egyptians in front of him, he drove his personal guard of 600 men in an oblique attack on the king's position. His horsemen charged into the king's cavalry bodyguard, commanded by Artagerses, and began a bloody fight. With the odds stacked firmly against him, Cyrus needed fortune to smile on him but Artagerses spotted him and immediately hurled his javelin, striking Cyrus. But his armour held strong and the missile fell to the ground. Cyrus quickly came to his senses and threw his own javelin at the retreating commander, penetrating the base of his neck and out through his collar bone.

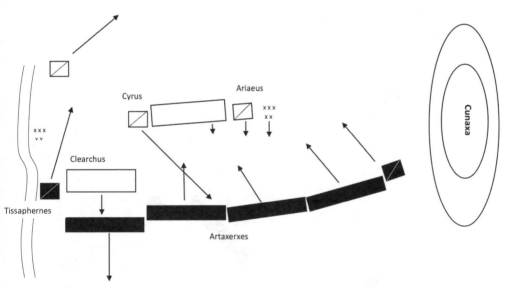

Map 17.2: Battle of Cunaxa, Phase 2.

With Artagerses dead, the bodyguard began to retreat, giving Cyrus first sighting of his brother. He rashly charged on, attacking the men directly in front of Artaxerxes and injuring the king's horse. Artaxerxes was swiftly given another steed, but Cyrus' next attack unhorsed him once more. By the third wave of assault, Artaxerxes felt no safer behind his protectors and moved forward to attack his insubordinate sibling. The fraternal duel was short lived, with Artaxerxes taking a minor wound to his body before swiftly escaping to the hill overlooking Cunaxa village with a large body of cavalry.

Cyrus soon became enveloped by his brother's men and, with one well-aimed javelin striking him through the temple and penetrating beneath the eye, he fell from his horse and died.[40] A close friend of the prince, named Artapatas, leapt upon his fallen body to protect it and, seeing that all was lost, pulled out a golden dagger and killed himself atop his liege.

Seeing Cyrus fall broke the resolve of Ariaeus, who fled with his cavalry, leaving his now-isolated infantry to be overwhelmed by the royal force's flanking manoeuvre to their left and the Egyptians to their right. As the royal forces broke through, many of them chased the broken ranks back to the Greek camp. But only Ariaeus' horsemen were fast enough to continue fleeing back to their original bivouac site, from which they had marched earlier that morning.

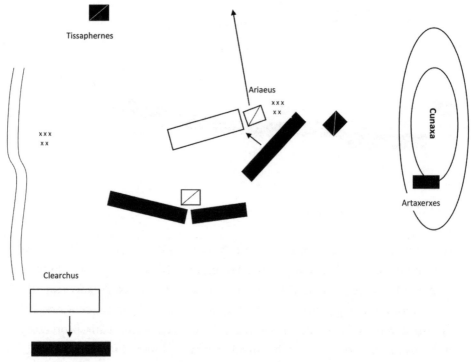

Map 17.3: Battle of Cunaxa, phase 3.

In the Greek camp, the men of Artaxerxes became enamoured with the plunder and women available to them. A plucky resistance from a handful of Greeks managed to save Cyrus' youngest concubine, but did little to resist the awesome power of their enemy. Back on the hill overlooking Cunaxa, Artaxerxes had been patched up by his physician, Ctesias, and was awaiting reports from the battle.[41]

Thirty messengers came bursting onto his position to give him the news: Cyrus had fallen, the Greeks had left the field, and Artaxerxes had won the day. Elated by his success, Artaxerxes ordered the troops with him on the hill to accompany him down to the battlefield. As he descended, more and more of his forces began to regroup around him. When Artaxerxes' men finally took control of the body of Cyrus, the head and right hand of Cyrus were unceremoniously hacked from his corpse in accordance with Persian law. The king was handed the head of his brother, which he held aloft as a symbol of his victory. The bloody scene attracted more of his disparate forces to gravitate around him, but news came that disrupted the victory celebrations: the Greeks had stopped their pursuit.

As the fraternal battle had been fought and the rout completed, Clearchus finally reconstituted his forces; their chase had taken them 5km away from the army of Artaxerxes. Believing that they had won the day, the Greeks relaxed, but word reached them that their baggage camp was being raided by the king's men. Clearchus spoke with Proxenus, one of the mercenary commanders, and debated whether to send a detachment to help defend the camp or to go in full force. But, before a decision could be made, a new message arrived warning of the approach of Artaxerxes' army.

Clearchus turned his army about-face to meet the royal army, but became concerned that he would be quickly outflanked on his new right wing. He hoped to peel back Meno's men and turn the entire army ninety degrees with the river to their backs, but the king's army was progressing too fast to do it safely. The late afternoon sun was quickly fading and neither army wished to fight in the dark, but each planned to deal with it differently. Artaxerxes ordered his army to return to the hill above Cunaxa and set up camp. The Greeks, on the other hand, saw only one way to survive this day and ordered the *paean* to be chanted and the army to advance.[42]

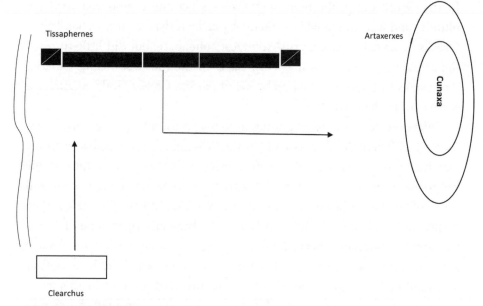

Tissaphernes

Artaxerxes

Cunaxa

Clearchus

Map 17.4: Battle of Cunaxa, phase 4.

The disorder of the royal lines caused by the retreat was compounded by the sight of the Greek advance, quickly turning into a rout. The Greeks chased them as far as the village of Cunaxa, but the king's cavalry had regrouped on the hill to protect the continuing retreat of the infantry. The Greeks were brimming with confidence and continued their advance up the hill, with the Persian cavalry swiftly following their infantry counterparts down the other side of the plateau. Clearchus stopped the pursuit before it reached the summit, sending some scouts to check the situation from the top. Once word was received that the Persians had fled and set up camp, the Greeks finally rested knowing that the day was over and their battle won.

Losses on either side are unknown, but the king's forces may have lost somewhere in the region of 9,000 men in total.[43] The Greeks ostensibly lost no men, with only one injury noted due to the chariots and one more due to an arrow. Cyrus' near-eastern forces are unaccounted for.

The Aftermath

The Greeks returned to the baggage camp, which had been sorely raided by the Persian army. As night enveloped their camp, they began to question where Cyrus was, presuming that he had continued a pursuit, or perhaps he had taken up a strategic point nearer to Babylon; either way, they were not concerned.

By the next morning they were more perplexed, Cyrus had still not sent a messenger with orders of what to do. They decided to continue with the original plans to march on Babylon, and hope Cyrus sent them instructions along the way. As the sun fully rose above the horizon their preparations for departure were interrupted by two riders who had come from Ariaeus with the news of Cyrus' death.

Cut off and alone in the heart of the Persian Empire, the Greek army embarked on their famous journey home.[44]

Part V

Conclusions

The classical Greek world was particularly fascinated with war. It was not their only interest of course, but so much of their writing, their drama, their poetry, their philosophy, and their rhetoric was influenced by the actions and behaviours of people in war. From combatants on the front line, to their wives at home, the Greeks were interested in the wider picture that prolonged warfare can paint for a society.

When it came to Greek battles, the image was anything but static. Rather than visualizing a set block of formations crashing into another block, we see a complex, nuanced approach to battle which incorporated the multi-faceted make up of their armies. The classic image, of battle being decided by a clash of phalanx-against-phalanx, can only be seen in a small handful of battles (First Mantinea, Coronea, Nemea and Leuctra), with every other example described within this work containing an important divergence from this model. This raises the question: how valid is the traditional model, as a reflection of Greek warfare?

The importance of light infantry can be seen from the very start of the Peloponnesian War, at Olpae and then at Sphacteria, all the way through to the supposed mastermind of their incorporation into Greek tactics, Iphicrates at Lechaeum. By the time of the Second Battle of Mantinea, their impact within a joint force with cavalry is plain to see. Unfortunately, as it is just as plain to see in the battle maps, they go missing from the battle narratives unless they specifically impacted the outcome of battle, which means that they are left to wander the imaginary battlefield without direction.

The role of cavalry is just as easily overlooked. From as early as Marathon it can be seen that the Greeks held a healthy respect and fear for the organized Persian cavalry force. Yet the Greek cavalry held a similar capability, as was seen by the Spartans when they were repulsed by a Thessalian cavalry force in 510 BC, and again at Plataea when the Boeotian cavalry wiped out 600 fellow Greeks in a single charge. By the battle of Delium they are shown as a useful tactical arm for the commander, and at Lechaeum their incompetence reveals the important role cavalry was expected to play as a screening force. By far their most common role was to pursue and cut down the enemy as they fled the battlefield, something the phalanx couldn't do without breaking their own formation and becoming vulnerable to counterattack.

The traditional image of battle also negates the role of individual commanders, or groups of commanders, who showed themselves to be uniquely minded in resolving the persistent problems that arose from battle. Demosthenes was able to learn from his humiliation in Aetolia by utilizing the light-armed troops, who had so efficiently destroyed his own forces, to overcome the dominance of the Spartans on the battlefield, not once but twice. At Delium, Pagondas pre-empted the loss of his left wing and split his cavalry force to surprise the Athenian right wing before it could reinforce the remainder of their army. Iphicrates and Callias masterminded the victory at Lechaeum by studying their enemy and predicting their behaviours, timing their attack to perfection, and the same was true of Miltiades at Marathon.

The Spartans seem to have had a general battle plan, based upon the exploitation of Greek battlefield habits, which resulted in a similar manoeuvre in each battle. They would try to outflank the enemy, wheel around and sweep up the rest of the field, and it worked time and again with devastating results. However, the Spartans were also capable of adaptation. At Olpae, Eurylochus switched the strongest wing to the left hand side, so that he could direct his attack on Demosthenes in person. Brasidas, at Amphipolis, planned an ambush from inside the city, which had a horrific result on the Athenian army that was marching past. Later still, Praxitas in the Long Walls of Corinth chose to fortify his position on a narrow battlefield and use his cavalry force as a mobile reserve. Once battle was under way, he waited until it was most opportune and enacted the standard Spartan tactic of pushing forwards, wheeling his formation and sweeping up the field – indeed this is the main reason why the battle has not been classified as a siege here.

The Theban general Epaminondas was equally adept at changing his tactics. Whilst very few of his ideas were unique, he was able to learn the lessons from battles over the past 100 years to great effect. His displacement of the deep Theban formation to the left wing, his use of cavalry and light-armed troops, his oblique march on the enemy formation: all evidence of an ability to adapt away from the 'classic' model.

What is also quickly apparent is that a battle was not decided solely on the battlefield. The background to a battle, with all of its minor skirmishes, false starts of combat, diplomatic wrangling, and wider campaign objectives, creates a more complex image of the morale and the mind-set of the men involved in the battle. Similarly, many battles ended not in a rout, but in a siege situation. At Plataea and Delium, as well as the unmentioned Potidaea, a ferocious battle was ended with a bloody siege.

Sieges themselves took a variety of forms. There were classic sieges of cities like Syracuse and Plataea, but there were variances such as the siege of an island like at Sphacteria, or the siege of fortified military positions like at Pylos and the Persian fort at Plataea. We are also fortunate to have the detailed account of a siege against a foreign city, the Drilae, which highlights one of the weaknesses of a Greek siege, the discipline of their men. The image of Greek siege warfare is not one of finesse, but of pragmatism. The methods, and counter methods, of sieges were not always sophisticated, but they were effective, and the overarching battle was not always a physical one, with morale being the most important factor in a siege's outcome.

The Greco-Persian conflicts have been dealt with separately from the main Greek narrative. This has allowed for a more rounded image of the conflict to appear, by removing such an emphasis on Greek military practices, which had already been covered. The subsequent narrative shows the Greeks and Persians to be equally adept at tactical adaptation and, at times, innovation.

The Athenian victory at Marathon was no less impressive a feat even when the Persian numbers, and their campaign motives, have been altered from Herodotus' account. Miltiades was able to exploit a weakness he studied in the Persian behaviour, and implement a charge which seems to have had a very powerful psychological impact on the Persians who faced it. By the Battle of Cunaxa, it was the Persian commander Tissaphernes who had studied his enemy. By exploiting Greek battlefield behaviour, the Persians were able to nullify their impact on the battle and remove them as an imminent threat.

The overall image of Greek warfare cannot comfortably fit into a model, because it was not a set process. While there are common threads throughout, the most dominant aspect of any battle is how one, or both, sides adapted to the changes in circumstances to try to achieve victory.

Following the uneasy stalemate after the Second Battle of Mantinea, Greece became devoid of any singular power or authority. This impotence was brought to light in 356 BC, when the collective group that held responsibility over the Panhellenic site of Delphi, the Amphictyonic League, was unable to punish the *polis* of Phocis for the sacrilegious cultivation of sacred lands. The dispute broke out into war, now known as the Third Sacred War, and it lasted for ten years. This was an impressive feat for Phocis, as the council had some seemingly powerful *poleis*, such as Thebes, in its membership. It was not until the intervention of an external power that the conflict was brought to an end. But in a historical twist that foreshadowed the coming epoch, it was not the Persians who became involved in this dispute, but King Phillip II of Macedonia.

Phillip's presence begins the period of Macedonian influence, and later control, over the Greek city-states. With the battle of Chaeronea in 338 BC, Greek resistance to Macedonia was conclusively beaten, bringing an end to the classical Greek world and ushering in the new Hellenistic world.

Notes

Chapter 1: The Battle of Olpae (426/5 BC)

1. Whilst land battles had already been fought – such as the Corinthian defeat at Megara, the Athenian victory outside the walls of Potidaea, the Athenian defeat at Spartolus – the two spheres of activity that engage the most of Thucydides' attention were two sieges, Potidaea and Plataea (See Part 3: Siege Warfare and Chapter 11 in particular). The Battle of Olpae is the first, large scale, hoplite battle which Thucydides gives a detailed account of.
2. Melos had up until now refused to join the Athenian confederacy or become subjects of Athens.
3. These Messenians had been settled in Naupactus by the Athenians in the aftermath on the *helot* revolt in Sparta (465–457/6 BC)
4. An undeniable driving force for the young Demosthenes was his own quest for glory, this will not be the last time he makes plans to act without the necessary support from Athens.
5. We do not know the size or make up of this polyglot force, but the description of the subsequent fighting implies they were mostly hoplites, with a force of archers in their midst.
6. The Aetolians were known to be very numerous and warlike, but lightly armed and widely dispersed in their un-walled villages. (Thucydides, III.94.4).
7. A minor point but an important one in grasping the character of Demosthenes, he was not let down by his allies, as suggested by Roisman, but was too eager for action and too easily manipulated by the Messenians. J. Roisman, *The General Demosthenes and His Use of Military Surprise* (Stuttgart, 1993), p. 26.
8. The Athenian army did have a guide, Chromon the Messenian, but he died in the earlier stages of the battle.
9. Almost half of the original 300 Athenians in the army. Thucydides (III.98.4) describes them as by far the best men in the city of Athens that died during the war, perhaps indicating that he knew some of them.
10. Note that this did not include a fighting force from Sparta itself, they only supplied a commander and two other *spartiates*, Macarius and Menedaius.
11. Eurylochus purposefully targeted the Ozolian Locrians because they were an ally of Athens. Without the immediate use of force he was able to intimidate many of the cities in the region to offer hostages or join his army.

12. Amphilochian Argos was so called to differentiate it from the more widely known Argos in the Peloponnese, in this chapter only it will hereafter be referred to as Argos.

13. N. Hammond, 'The Campaigns in Amphilochia during the Archidamian War', in *The Annual of the British School in Athens*, 37 (1936/7), p.129 (fig.1).

14. If Hammond is correct in his placement of Metropolis then the geography of the area explains why the ravine was not mentioned within the battle narrative, when the Peloponnesians routed they headed due west to Olpae so it was never an obstacle.

15. This was, after all, supposed to be a precursor to a greater offensive that would secure Spartan influence in the region.

16. The attribution of this ambush to Demosthenes is a controversial topic, focussing on whether or not he envisioned this ambush all by himself. Whilst it is undoubtable that he would have learned from his experiences in Aetolia the year before, he was not ever ambushed (as far as we know) by a joint force of hoplites and light-armed troops. The distinctive use of hoplites within this ambush shows that, whilst this may not have been a unique idea, from looking at his own experiences, he had adapted it to fit within the formal setting of a hoplite battlefield. Cf. J. Roisman, *The General Demosthenes and His Use of Military Surprise* (Stuttgart, 1993), p. 29.

17. This is contrary to 'traditional' hoplite battle models which place the direction of attack on the right wing, possibly due to the inclination of the men to hide behind the shield to their right creating a drifting effect in that direction. The most intriguing element is not that the Spartan commander diverged from accepted protocol, but that Demosthenes anticipated this unusually strong left wing and hid the small force there to help protect him from it – bringing into question how unusual the tactic really was in Greek warfare.

18. A classic, and stereotypically Spartan manoeuvre which demonstrates that Eurylochus must have drilled his allies to achieve this very complex action in the field.

19. Mendaius was the third choice of command. Not only had Eurylochus died in battle, but also the Spartiate Macarius who was second in command.

20. Amazingly these were the reinforcements that were called for by the Ambracian army, before Eurylochus had even arrived at Olpae.

21. Ancient Greek, like many modern languages, was spoken in a variety of dialects that were well known. Different groups shared dialects, such as the Messenians and the Spartans. If an Athenian had led the army and spoken his native tongue he would have been recognized as speaking Attic Greek, and could not be confused for being a Spartan.

22. Thucydides (III.113.6) states that the numbers of Ambracians dead, as given to him by his source (possibly Demosthenes himself), was out of proportion with the size of the *polis* of Ambracia and therefore could not be considered credible.

Chapter 2: The Battle of Delium (424 BC)

1. For the sieges of Pylos and Sphacteria see chapter 12. Cythera lay off the south coast of the Peloponnese and was populated by *perioeci* from Laconia. It was an important landing place for trading vessels from Libya and Egypt. By taking the island, Athens had cut off trading income to Sparta. They had also established a second base, including Pylos, that allowed them to raid the Laconian countryside as they wished.

2. Athens had expulsed the Aeginetans from their island in 431 BC, blaming them for being part of the decision of the Peloponnesians to join the war with Athens.

3. Amazingly, considering the dire situation in which Sparta found itself in 424 BC, it never experienced the loss of allies or the dreaded *helot* revolt that it so greatly feared. V. D. Hanson, *A War Like No Other: How the Athenians and Spartans Fought the Peloponnesian War* (New York, 2005), p.123.

4. A 'popular party' was a group who wanted to invest the Greek concept of democratic rule in a given city; it was usually necessary for this party to overthrow either a tyrant or an oligarchic regime (as in the case of Megara).

5. This was the same Demosthenes who won the victories at Olpae and Pylos (see chapters 1 & 12 respectively)

6. It is interesting that the ruling authority needed to be cautious in its dealings with Athens through fear that the very people they were meant to represent might resist. Their assumption that the city would capitulate to the Athenians without resistance shows a gross underestimation for underlying animosities.

7. *Peripoloi*: almost nothing is known about the *peripoloi* other than they may have served as a frontier guard or territorial police. The idea that they might have been young Athenian recruits is taken from A.W. Gomme, *A Historical Commentary on Thucydides*, vol. iii, (Oxford, 1956), p. 539.

   Enyalius was a war god, akin to Ares. The location of the sanctuary is still unknown, but we can assume it was still on the island of Minoa.

8. Diodorus' account (XII.66.1–4) differs from Thucydides in that he suggests that the walls which were originally breached were not the long walls but the city walls of Megara, meaning that the Athenians were inside Megara when they laid siege to Nisaea. I have preferred to use Thucydides' account because it is more in depth and gives a more rounded version of events, namely the lack of popular support held by the popular party.

9. The same Brasidas who fought bravely at Pylos (see Chapter 12), and who would go on to fight at Amphipolis (see chapter 3).

10. This included 2,700 Corinthians hoplites, 400 Phleiasians, 600 Sicyonians, 2,200 Boeotians, and 600 Boeotian cavalrymen.

11. For Athens they were outnumbered, their original force of 600 hoplites in Hippocrates' original detachment, had been joined by 4,000 hoplites from Eleusis (Thucydides, IV.68) and the small group of lightly armed troops from Demosthenes' original fighting force. As for Brasidas, he could realistically have

engaged in the battle expecting victory, he had taken the better position and he had the larger army, but the loss of life was unnecessary if he could intimidate the Athenians into not engaging in battle.

12. For the invasion of Thrace see Chapter 3.

13. Contrary to some reconstructions, there is little evidence that the plan involved a large-scale pitched battle that would 'decide' the issue in Boeotia, namely the democratization of the region. Cf. V. D. Hanson, *A War Like No Other: How the Athenians and Spartans Fought the Peloponnesian War* (New York, 2005), p.125.

14. The splitting of the forces is not a suspicious act. The close proximity to Athens would have made a strong appeal to people wanting to return home and back to work. For the richer hoplites it is possible that the lure was less strong to return home, but it is more likely that they had more to carry and so needed the rest in camp.

15. According to *Hellenica Oxyrhynchia* (XVI.4) each *boeotarch* would have brought a division of 1,000 hoplites each and 100 cavalry, so in this respect the Theban army was grossly undermanned. Diodorus (XII.69.3–4) gives an overall figure of just under 20,000 men, and 1,000 cavalry, but he does not specify if the infantry were all hoplites, in which case his figure is not that different from Thucydides'.

16. The Athenian cavalry may even have been in greater number than the Boeotians, as Hippocrates felt secure enough to leave 300 of his cavalry at the fortified sanctuary, despite knowing he would be facing some of the best horsemen in Greece. G. Bugh, *The Horsemen of Athens* (Princeton, 1988), p. 87–8.

17. The sanctuary was technically in the lands of the *polis* Oropus which was a border town between Attica and Boeotia. The comment is made all the more absurd because Thebes and Athens so often challenged each other for control of it (Pausanias I.34.1).

18. The sacrilege of destroying sacred property and fortifying the sanctuary at Delium.

19. Hippocrates' early death is commented on by Pausanias (III.6.1).

20. It is said that the famous philosopher Socrates was present at the battle and received many plaudits for his behaviour during the rout (Plato, *Symposium*, 221a-b). However, Thucydides' failure to mention him did cause some scepticism of these claims, with some people accusing Socrates or his followers of making it up (Athenaeus, *The Deipnosophists*, 5.pos=392).

21. There was no greater taboo than the refusal to properly care for the dead and Boeotia's answer would have been greatly distressing for the Athenians.

22. The complexity of the argument is brilliantly presented by Thucydides (IV.97–99) and is a must-read for anyone interested in the 'rules' of Greek warfare. The argument is not given by Diodorus at all, nor does he mention the withholding of the corpses. For a fascinating analysis of the two writers and their accounts of Delium's aftermath see S. Nevin, 'Military Ethics in the Writing of History:

Thucydides and Diodorus', in (eds.) E. Bragg, L.I. Hau & E. Macaulay-Lewis, *Beyond the Battlefields: New Perspectives on Warfare and Society in the Graeco-Roman World* (Cambridge, 2008), pp. 99–120.

23. The full description of Thucydides is here summarized, for the original description see Thucydides, IV.100.2–4. A similar device seems to have been used by Brasidas at Torone, in the same year (see Chapter 3).

24. Thucydides earlier described the lack of light-armed troops for the Athenians at the battle, so this is either an oversight or a description of the deaths met on their independent march back to Athens.

Chapter 3: The Battle of Amphipolis (422 BC)

1. The Chalcedonian region's revolt against Athens began in 432, this gave rise to the siege of Potidaea which was the catalyst for the Peloponnesian War.

2. Lyncestis was a kingdom to the northern borders of Macedonia.

3. See Chapter 2: The Battle of Delium for the background regarding the Spartan concerns about the *helots*.

4. See Chapter 12.

5. Thucydides (IV.80.3–4) gives the figure of 700 *helots*, after describing an authorized massacre of a further 2,000. Diodorus (XII.67.3) gives the figure as 1,000 *helots* in Brasidas' army.

6. See Chapter 2 for a full explanation of the Siege of Megara.

7. The assumed autonomy of Brasidas during this campaign has been expertly criticized by S. Hornblower, *A Commentary on Thucydides: Volume II: Books IV-V. 24* (Oxford, 1996), p.51–3. The autonomy described here is not in contrast to Spartan orders or desires, but regarding his decision making and his ability to formulate alliances without correspondence with the leadership back in Sparta.

8. The act of marching through uninvited was enough for Thucydides to describe it as a 'delicate step to take' anywhere in Greece, but Thessaly had the added difficulty of having strong ties of friendship with Athens.

9. The manipulative nature of this rhetoric meant that the Thessalians, by not letting his army pass, were in essence acknowledging a conflict that the Spartans were not aware of – thus they would be causing a quarrel, and even a war, when there was not one to begin with. It is also an example of Brasidas' habit of making false statements of intent. He had no intention of stopping his army's march even without the opponent's approval.

10. Andros was an island off the coast of Athens. Although it was not Athenian, it was at this time a disillusioned member of the Delian League.

11. This was not the same army. The army he had in Megara was 6,000 strong and outnumbered the Athenians.

12. Although this was not directly a lie, the speed with which Acanthus was later handed over to the Athenians in 422/1 BC raises the question of whether

Brasidas already knew that Sparta would not protect the independence of any city in the region.

13. It is here that the narrative becomes more suspect because this is the same Thucydides who has been our venerable source for the entire Peloponnesian War and his writing appears to be an attempt to alleviate any blame from his name. Thucydides was exiled from Athens after the loss of Amphipolis. His experiences as a general give him both profound knowledge of the events but also an immeasurable bias that cannot be ignored. See J R Ellis, 'Thucydides at Amphipolis', in *Antichthon*, 12, (1978), pp. 28–35. To the credit of Thucydides, he tried very hard to not let his own experiences sully the integrity of his history covering this period.

14. Thucydides never tells us how long this took, but certainly implies it was all done with immediacy. It is unrealistic to believe that the fleet sailed the same day the message was received, as it was winter and during a storm. It has been postulated that Thucydides is purposefully vague to hide his own delay to act, something that was not treated kindly back in Athens. See G Wylie, 'Brasidas: Great Commander or Whiz-Kid?', in *Quaderni Urbinati di Cultura Classica*, 41:2, (1992), pp. 82–3.

15. Amphipolis governed an area which supplied Athens with much gold, silver and vital timber for its navy. The strategic position also gave greater protection to the crucial grain supply which came from Scythia, through the Black Sea.

16. This was a hugely symbolic resting point for any Spartan; the Dioscuri were the twins Castor and Pollux who were large cult figures in Sparta. They were given a special significance through their connection with the dual-kingship of Sparta.

17. See Chapter 2.

18. Interestingly this defence was already in place; maybe it was a hasty construction in the two day truce. What makes this interesting is that, ostensibly, the first appearance of this weapon was at Delium earlier that year. This means that the Athenians had already learned how to defend against it, and also that they were able to predict its most likely target within the siege (the defensive tower was built on top of a house, so it could not be moved). This implies a more thorough understanding of the weapon than we may expect from its contemporary appearance, or it implies that the weapon was not as novel as it appears in the sources.

19. Thucydides does not explain this decision, but maybe it was an attempt by Brasidas to secure more funding from the Macedonian king. G Wylie, 'Brasidas: Great Commander or Whiz-Kid?', p.86.

20. A lesson he may well have learnt from the diplomacy shown by Brasidas in the previous year.

21. This battlefield reconstruction is based upon the work of C. Koukouli – Chrysanthaki, 'Excavating Classical Amphipolis', in (eds) M. Stamatopoulou

and M. Yeroulanou, *Excavating Classical Culture: Recent Archaeological Discoveries in Greece*, BAR International Series 1031, (2002).

22. When the battle began Cleon was still waiting for more allies to arrive, but it is safe to say he was able to reinforce his men whilst in Eion.

23. The calibre of the troops from Lemnos and Imbros is attested by Thucydides who, as has been mentioned earlier, had strong connections with the area whilst commander of Amphipolis.

24. This anecdote is based upon a later Roman tradition related by Polyaenus (I.38.2) and Frontinus (I.5.23), the veracity of it is suspect but it makes for an interesting story and reflects Brasidas' arrogant character.

25. It is unlikely that this was Brasidas' actual plan, but rather an opportunistic pounce upon a fundamental military error by the Athenians.

26. This remarkably low loss of life for the army of Brasidas is explained by Thucydides (V.11.2) as the result of the irregular engagement, describing it as an affair of accident and panic, rather than a battle.

Chapter 4: The Battle of 1st Mantinea (418 BC)

1. The games at Olympia were held every four years and formed a temporary, religious truce during war.

2. Argos accused the authorities in Epidaurus of not sending an offering to Apollo Pythaeus, the temple of whom was managed by the Argives.

3. By taking Epidaurus it was hoped that Argos could force Corinth into a state of neutrality, which would open up the communication lines between Argos and Athens. It would also allow Athens safe passage into the Peloponnese with an army. As it was, they had to sail a long way round the point of Scyllaeum to enter Argive territory.

4. Perhaps signifying the trust, or power, held by Sparta with its allies, this force was so secret that the allied cities who supplied troops were not told the destination of intent. The Spartans were very diligent with their religious obligations, a negative divination would often override military sense.

5. In the opinion of the experienced military veteran Thucydides.

6. The exact number in this small army is not known, but we are told that the Corinthians alone supplied 2,000 hoplites so this would have been a substantial rearguard.

7. The third element of Agis' army, the Corinthian-Pellenian-Philiasian guard, had held their position after their skirmish and held the high ground, whilst the Boeotian-Megarian-Sicyonian force cut off the road back to Nemea.

8. Alciphron was one of five generals leading the army. A *proxenos* was a citizen of their state (in this case Argos) who was an official friend and representative for an external state (in this case Sparta).

9. It was considered a grave insult to the gods to harm someone who had taken refuge with them.

10. Tegea was the last major ally of Sparta in the lands of Arcadia.

11. D. Kagan, *The Peace of Nicias and the Sicilian Expedition* (New York: 1981), p.111–13.

12. For further information on the difficulties of this Thucydidean section see J.F. Lazenby, *The Spartan Army* (Barnsley, 2012), pp. 51–5.

13. Thucydides (V.68.1–2) says that although the Spartan army looked the larger of the two, it was hard to put down accurate figures for either host.

14. This elite force was specifically trained in war, making them an amazing commodity in ancient Greek warfare, and akin to the Spartan elite in ability and stature.

15. These figures are based on Lazenby, *The Spartan Army*, pp.154–6. The honest reasoning he uses in conjuring them is refreshing. His estimates also end with a figure that conforms to Thucydides' description that the Spartan force was the larger of the two, but not by a great deal. Cf. L. Tritle, *A New History of the Peloponnesian War* (Oxford, 2010), p. 124, who gives a larger figure of over 16,000 men for the Athenian confederacy but gives no reasoning behind this, completely contradicting Thucydides without explanation.

16. It is possible that this diversion of the waterways directed the river into another one, causing the levels of devastation described by Thucydides. Lazenby, *The Spartan Army*, p. 153.

17. The Spartans had a strict order of authority through which messages and orders were disseminated: Agis gave orders to the *polemarchs* who commanded the *morai*; they passed it on to the *lochagoi* who commanded the *lochoi*. From there the orders went down further through the minor officers called *pentecostyes*, *enomotarchs* and *enomoties* in order.

18. For all of the fear they were feeling, the confederates were not fleeing but were, in fact, able to maintain their march. If they were running the formation would have broken very quickly, which is not described by Thucydides. Cf. L. Tritle, *A New History of the Peloponnesian War* (Oxford, 2010), p. 124.

19. For this to make any sense Thucydides' use of the term *lochos* must here be an accurate one, otherwise Agis intended to move one third of his Spartan force just before the two lines clashed. Lazenby, *The Spartan Army*, p. 156–7.

20. This anecdote regarding Pharax is based upon Diodorus (XII.79.5–7) and receives no mention in Thucydides. We do not know how true the story is but it reiterates the challenge to Agis' decision making being made by his supposed inferiors.

21. Thucydides splits the Athenian figure between 200 for Athens and 200 for the Athenian island of Aegina.

22. For the Siege of Syracuse see Chapter 13.

Chapter 5: The Battle of the Nemea (394 BC)

1. For the background see Chapter 17: Cunaxa and Chapter 14: Siege of the Drilae
2. The force consisted of 1,000 freed-*helot* hoplites, 4,000 Peloponnesian allied hoplites and 300 Athenian cavalry. So, although this is numerically quite strong for a Greek army, it was by no means an elite force.
3. The role of command was not based on military merit but on a time frame. So Thibron was not replaced in the sense of being disgraced in the role but solely because his time was up.
4. Sisyphus was a mythical character from Corinth who was both notoriously cunning and incapable of being deceived, something that the historian Ephorus claimed was true of Dercylidas as well (70F71). Sisyphus was condemned by Zeus to spend eternity rolling a boulder up a steep hill only for it to roll back down before it passed over the brow. P. Cartledge, *Sparta and Lakonia: a Regional History 1300 to 362 BC* (New York, 2002), p. 235.
5. Ionia had been left undefended and the attack could not be ignored for the sake of ravaging Caria (Xenophon, *Hellenica*, III.2.14).
6. The force consisted of 30 fully fledged Spartiates, with 2,000 freed *helots* and 6,000 allies. For the unorthodox procedure that led to Agesilaus becoming king see Xenophon, *Hellenica*, III.3.1–3.
7. For Agesilaus' time in Persia see Chapter 6: Coronea (394 BC).
8. This alliance was not ever given a name in the ancient sources but, due to the role Thebes took in the Battle of Nemea and the Battle of Coronea which followed shortly after, the alliance shall be loosely named the Boeotian Alliance for the sake of relative ease (some historians also refer to it as the Grand Alliance).
9. *Hellenica Oxyrhynchia*, VII.2–3; Diodorus, XIV.82.2. For analysis of the various reasons given for the alliance see J.B. Salmon, *Wealthy Corinth: A History of the City to 338 BC* (Oxford, 1997), pp. 344–5.
10. Xenophon, *Hellenica*, IV.2.11–12.
11. Due to the lack of primary evidence this battlefield is based on conjecture combined with a thorough reading of the battle narrative. The model used here is based upon that posited by J.K. Anderson, *Military Theory and Practice in the Age of Xenophon* (Berkeley, 1970), p. 148. An opposite view is described by J.F. Lazenby, *The Spartan Army* (Barnsley, 2012), pp. 161–2 , in which he argues that the battlefield must have been to the east of the river and the riverbed described by Xenophon must be another river, not the Nemea. His argument is based upon the Roman geographer Strabo's description of the Nemea being the border into Corinth, and Xenophon's description of the Spartan force invading Corinth. Ultimately the issue arises around the location of the unknown town of Epieiceia and until this site is found the debate cannot be settled.
12. The 6,000 Lacedaemonian hoplites most likely included the 300 Hippeis, 600 Sciritae, 1,500 freed *helots* and somewhere between 3,500–4,500 from

the Spartan *morai* (2,500 *perioeci* and 2,000 Spartiates). Cartledge, *Sparta and Lakonia*, p. 239–40.

13. Xenophon mentions 'Achaeans' in the battle narrative, which might mean the Sicyonians, or the Pellenes he also names, or it could mean that there are yet more allies he has failed to mention (or did not know the names of).

14. Xenophon was himself quite sceptical of the figure for the Argives and reports it more like hearsay. These figures show how unlikely it was that the unknown elements of the Spartan army amounted to 9,500. For that would mean that the cities of Tegea, Mantinea and Pellene could accumulate a force larger than all of Euboea and Boeotia combined, or alternatively more hoplites than Athens and Corinth.

15. This was an assertion which was shown to be true by later battles in which the Thebans fought, most famously at Leuctra (see Chapter 9).

16. This passage of time, even if it was just a day, confirms the assertion by Anderson that the proceeding tactics were not spur of the moment accidents but most likely planned strategies, especially in the case of the Spartans. Anderson, *Military Theory and Practice*, pp. 144–5.

17. Xenophon does not give the exact depth but, if the Battle of Delium is anything to go by, then it could have been anywhere around twenty-five men deep.

18. Once the maths has been done this means that the Spartans had over half of their own men facing no opposition at all. What is more, this would have been the far right of the line, meaning that this was the elite of the Spartan force. Anderson, *Military Theory and Practice*, p. 145.

19. A similar event occurred in the medieval Battle of Bannockburn, with equivalent results.

20. It was a tactical strategy that Xenophon described on a couple of occasions, notably at Leuctra (see Chapter 9) and in his fictional work the *Cyropaedia* VII.1.5.

21. Xenophon only mentions that the enemy losses were high and that Sparta's allies lost a substantial amount as well. Xenophon, *Hellenica*. IV.3.1.

22. Diodorus, XIV.83.2.

Chapter 6: The Battle of Coronea (394 BC)

1. For the background surrounding Agesilaus' arrival in Persia see Chapter 5 Battle of the Nemea.

2. Lysander was older than Agesilaus and chose the young prince as a lover, in keeping with the Spartan educational norms of pederasty.

3. Agesilaus liked to think of himself as a new Agamemnon, uniting the Greeks to defeat the Asian enemy.

4. This was an act that Agesilaus would never forgive the Boeotians for, harbouring a disdain that would last his entire life and something he passed on to Xenophon, who is our main source for the period.

5. The duration is not given in *Hellenica* but Xenophon describes it in his *Agesilaus*, I. 10, as lasting this length of time.

6. Xenophon, *Agesilaus*, I.12.

7. If Diodorus is to be believed the troops thus raised amounted to 4,000 more infantry (XIV.79.1–3).

8. The valley was the last piece of land which suited his cavalry before the less hospitable environs of Caria were reached.

9. The Pactolus River runs north to south past Sardis.

10. Xenophon (*Hellenica*, III.4.24) describes the event of Agesilaus bringing these camels back to Greece in a manner which implies that it was a well-known event for his readers.

11. A more detailed account of this period of action is described by the *Hellenica Oxyrhynchia*, XXI.1–6.

12. Xenophon describes these chariots in greater detail in his work *Anabasis* (I.8.10).

13. *Anabasis* was a word used to describe going 'up country' or more specifically 'in land'. As this was the word chosen by Xenophon, himself the author of a work entitled *Anabasis*, we can assume it was a deliberate description of Agesilaus' plan. Xenophon was most likely trying to allude to the idea that Agesilaus was on the verge of formulating a campaign akin to the one Xenophon had written about, in which a Persian rebel army marched from Ionia into what is modern-day Iraq and fought the Persian king at the Battle of Cunaxa (401 BC).

14. For the opposition to the Spartans, see Chapter 5: The Battle of the Nemea.

15. The prizes ranged from the best hoplite equipment made by master craftsmen, the very best in cavalry arms, and gold crowns. Agesilaus was smart enough to not give out the prizes until the army had crossed from Asia into Europe and the men were fully committed to the expedition.

16. Xerxes' march is described by Herodotus, *Histories*, VII. 105–132.

17. Agesilaus was at Amphipolis when he received the Spartan commander Dercylidas who had fought in the battle. For the Battle of the Nemea see Chapter 5.

18. The very specific date is rather unusual for ancient Greek history but we know it because we are told by Xenophon that this happened on the same day as a solar eclipse which left the sun in the shape of a crescent moon (Xenophon, *Hellenica*, IV.3.10).

19. This was, at least, half true. P. Cartledge, *Sparta and Lakonia: a Regional History 1300–362 BC* (New York, 2002), p. 240.

20. Although prepared for battle, he was ordered by the *ephors* to invade Boeotia earlier than he had intended; but this did not deter him. (Plutarch, *Life of Agesilaus*, 17.1)

21. Xenophon actually describes it as such twice, in *Hellenica*, IV.3.16 and *Agesilaus*, 2.9.

22. The figures below are based on those posited by J. F. Lazenby, *The Spartan Army*, (Barnsley, 2012), pp. 169–70, with relevant discussion and divergence contained within the notes below.
23. Xenophon, *Hellenica*, IV.3.15.
24. Assuming it was at full campaign strength, see Lazenby, *The Spartan Army*, p.169. This would not have been made up of just Spartiates but also *perioeci* and quite possibly more freed *helots*.
25. Depending on the desertion rate this could be anywhere from 5,000 to 8,000 strong, as we know that the mercenaries had just over 8,000 men towards the end of Xenophon's account in *Anabasis* (V.3.3).
26. Lazenby, *The Spartan Army*, p. 170, asserts that the Spartans were outnumbered by roughly 5,000 hoplites, giving the Spartans a hoplite force of 15,000 men or less, but he uses nothing more than conjecture to arrive at this conclusion. He is also assuming the enemy were 20,000 strong (see below). Whilst Xenophon is clear when he says '[Agesilaus] took to the field with a force of at least the same size as the enemy's' (*Agesilaus*, 2.7), this does not allow us to dismiss the idea that Agesilaus was outnumbered by hoplites, just that his army was not numerically inferior overall.
27. Due to the close proximity of Athenian territory to Boeotia it is likely they sent a similar force to the one they sent to the Nemea; however Lazenby is probably correct when he says they could easily have sent a slightly smaller force due to concerns for the safety of Athens herself. Lazenby, *The Spartan Army*, p.170.
28. This is the only way that Lazenby's figure of 20,000 hoplites is plausible.
29. This would have been a very strong section of his army but they do not appear at all in the battle narrative.
30. The silence is mentioned in two separate versions by Xenophon: *Hellenica*, IV.3.17 and *Agesilaus*, 2.10.
31. Xenophon, *Agesilaus*, 2.7–8. The bronze is reference to the shining armour that Agesilaus was at such pains to outfit his army with. The red is a reference to the characteristic red cloak worn by the Spartans, a cloak which the mercenaries under Herippidas had already begun wearing back in 401 BC.
32. Xenophon's accounts are clearly an attempt to hide this error by Agesilaus, due to his friendship with the king. Xenophon's description certainly implies it was the obvious decision to make, and it is reminiscent of the tactics used at the Nemea, but Xenophon tries to disguise it by claiming that Agesilaus chose a more courageous option. For a counter argument to this, and a defence of Agesilaus' decision, see Lazenby, *The Spartan Army*, p. 171–2.
33. Xenophon, *Hellenica*, IV.3.19.
34. Xenophon, *Agesilaus*, 2.13. This is an important point because it is the only evidence we have for the variety of weapons that were used in the battle. This implies that not only swords and spears were used but also arrows, javelins and

stones, therefore showing that the light-armed contingents did participate in the combat.

35. This description is based on Xenophon's own, *Agesilaus* 2.14. It highlights just how vivid a scene it must have been for it to make such a lasting impression on such an experienced warrior as Xenophon.

36. Lazenby, *The Spartan Army*, p. 172, denies that it was a victory for Agesilaus but he downplays the importance of Greek perception. The erection of the trophy and the Theban request for the dead show that Thebes believed itself to have been beaten. Furthermore Athens also considered it a categorical defeat at the hands of Sparta: Andocides, *On the Peace*, 3.18.

37. Plutarch, *Life of Agesilaus*, 18.4.

Chapter 7: The Battle of the Long Walls of Corinth (392 BC)

1. The naval commander had won the sea battle of Cnidus with the support of the Persian *satrap* Pharnabazus.

2. For a mercenary force at Corinth: Aristophanes, *Plutus*, 173. For the presence of Iphicrates as their commander: Demosthenes, *Phillipics*, 4.24; Androtion, FGrH 324 F 48 = Philochorus, FGrH 328 F 150; P.J. Rhodes, *A History of the Classical World: 478–323 BC* (Oxford, 2010), pp. 138–9.

3. For a larger exploration of the discontent felt in Corinth see G. Grote, *History of Greece*, vol.9 (London, 1854), pp. 326; D. Kagan, 'Corinthian Politics and the Revolution of 392 BC', in *Historia: Zeitschrift für Alte Geschichte*, 11:4 (1962), pp. 447–57.

4. Xenophon, *Hellenica*, IV.2.23; Demosthenes, *Against Leptines*, 20.53.

5. They hoped to capture more men in the *agora* during the festivities.

6. Whilst the vivid image portrayed by Xenophon is worthy of replication here, it should be noted that the extra stress Xenophon places upon these sacrilegious acts is a little suspect. There is no question that his sympathies lay with the victims, no doubt in part due to their later action in conjunction with Sparta. Diodorus (XIV.86.1–2) gives a simpler and less vivid account of the same event which does not include all of the impiety. He does confirm the timing of the purge to be during a festival, so there was an impious edge to the events even without Xenophon's hyperbole.

7. While Xenophon does not describe a gymnasium it is most likely that there was one because a) there was a famous (old) gymnasium there in later centuries as described by Pausanias (II.4.5), and b) a gymnasium would be a logical place for the young and 'best' of Corinthian men to spend time. J. Wiseman, 'Ancient Corinth: the Gymnasium Area', in *Archaeology*, 22:No. 3 (June, 1969), pp. 216–25; J. Delorme, *Gymnasion: Étude sur les monuments consacrés à l'éducation en Grèce (des origines à l'Empire romain)* (Paris, 1960), p. 333.

8. The Acrocorinth (the acropolis of Corinth) was a very steep and very high hill that overlooked the ancient city. The suitability for a defensive resistance to be

maintained there is highlighted by the fact that these men chose to run through the city (north-to-south), past the *agora* and the theatre, to reach it.

9. Some 500 men fled into a self-imposed exile (Diodorus XIV.86.1–2.).

10. For the debate that surrounds the nature of this 'union' between Corinth and Argos see J.B. Salmon, *Wealthy Corinth: a History of the City to 338 BC* (Oxford, 1997), pp. 357–64.

11. *Metics*, a Greek word describing resident aliens, usually held no rights of citizenship, but in this case they most certainly did.

12. Whilst J.B., Salmon, *Wealthy Corinth* , p.357, is probably correct in his challenge to the veracity of Xenophon's account that describes the state of Corinth after the revolution, it is no less valid, then, to accept this bias as an accurate reflection of the beliefs of the exiles in question. So, whilst it is unlikely that this is an accurate description of Corinth at the time, the exiles believed this to be the case.

13. Xenophon, *Hellenica*, IV.4.7, implies that this trust came from an earlier dealing between them, but does not expand upon this.

14. The description given by Xenophon of the gate, and trophy, should also be considered when the debate regarding the location of the battle of the Nemea is being had. For the debate see Chapter 5: Battle of the Nemea, n. 11. This could support Lazenby's argument for the identification of a more eastern river, nearer to the city.

15. Information taken from http://corinth.sas.upenn.edu/corinth.html (03/11/14; last accessed at 13.20).

16. Trying to numerically define a standard Spartan *mora* is notoriously difficult as the ancient sources never seem to agree. For arguably the most influential debate on the matter, and the provider of the highest possible number of 1,120 men, see Lazenby, *The Spartan Army*, pp. 8–12. Cf. J.K. Anderson, *Military Theory and Practice in the Age of Xenophon* (Berkeley, 1970), p. 155, who uses a much smaller figure of 600 Spartans for a Spartan *mora*.

17. Anderson, *Military Theory and Practice,* (Berkeley, 1970), p. 155; Cf. F.E. Ray Jr., *Greek and Macedonian Land Battles of the 4th Century BC: A History and analysis of 187 engagements,* (Jefferson, N.C., 2012), p.31.

18. Whilst it could be said that the Corinthians should not have been expected to attack without their allied reinforcements, it is still surprising that we do not hear of any skirmishes or even just some military posturing. Corinth did have a force of *peltasts* under Iphicrates who could realistically have caused damage to the Spartans during this wait, if only to their morale.

19. The placement of the *peltasts* on the right wing contravenes the traditional view of Greek armies, where the strongest, most influential, contingent is given this place of honour – we may have expected it to be held by the 'home' army of Corinth. There are numerous examples of this being contradicted, Olpae being a good example (see Chapter 1), and the positioning in this battle seems to

continue this tactical shift. However, it seems that the idea posited by Anderson, *Military Theory and Practice*, pp.121–2, that the positioning of the *peltasts* was in keeping with the Greek military habit of leaving light-armed troops on the flanks of armies, away from the hoplite fighting, is somewhat flawed because the impediment of the walls was always going to force the flanks to be a part of the 'hoplite' battle.

20. The Corinthians charging the Sicyonian position is based upon the translation of Xenophon by Strassler, of a notoriously difficult passage which only says 'they charged', whoever 'they' are. I have found that Strassler's translation can be seen to make sense with a few adaptations, and that this reading best explains what happens to the Corinthians who are otherwise completely absent from the battle narrative. Anderson, *Military Theory and Practice*, p. 155. The charge of the Corinthians may also explain the placement of Iphicrates' men on the right wing, as it could be seen that the plan was for the Corinthians to lead the attack from the left whilst the far right wing was to remain in position – in effect creating an oblique line similar to that seen at Leuctra (see Chapter 9).

21. This fighting with the Spartans is not described in any of our sources which seem to ignore the Corinthians almost entirely in the narrative, and the Spartans are left doing nothing - which seems highly unlikely. This supposition is based upon my belief that the confederate army line must have stretched the full width of the Spartan line, or else the Spartans were left completely unopposed which again seems unlikely.

22. This manoeuvre is a perfect replication of the one used at the Battle of Mantinea, with identical results. It should be noted that the text of Xenophon is not clear here, as it describes this action as one to help the Sicyonians but the description of the stockade remaining on their left-hand side does not make any sense. It is postulated here that the way Praxitas was going to save his allies was by creating a new front in the battle.

23. There has been some speculation that the walls described here are proof that Lechaeum was a walled harbour, see J. Wiseman, *The Land of the Ancient Corinthians*, (Studies in Mediterranean Archaeology, vol. 50), (Goteborg: 1978), p. 95 n.69. But there is no reason to see Xenophon as describing a defensive position, the men are fleeing to the walls rather than taking a strong position to repel an attack.

24. Xenophon, *Hellenica*, IV.4.12.

Chapter 8: The Battle of Lechaeum (390 BC)

1. Polyaenus, III.9.49.

2. Something they had hitherto refused to allow due to their concerns that Sparta would reinstate exiles from the city who were sympathetic to the Spartans. The fact that these fears were superseded by that of Iphicrates' men shows just how intimidating they really were.

3. This was not a new tactic to Sparta, it was well utilized by Brasidas who may well have learned it from the Thracians who, according to Thucydides, used it against Theban cavalry after the sacking of Mycalessus. J.K. Anderson, *Military Theory and Practice in the Age of Xenophon* (Berkeley, 1970), p.123.

4. 'Spindle-throwers': a description I have adapted from a Spartan quip about archers after the defeat at Sphacteria. The gist being that long-range weapons were seen as unmanly, like women's spinning spindles. (see Chapter 12).

5. The bogeyman, in this instance, is actually a bogey woman called Mormo. She was a bad spirit which was used as a scary story to stop children from misbehaving

6. Xenophon rather confusingly describes the *mora* coming out of Lechaeum but later on in the narrative implies that the harbour is taken by a Spartan fleet (*Hellenica* IV.4.19; Plutarch, *Life of Agesilaus*, 21.1) which would not be necessary if they already had it in their control. It seems that J.B. Salmon, *Wealthy Corinth: a History of the City to 338 BC* (Oxford, 1997), p. 364, is right in suggesting that the harbour town must have been retaken by the confederates, but there is no way to determine when. Salmon suggests that the rebuilding of the Long Walls is indicative of a lack of Spartan presence at Lechaeum. This makes sense, but occurs directly after the Spartan show of force that Xenophon describes coming from the harbour.

7. This siege is not mentioned in Xenophon, but it is alluded to in Diodorus (XIV.86.4). The presence of a siege would resolve both of the issues presented by Salmon, but it does not necessitate the need for Xenophon to have omitted the loss of Lechaeum for the Spartans. The idea of a siege has one major flaw, which is that Lechaeum was not a walled harbour (see Chapter 7, n. 23). However, it is my belief that the Spartans would have constructed a temporary wall of their own just as they did before the Battle of the Long Walls. If they had not, then they were sitting ducks waiting to be attacked at the earliest show of weakness.

8. Xenophon, *Agesilaus*, 2.17. The Hyacinthia was a festival dedicated to Apollo and was celebrated in the village of Amyclae.

9. Xenophon, *Agesilaus*, 2.18. The Athenians' use of the area is not commented on by Xenophon but is a logical extrapolation. By taking the Peiraion, Sparta would finally close off the Isthmus from their biggest threat of Thebes and Athens. Salmon, *Wealthy Corinth*, p. 365.

10. Xenophon, *Hellenica*, IV.5.3. What this actually means is not described in the sources, but evidently there was a way to act when threatening a city and Agesilaus was not conforming to it.

11. The ridge was very cold at night and it is said to have rained, and even hailed. The gesture that Xenophon dwells upon, of Agesilaus sending fire up to his men, does little to undermine the fact that he spent time next to a luxurious thermal spring whilst many of his men shivered the whole night through!

12. For the massacre at Corinth see Chapter 7.

13. This narrative is not in chronological order, it purposefully mimics the same literary device used by Xenophon in his *Hellenica* when recounting the episode. For more see V. Grey, *The Character of Xenophon's Hellenica* (London, 1989), p.157; and B. Burliga, 'Did they Really Return upon Their Shields? The Hubris of the Spartan Hoplites at Lechaeum, 390 BC', in (eds.) N. Sekunda & B. Burliga, *Iphicrates, Peltasts and Lechaeum* (Gdansk, 2014), pp.72–3.

14. The precise date is hard to pin down because it involves the absolute dating of two different festivals: the Isthmian Games and the Hyacinthia. For a good discussion and argument for a date in June of 390 BC see A. Konecny, '"Κατέχοψεν την μόραν 'Ιφιχράτης"', The Battle of Lechaeum, Early Summer, 390 BC', in (eds.) Sekunda & Burliga, *Iphicrates, Peltasts and Lechaeum*, p.20–1, n.52.

15. The name of the *polemarch* is unknown, possibly an indictment of how little Xenophon thought of him. It has been recently suggested by Burliga that this was the commander that Plutarch named as Bias (*Sayings of the Spartans*, 22.1), but the saying captured by Plutarch is almost identical to that which Xenophon gives to a separate Spartan commander who was, likewise, caught in an ambush by Iphicrates, named Anaxibius (*Hellenica*, IV.8.38). It is more likely that Plutarch has got the name wrong when relaying the story. B. Burliga, 'Did they Really Return upon Their Shields?', p. 67.

16. The description of the allies guarding a wall (singular) gives credence to the idea that the Spartans had constructed a temporary fortification to defend the harbour. If the wall being described was actually the Long Walls, as inferred for instance by R. Rothaus, 'Lechaion, Western Port of Corinth: a Preliminary Archaeology and History', in *Oxford Journal of Archaeology*, 14: 3 (1995), p.301, then there are two problems which would need to be addressed: i) if the garrison was going to defend one of the walls then they are just as likely to defend both of them, but Xenophon (*Hellenica*, IV.5.11) uses a singular noun ii) The Long Walls were not a strong position for defence because they ran parallel to the harbour rather than obstructing it from Corinth. An exception to this would be if the allies had a strong missile-based contingent but this was certainly not the case. For these reasons it should be discounted that the Long Walls are being described here.

17. It would take the Amyclaeans approximately 5–6 days to reach Sparta from their starting point at Lechaeum.

18. The exemplary work by Konecny on the Battle of Lechaeum as a whole, and the topography of the battlefield in particular, is the basis for the reconstruction here. Konecny, 'The Battle of Lechaeum', pp. 12–18.

19. '[A] small hill about two *stades* distant from the sea and about sixteen or seventeen *stades* from Lechaeum', Xenophon, *Hellenica*, IV.5.17.

20. For numbers see Konecny, 'The Battle of Lechaeum', p. 19; J. F. Lazenby, *The Spartan Army* (Barnsley, 2013), p. 16; I.G. Spence, *The Cavalry of Classical Greece: a Social and Military History* (Oxford, 1993), p.3. Konecny cites the cavalry's poor performance as a factor in choosing a smaller figure of nearer sixty horsemen. The same figure, but without explanation, is given by Anderson, *Military Theory*, p.123.

21. Konecny uses a range of 500–700, but it seems unlikely, to me, that a Spartan force that was so arrogant in its manner would not face off against an inferior sized force. Konecny, ' The Battle of Lechaeum', p. 20.

22. The figure of 1,200 comes from Xenophon's description of Iphicrates being sent to the Hellespont in the following year with that many peltasts, the majority of which served under him in Corinth. Xenophon, *Hellenica*, IV.8.34.

23. Konecny, 'The Battle of Lechaeum', p. 20–1. This is supposition, but it makes more sense that the almost divine inspiration that would have been needed by Iphicrates to plan his assault, convince his commanding officer to let a subordinate take the lead, prepare his men tactically, and then execute the plan in just a matter of hours.

24. It is easy to forget that Iphicrates was not the official leader of this battle, as it was most often his name that was associated with the victory (eg. Aeschines, *Against Ctesiphon*, 3.243). Callias deserves greater credit for his decision to allow Iphicrates to take the lead on a tactical level, and for putting his hoplites in potential danger against a superior fighting force to support the young commander's venture.

25. Konecny, 'The Battle of Lechaeum', p. 23

26. It is possible, from Xenophon's silence regarding the commander of the *mora*, that he had died in the retreat or else on the hill, which could partly explain the inclination to run.

27. Using the postulated figures given by Konecny, 'The Battle of Lechaeum', p. 29 n.98.

28. Cf. P. Cartledge, *Sparta and Lakonia: A Regional History 1300–362 BC*, (New York, 2002), p. 244, who says this number is surprisingly low and puts forward the suggestion that Xenophon was only counting full Spartiate hoplites.

Chapter 9: The Battle of Leuctra (371 BC)

1. The festival was celebrated by women only, and took place in the Theban acropolis, the Cadmeia, which had forced the Assembly to relocate to the market.

2. There is a suggestion by Plutarch (*Life of Pelopidas*, 6.1) that Phoebidas was fined for his actions to the sum of 100,000 drachma.

3. The year 379 saw the end of the fighting with Olynthus in Chalcidice and also the subduing of Sparta's ostensible ally, Phleious. For a full description of the Spartan situation and the authority it now held see Xenophon, *Hellenica*, V.3.27.

4. Pelopidas is not mentioned by Xenophon in his entire account of the build-up to, and the battle of, Leuctra. Pelopidas' position here is derived from the account by Plutarch's *Life of Pelopidas* but he was somewhat of an admirer of the young man, and Pelopidas' exacting role put forward should be taken with a pinch of salt.

5. The most vivid account of this entire plan is given by Plutarch, *Life of Pelopidas*, 7–11; but it does have some discrepancies with Xenophon's own account, *Hellenica*, V.4.1–7

6. The descriptions of murder, beyond those of the magistrates, is not described by the Boeotian writer Plutarch, but is prevalent in the anti-Theban writer Xenophon. This makes it difficult to discern which of the two biased accounts is accurately reflecting the real events. As the description of the coup and counter-coup is in keeping with the bloodiness that Xenophon used to describe a similar affair in Corinth (see Chapter 7), I have been tempted to lean more toward his account.

7. The acquittal of Sphodrias was denounced by Xenophon, who gives a long explanation for the decision which rested upon the influence of the king, Agesilaus (*Hellenica*, V.4.25–33).

8. Within the term 'Athens' we must of course include here the 2nd Athenian League which constituted all of Athens' own allies.

9. R. Buck, *Boiotia and the Boiotian League, 432–371 BC* (Edmonton, 1994), pp. 98–9.

10. The date of the battle is most likely to be around 375 BC. Its importance is attested in the ancient sources and a great account is given by S. Sprawski, 'Battle of Tegyra (375 BC). Breaking through and the opening of the ranks', in *Electrum*, 8 (2004), pp.13–26.

11. Diodorus gives a very different, and confusing, account of the cause of this short peace to that of Xenophon, placing the Persian king at the heart of the negotiations. I have continued with Xenophon's account in keeping with Buck, *Boiotia and the Boiotian League*, pp. 101–3.

12. B. Craven, *Dionysius I: War-Lord of Sicily*, (London, 1990), pp. 202–3.

13. The same commander who won the famous victory at Lechaeum (see Chapter 8).

14. Thebes took control of both towns and inflicted great damage on then. Plataea: Diodorus XV.46.4–6; Thespiae: Diodorus XV.86.

15. These three alliances were long established, verging on sacred to the Athenians. Plataea had stood by them during the Battle of Marathon (see Chapter 15), whilst Thespiae had been present at the Battle of Thermopylae, hence Xenophon's description of them as allies of Athens during the Persian Wars (*Hellenica*, VI.3.1). Phocis was an alliance that was well established by the outbreak of the Peloponnesian War.

16. The speeches are very long-winded but focused upon the fact that neither side disagreed on the more important matters like Hellenic autonomy. (*Hellenica*, VI.3.4–17).

17. The following scene comes from Plutarch, *Life of Agesilaus*, 28.1–2. It is not described by Xenophon, who actually omits Epaminondas from all of the narrative in the lead up to Leuctra, and even the battle itself.

18. Pausanias (IX.13.3) mentions an earlier altercation between Cleombrotus and a Theban force led by Chaereas which was under orders to guard a pass, but no specific location is given. The battle ended in a Theban massacre, but no details are given. For a reconstruction of the march which attempts to include the extra information given by Pausanias see J. F. Lazenby, *The Spartan Army* (Barnsley, 2012), p.177–8.

19. The separation of the *hippeis* as an extra 300 men is not accepted by J.K. Anderson, *Military Theory and Practice in the Age of Xenophon* (Berkeley, 1970), p. 196, who thinks it is more likely to have been incorporated into the numbers of one of the *morai*. I have kept them separate following the guiding logic of Lazenby, *The Spartan Army*, pp. 14–15 and 178.

20. Lazenby, *The Spartan Army*, p. 179. Pausanias, VIII.6.2.

21. Plutarch, *Life of Pelopidas*, 20.1. For unrealistic figures ranging from 24,000 hoplites to 40,000 men see Frontinus (IV.2.6) and Polyaenus (II.3.8) respectively.

22. Anderson, *Military Theory and Practice*, p. 196–7. For a full breakdown of the hypothetical numbers involved see Lazenby, *The Spartan Army*, p.178–9. Diodorus, XV.52.2 is the one source for the battle itself. Frontinus, IV.2.6, does give a figure of 4,000 men and 400 cavalry which seems to be a fair reflection of the Theban figures within the Boeotian army, when compared to Diodorus' figure.

23. This organization is in keeping with the description of the Boeotian constitution given by *Hellenica Oxyrhynchia*, XVI. 3–4.

24. *Ibid.* See: Lazenby, *The Spartan Army*, p.179; Anderson, *Military Theory and Practice*, p. 197.

25. Diodorus, XV.53.4; Xenophon, *Hellenica*, VI.4.7; Frontinus, I.11.16. Polyaenus, II.3.8, gives a slightly different tradition to the story but the impact remains the same.

26. The importance of this monument, and the associated story, for the psychology behind the Theban desire to fight against greater numbers is emphasized by the fact that it appears in all of our sources for the battle: Xenophon, *Hellenica*, VI.4.7; Diodorus XV.54.3; Plutarch, *Life of Pelopidas*, 20.3; Pausanias, IX.13.5–6. For a telling of the story in more detail see Plutarch, *Love Stories (Amatoriae narrations)*, 3.

27. Only Diodorus and Pausanias give mention to this conference. Diodorus places it before the manufactured omens, while Pausanias places it afterwards. I have followed Pausanias' timeline because it seems more plausible that Epaminondas would have tried to rouse the spirits of his men and use their enthusiasm for

battle as support for his view to fight, rather than convince the commanders of battle without making sure his own men were up to the challenge.

28. This revelation comes from Xenophon (*Hellenica*, VI.4.1) and, assuming it is true, could either reflect their own arrogance regarding their superiority or it may have been an attempt to cover their own fears for the impending battle. I am more inclined to the latter as it fits the narrative of Xenophon regarding the misgivings Cleombrotus had for battle and which must have filtered down into his army.

29. Xenophon, *Hellenica*, VI.4.9; Pausanias, IX.13.8; Polyaenus, II.3.3. Pausanias and Polyaenus both specify that it was the Thespians who left, but no known earlier source corroborates this.

30. V.D. Hanson, 'Epameinondas, the Battle of Leuktra (371 BC), and the "Revolution" in Greek Battle Tactics', in *Classical Antiquity*, 7:2 (1988), pp.195. There is never a reason given for this tactical decision by Cleombrotus, but it seems to me like it was a screening position to allow the Spartans to shift formation if need be without fear of attack, the likes of which almost ended in disaster at Mantinea (418 BC). The Spartans must have known that the Thebans would have formed a deep formation, giving their line a narrower front, so a manoeuvre to extend the line was always possible once the two phalanxes had formed, and a tactical assessment could be made. For a presentation that argues that the Spartan cavalry was placed in reaction to the already positioned Theban cavalry see J. Buckler, 'Epaminondas at Leuctra, 371 BC', in (eds.) B. Campbell and L. Trittle, *The Oxford Handbook of Warfare in the Classical World* (Oxford, 2013), p. 667.

31. The positioning of the Sacred Band has been a point of debate for over a century but it is finally becoming accepted that the positioning at the front makes the most sense in light of the available evidence. For a good review of the debate and a strong arguing for the positioning at the front see V.D. Hanson, 'Epameinondas, the Battle of Leuktra', pp.196–7.

32. The snake analogy is described by Polyaenus, II.3.15. The sentiment echoes the assessment of Xenophon, *Hellenica*, V.4.12.

33. Spartan tactics are not really discussed in Xenophon's account, so any reconstruction must rely heavily upon the later sources. This simple reconstruction of the Spartans meeting the Thebans head on, without any specific tactical manoeuvres, is based upon the description of Polybius who says that 'the Battle of Leuctra was straightforward' (*The Histories*, XII.25.f).

34. Frustratingly we hear no more of the Boeotian cavalry, so we do not know where they went or if they took any further part in the battle.

35. The only mention of Spartan allied losses is in Pausanias (IX.13.12) who simply implies the losses were minute, emphasizing the point that the fighting really did lie between the Thebans and the Spartans.

36. Plutarch, *Life of Agesilaus*, 30.2–3. The penalties enforced on the *tresantes* were mainly social rather than financial.

254 Great Battles of the Classical Greek World

Chapter 10: The Battle of 2nd Mantinea (362 BC)

1. The size of the force is given in Plutarch, *Life of Agesilaus* (31.1), *Life of Pelopidas* (24.2), and Diodorus (XV.81.2) at 70,000 strong, with 40,000 hoplites. Whilst not impossible, these figures are astronomically high.

2. Megalopolis, roughly translated, means Big City. The date of its founding is a contentious matter, due to a split of opinion in the later tradition: Pausanias (VIII.27.8) dates the founding to a few months after the Battle of Leuctra (371 BC), as I have here, but Diodorus (XV.72.4) places it after the 'Tearless Battle' (see below) which occurred two years later. To confuse matters more, there is epigraphical evidence for a dating of 370 or 369 BC from the Parian Marble at the Ashmolean Museum in Oxford (Fr. 72, translated for free access on their website). See S. Hornblower, 'When Was Megalopolis Founded?', in *The Annual of the British School at Athens*, 85 (1990), pp. 71–7.

3. For Epaminondas' reticence to invade Sparta see Xenophon, *Hellenica*, VI.5.24. Cf. G. Cawkwell, 'Epaminondas and Thebes', in *Classical Quarterly*, 22:2 (1972), p. 266, who argues that Epaminondas had very good reason to invade Laconia and that it was his intention all along.

4. Xenophon says the army was split into two, the Thebans (Boeotians) and the Arcadians (*Hellenica*, VI.5.25–27). However, Diodorus (XV.64) describes the army as being split into four groups: the Boeotians went to Sellasia, the Argives entered through the borders of Tegea, the Arcadians invaded the Skiritis region, and the Eleians marched through unguarded territory towards Sellasia.

5. This is almost certainly a purposeful contrast with the behaviour endorsed by Agesilaus in his earlier invasion of Arcadia (Xenophon, *Hellenica*, VI.5.12).

6. The women of Sparta are shown to have been especially shocked by the experience, having never seen warfare that close before. Xenophon, *Hellenica*, VI.5.28; Plutarch, *Life of Agesilaus*, 31.4.

7. Diodorus (XV.65.6) states there were only 1,000 *helots* who were emancipated. It is possible that this is due to a corruption of the text, but ultimately we do not know whether Xenophon's much larger figure is correct.

8. Plutarch (*Life of Agesilaus*, 32.8–33.1) gives a variety of possible reasons for the departure, according to his different sources, including the cold weather, the length of their campaign, and even the possibility that the Spartans bribed them to move on.

9. The repopulation of Messene and the founding of Megalopolis are both absent from Xenophon's account of the period, which is an oversight that betrays his personal affiliation for Sparta, which suffered humiliation on account of both events.

10. Xenophon (*Hellenica*, VII.1.25) shows his own admiration for their abilities, describing their fortitude and determination. He says they believed themselves to be the strongest of all the Greeks.

11. Xenophon names the *satrap* Ariobarzanes as the instigator, but Diodorus is surely correct in saying that Artaxerxes was responsible, with the *satrap* acting on his behalf.

12. Interestingly, Xenophon (*Hellenica*, VII.1.27) says it was the Spartan reluctance to give up Messenia (hitherto unmentioned in his account) that forced the negotiations to break down. But Diodorus (XV.70.2) makes the claim that it was the Thebans' refusal to release the Boeotian towns from their confederacy that was the cause of the break down.

13. The small force was sent by the tyrant of Syracuse, Dionysius I. It was the second force he had sent to aid the Spartans, the first having arrived just the year before in 369 BC.

14. Xenophon focuses his attention throughout this period in the Peloponnese, ignoring the expedition of the Theban commander Pelopidas into Thessaly to assist them in their defence against the tyrant Alexander of Pherae (Plutarch, *Life of Pelopidas*, 26–32.7).

15. Xenophon (*Hellenica*, VII.1.28) does not state whether these killings were only of men of age, or all of the males, or if they killed all genders and ages indiscriminately.

16. Diodorus (XV.76.3) actually describes this peace treaty as signifying the end of the Boeotian-Spartan war, but I have followed Xenophon's account which shows quite the opposite.

17. Xenophon (*Hellenica*, VII.4.25) implies that the battle could have continued, before the two sides decided to end it. However, the Spartans are said to have collected their dead and the Arcadians to have erected their trophy – both of which are signs that the Spartans accepted it as a defeat.

18. Diodorus (XV.78.2–3) described the battle, but reverses the roles of the two armies. He states that Elis was trying to run the games and Arcadia, with Pisa in support, marched in full arms. Both Diodorus' and Xenophon's account are plausible, but I have chosen Xenophon's account due to his description of the Eleians. He chose this instance to describe the men of Elis as being brave and capable fighters (*Hellenica*, VII.4.30), but surely for a writer so engrossed in the details of religious sanctity this prestige from battle would have increased had Elis been the wronged party i.e. the Arcadians had been the ones to break the religious amnesty. I find it hard to believe that Xenophon would have neglected the opportunity to add further credit to the Eleians, if the situation had allowed it.

19. Diodorus (XV.82.1), once again, reverses the account of Xenophon, claiming that the Mantineans were trying to maintain the use of the misappropriated funds.

20. Diodorus (XV.82.2–3) describes violence breaking out between Tegea and Mantinea, under the illusion that Mantinea was to blame for the use of sacred funds. It is possible that his confusion arose from this encounter in Tegea, but it was the Boeotians and not the Tegeans that were the opposing faction.

21. Cretan runners: Diodorus (XV.82.6) explains that there were numerous Cretan runners sent out from Sparta to alert Agesilaus to the danger. Spartan regiments: I have here refrained from using the term *mora* that I have used regarding the Spartans up until this point because, after their defeat at Leuctra, Xenophon stops referring to *morai* and instead uses the pan-Greek term for the smaller army units, *lochoi*.

22. Diodorus (XV.84.1) is our clearest source for the movement of the Mantineans in support of Agesilaus. The numerical advantage is so large that it is often considered false by modern commentators who present their own numbers. Whilst they are most likely correct (the Greeks rarely fought an even battle when they were so heavily outnumbered), any other set of figures is pure guesswork so I have stayed with Diodorus. The issue is not something that Xenophon ever explicitly states.

23. Pausanias (VIII.11.5). Philip Sabin, *Lost Battles: Reconstructing the Great Clashes of the Ancient World* (London, 2009), pp. 121–2; R. Gaebel, *Cavalry Operations in the Ancient Greek World* (Norman, 2002), p. 139.

24. Only Diodorus (XV.84.4–85.3) gives the relative military strengths of each army. His reliability cannot be assumed, but Xenophon is frustratingly silent on the issue.

25. The review of the phalanx, after the march in battle order, ensured to Epaminondas that all of his men were exactly where he wanted and needed them to be.

26. The passage in Xenophon (VII.5.22) is notorious for its lack of explanation.

27. A paraphrase from a poignant, yet insightful comment from Xenophon (*Hellenica*, VII.5.22) about the nature of the men who were fighting in these battles.

28. The entire episode of Epaminondas' death comes from Diodorus (XV.87.1–2), who is otherwise unused in this battle narrative. Xenophon only remarks on the commander's death without any further description. The weapon that caused his death is said to have been a spear by Diodorus, but the sword is described by Plutarch (*Life of Agesilaus*, 35.1–2) who was drawing on not only the later Spartan tradition, but also the Boeotian tradition regarding one of their greatest historical figures.

29. Diodorus' account of the entire battle emphasizes the conflict between the cavalry over the infantry. But if the cavalry were that important I find it hard to believe that Xenophon would not have mentioned it, as an avid horseman himself.

30. Diodorus XV.89.3. It was not just Xenophon who ended his narrative of the *Hellenica* immediately after the battle, so did Anaximenes of Lampascus in his work *First Enquiry of Greek Affairs*, and Philistus ended his history of Dionysius the Younger in this same year following Epaminondas' death.

31. For the difficulty of dating the Third Sacred War see F-D. Deltenre, 'La datation du début de la troisième guerre sacrée. Retour sur l'interprétation des comptes de Delphes', in *Bulletin de Correspondance Hellénique*, 134 (2010), pp. 97–116.

Chapter 11: The Siege of Plataea (429–427 BC)

1. This was due in part to its illustrious role in the defeat of the Persians (see Chapter 16: Battle of Plataea). Its independence was also aided by its long-standing alliance with Athens (Herodotus, VI.108), something that was established even before the Battle of Marathon (see Chapter 15), as shown by them fighting side by side in the first Persian invasion.
2. Some of the largest, internal tensions within any given *polis* during the classical Greek period were often down to a division between oligarchs and populists (advocates of democracy).
3. D. Kagan, *The Archidamian War* (New York, 1974), p. 44.
4. Or perhaps, more cynically, these people wanted to see the instigation of an oligarchy, where only those who were rich enough had any political power.
5. Neither Thucydides nor Diodorus explain how the citizen became aware of this, as they are described as hiding in their houses. Perhaps many were on their roofs watching the proceedings, and then spread the word.
6. Thucydides (II.4.2) describes women and slaves doing the throwing, whereas Diodorus (XII.41.6) describes children and slaves. I have kept both elements to give the underlying feeling of the action, everyone got involved in trying to overcome the Thebans. This was a desperate dog-fight for the independence of Plataea.
7. This number included Eurymachus, the Theban through whom the Plataean conspirators had orchestrated the failed coup.
8. Diodorus (XII.41.7) claims that the Theban reinforcements killed many of the Plataeans who lived outside of the city in the surrounding countryside. But it seems unlikely that Thucydides, an Athenian who may well have received much of his information from surviving Plataeans, would omit this piece of information (II.5.1–4).
9. Plataea always maintained that this release of prisoners was never agreed under oath. Thucydides' account (II.5.5–2.6) shows his disapproval of the Plataean decision. Strangely, Diodorus' account (XII.42.1) claims that the Plataeans did not kill the prisoners but returned them under the agreed truce, but preference is given here to the contemporary source of Thucydides. For a modern assessment of the morality of the event see P. Kern, 'Military Technology and Ethical Values in Ancient Greek Warfare: The Siege of Plataea', in *War and Society*, 6:2 (1988), pp. 5–6.
10. What Diodorus (XII.42.2) rather eloquently describes as a rabble.

11. The Siege of Potidaea lasted three years and had cost the Athenians an extortionate amount of money to fund (Thucydides, II.13.3, 70.2; Diodorus, XII.40.2).

12. Pausanias was the leader of the Greek army at the Battle of Plataea (see Chapter 16), so the Plataeans were pointing towards their role in the resistance to the Persians.

13. Implying, of course, that the protection offered by Sparta would mean that Sparta would instate a presence in the city.

14. The psychological impact on the Plataean force as they watched their food sources and agricultural labours destroyed in a matter of days should not be ignored.

15. It seems very unlikely that this would have been attempted at every point along the wall, so I have followed Konecny's topographical argument for their position and placed them by the south wall according to his own projection of the possible archaic/early classical fortifications (but he does state that the east wall is also a possible ramp location); A. Konecny, V. Aravantinos & R. Marchese, *Plataiai. Archäologie und Geschichte einer boiotischen Polis* (Vienna, 2013), pp.58–62, 377; G. Grundy, *The Topography of the Battle of Plataea: The City of Plataea. The Field of Leuctra* (London, 1894), p. 65.

16. The mine would have started inside the city and never extended beyond the siege mound, meaning that the Peloponnesians would have been unable to utilise the method of detecting mines, if they were suspected, by tapping the ground with a bronze shield (Herodotus, *Histories*, IV. 200).

17. Plutarch (*Life of Pericles*, 7) does describe battering rams being used in the siege of Samos, 440 BC but he wrote centuries later. Thucydides is the earliest known source to describe their usage in Greek warfare.

18. How true this is cannot be said, but it does give a real idea of just how dramatic a flame this must have been.

19. We do not know if the Peloponnesians were also aware of the poisonous gasses they were producing, utilizing the deadly aspects of sulphur to engage in one of the earliest forms of chemical warfare, so this may just as easily be an unexpected bonus rather than being a specific design.

20. These simultaneous undertakings suggests that the force that was left was still very sizeable.

21. This gives us a better idea of how far the wall was from the city as it was close enough to see the individual bricks by plain sight, say no more than 100 metres.

22. This interesting passage from Thucydides (III.23.2–4) shows the use of the bow in a short-range environment.

Chapter 12: The Sieges of Pylos and Sphacteria (425 BC)

1. See Chapter 2: The Battle of Olpae for a full background to this period.

2. The bloody revolt at Corcyra and the ensuing civil war are described, and condemned, by Thucydides (III.70–85). The exiles were removed by Athenian

support, but they took up fortified positions in the surrounding countryside. Once the Athenian presence left the island the exiles began marauding, whilst simultaneously canvassing for support from Sparta and Corinth.

3. Whilst Diodorus' account of the battle describes one that was well planned and thought through, I feel this campaign must be understood in the Thucydidean tradition of Demosthenes' personal opportunism. The subsequent narrative was not planned by Athens, but was based upon on-the-spot decision making by Demosthenes. Cf. W. Shepherd, *Pylos and Sphacteria 425 BC* (New York, 2013), p. 33.

4. Thucydides gives us a very detailed and vivid account of the sieges, and he is very definite in his descriptions of the location. These are corroborated by other ancient authors like Pausanias and Diodorus, so we can be safely certain in our location being the modern island of Sphacteria and the land mass above it being the location of Pylos, and the harbouring Navarino Bay which lies to the east of the island.

5. Sparta lived in a constant fear of *helot* revolt. Roughly outnumbered 10–1 by the *helots*, this was not an unjustified fear. Furthermore, Sparta's enemies knew that if a revolt could be incited then Sparta would choose to abandon all foreign policy in exchange for securing their own dominion.

6. It is easy to think of Greek soldiers as trained and disciplined veterans of war, but these were civilian conscripts who did not consider their commanding officers to be superior to them. So when Greek soldiers got bored, there was little their commanders could do to stop them relieving that boredom.

7. Whilst the force was around 1,000 men, this would have included only a small number of hoplites, maybe 75, and 20–30 archers, but the remaining forces could be relied upon as light-armed troops (*psiloi*) and even make-shift hoplites if necessary. Shepherd, *Pylos and Sphacteria*, p. 35.

8. This was not due to a need for reinforcements to face Demosthenes, as much as their fear of leaving Sparta under-protected against attack or *helot* uprising.

9. The size of the Spartan force at the siege is only given by Diodorus (XII.61.2) who claims it was 12,000 strong. Whilst this figure is a reasonable estimate, we do not know if this was the original force sent out of Sparta or the size once the various contingents converged around Pylos. J.F. Lazenby, *The Spartan Army* (Barnsley, 2012), p.142.

10. The distances Thucydides gives for these entrances are 2–3 ships' width for the entrance between Sphacteria and Pylos, which is a reasonable estimate based on the modern topography, and 8–9 ships' width for the entrance between Sphacteria to the south and the mainland, this is a distance of well over 1km and cannot be trusted as an estimate. It is not the only mistake Thucydides makes in describing the topography, as he erroneously describes the island of Sphacteria as being roughly half its actual length. R. Strassler (ed.), *The Landmark Thucydides* (London, 1996), p.227, n. 4.8.6b; M. Sears, 'The Topography of

the Pylos Campaign and Thucydides' Literary Themes', in *Hesperia*, 80 (2011), pp.158–60.

11. This force numbered 420 hoplites and an unknown number of *helot* attendants. They were commanded by Epitadas.

12. The shield was captured by the Athenians and formed the basis of the trophy they finally erected in victory after the fighting ended. It says a lot for the actions of Brasidas that after committing the great hoplite sin of losing one's shield, he was not punished or chastised. In fact, his career exploded in an upward trajectory and he became arguably the greatest Spartan commander of the Peloponnesian wars.

13. The equipment is not defined by Thucydides but would have included ladders and most likely battering rams.

14. These ships were to be returned in the same condition at the arrival of the envoys after their negotiations in Athens.

15. It is pertinent to understand that our main source, Thucydides, hated Cleon and this should be taken into account any time the latter's name arises in his narrative. For an excellent review of the issues surrounding Thucydides' representation of Cleon see A.G. Woodhead, 'Thucydides' Portrait of Cleon', in *Mnemosyne*, 13:4 (1960), pp.289–317.

16. In a very amusing episode of Thucydides (IV.27.4–28.5) it can be seen how the shame culture in Athens really manipulated even the most powerful of citizens. Cleon, for all his posturing, had no intention of leading the expedition but the Athenian assembly blamed him for their predicament and, with the false humility of Nicias, they were able to force him into taking command.

17. This was a smart political move for Cleon, as the prospect of losing more Athenian citizens was neither popular nor prudent in a *polis* that was still recovering from the devastating death toll of a plague.

18. See Chapter 2: The Battle of Olpae.

19. The Spartans did not attempt a resistance similar to Demosthenes' on the beach outside of the fort at Pylos, most likely due to their small numbers and the indeterminable amount of landing points available to the Athenians. Lazenby, *The Spartan Army*, p.146.

20. The Spartan helmet was called a *pilos*, it was a conical and open bronze helmet which substituted greater protection for better vision and hearing.

21. This was an accurate appraisal of the situation if the Athenians were manned solely by hoplites, as the heavy armour would be far too impractical to attempt to traverse the cliff.

22. Pausanias, IV.26.2. D. Kagan, *The Archidamian War* (New York, 1974), pp.246–7.

Chapter 13: The Siege of Syracuse (415–413 BC)

1. Syracuse was originally a colony of Corinth, and from the outbreak of the Peloponnesian war offered aid to the Peloponnesian faction.

2. A more extensive account of the conflict between Egesta and Selinus can be found in Diodorus (XII.82.3–83.6).
3. This amazing anecdote of deception is confirmed by both of our main sources for the conflict: Diodorus, XII.83.4, and Thucydides, VI.46.3–5.
4. The Leontines had been thrown out of their city by Syracusan forces in 427 BC, after the failed Athenian attempt to exert influence over Sicily.
5. As Athens had finally begun to recover from the plague that had hit it so hard during the war with Sparta, the younger generation were numerous enough to fulfil this recruitment quota.
6. In the words of Thucydides (VI.31.2) it was the 'most splendid force that had ever been sent out by a single city up to that time'. There is an interesting analogy that has been made by B. Jordan, with the non-existent farmhouses created by Potemkin to conceal poverty from Catherine the Great's great tour. Jordan argues that much of this fleet was about putting on a show of strength to the Athenian people, rather than a reflection of how well prepared they were for the expedition. B. Jordan, 'The Sicilian Expedition was a Potemkin Fleet', *The Classical Quarterly*, New Series, 50:1 (2000), pp.63–79.
7. Whilst the Athenian fleet was originally being prepared for the expedition, all of the Hermae (statues of Hermes which resided outside most households and temples) were mutilated. Alcibiades was accused of being involved, but his popularity was too high for his enemies to want to take him to trial immediately. They chose to bide their time before having him recalled to face the accusations. He never made it home, instead he disappeared in Italy before reappearing in the Peloponnese as an enemy of Athens.
8. Much is often made of Nicias' decision to delay the assault on the city of Syracuse. He encamped over winter (415/4 BC) at Catana, and this is something that Thucydides later criticizes him for (Thucydides, VII.42.3). But this ignores two important elements. Firstly, Nicias was not sole commander and it was not his decision alone. Secondly, Syracuse was a major city with strong defences. Greek sieges were rarely settled by a single assault but by longer term plans and the cutting off of supplies. To expect Syracuse, no matter how low their morale, to simply give up in the face of an unexpected threat undervalues the strong position Syracuse actually held, and the strong military tradition it had forged for itself in its campaigns to dominate Sicily.
9. Gylippus was not a full Spartiate, but a Spartan who had fallen from the highest echelon of their society (*mothax*). Reasons for this fall in social standing had various causes, but in the case of Gylippus it was due to his father being sent into exile. D. Kagan, *The Peace of Nicias and the Sicilian Expedition*, (New York, 1981), p.258.
10. This is a phenomenal loss in Greek warfare, equalling 50 per cent of the strength of a force.

11. I have followed the interpretation of the wall in R. Strassler (ed.), *The Landmark Thucydides: A Comprehensive Guide to the Peloponnesian War* (New York, 1996), p. 419.

12. In addition to the 300 were an unknown number of light-armed troops and archers from their allies. We do know that some of those who died in this small venture were Argives, but we do not know any more specifics.

13. Lamachus' died in battle as part of an isolated group of light-armed troops and archers. Plutarch gives a particularly Homeric account of his death, including a heroic duel against a great warrior named Callicrates (*Life of Nicias*, 18.2)

14. With the death of Lamachus and the recalling of Alcibiades, Nicias was the sole commander of the army for now.

15. Kagan convincingly argues that the force of Gylippus reflected a negative outlook from the Spartans on the chances of saving Syracuse. Gylippus himself was said to have thought Sicily lost, and that his man aim was to save Italy (Thucydides, VI.104.1). D. Kagan, *The Peace of Nicias and the Sicilian Expedition*, pp.257–9.

16. It is alleged that this defeat was manufactured by Gylippus, who informed the Athenians of the initial plan (Polyaenus, I.42). According to this tradition, Gylippus did this to undermine confidence in Syracusan commanders and encourage the authorities to hand full command over to him. This contradicts Thucydides who explicitly describes the plan as being Gylippus', and that he apologized to his troops for his failures. Whilst this speech may have been an attempt to revive morale, removing blame from the soldiers to the commander, it seems a more likely account of what happened than the sacrifice of men to gain control of an army that he seems to have had full control of already. Plutarch (*Life of Nicias*, 19.4) shows the likely scenario where the Syracusans derided the Spartan for his harsh way but soon accepted his authority due to his experience and abilities as commander.

17. For Demosthenes' exploits in masterminding the victories at Olpae and at Pylos, which ended with a Spartan surrender, see Chapters 1 and 12 respectively. As well as Demosthenes, the Athenians sent Menander and Euthydemus to help Nicias.

18. Demosthenes' plan was to retake the high plateau and immediately fortify themselves in position. Thucydides (VII.43.2) tells us that he took masons and carpenters on the expedition. He also mentions that they took five days' provisions and arrows, the latter a small acknowledgement of the known presence of archers in the Athenian army.

19. Only Diodorus (XIII.11.3) gives us this figure.

20. In the early summer of 413 BC Sparta had invaded Attica and fortified a permanent position in Athenian lands at Decelea. This position was roughly 14 miles from Athens and allowed access to some of the richest parts of the country

(Thucydides VII.19.1–2). Interestingly it seems this strategy was adopted on the advice of the Alcibiades.

21. Diodorus (XIII.12.6) claims it was only a three day wait, but this does not allow Gylippus time to utilise the pause in fighting for his own cause.

22. This was a heinous act of sacrilege, as well as defying one of the few 'rules' of Greek warfare. To not collect your dead comrades was a large taboo, and the Athenian inaction here cannot be overstated.

23. This would have been an honour of particular significance as Demosthenes was responsible for the defeat at Pylos (see Chapter 13) and the subsequent parading of Spartiates as prisoners in Athens.

Chapter 14: The Siege of the Drilae (400 BC)

1. Xenophon (*Anabasis*, II.6.1–16) gives a fascinating biography of Clearchus describing his many personality traits including being a lover of war, as well as a harsh man to serve under. For a modern interpretation of Clearchus' character as reflected by the modern diagnosis of PTSD, see L. Tritle, *Melos to My Lai: War and Survival* (London, 2000), pp.59–74.

2. Clearchus lived for roughly a year in a Persian prison before he was executed. The last to be killed was Menon the Thessalian.

3. A rough estimation for the distance given at 10,000 stades.

4. Rhodes was famous for its slingers, and it is interesting that these Rhodians were not only simply assumed to be able to use a sling with unrivalled proficiency, without any evidence to support this, but that they actually performed to a high standard.

5. This small skirmish is easily forgotten in the grand scheme of Greek warfare, but it had two important elements that are worth noting: 1) the painless adaptability of the troop types when the situation required it; 2) after this battle the Greeks who had chased the Persians down did something very unusual in Greek warfare – they mutilated the bodies, we are told it was to scare the Persians into not trying an attack again (Xenophon, *Anabasis*, III.4.5).

6. These mountains held a reputation of fear and dread within the Persian psyche. One story says that a Persian king sent an army of 120,000 men into these mountains to subdue the Carduchians, and not one man returned alive. (Xenophon, *Anabasis*, III.5.16)

7. This was only a betrayal in the eyes of the Greeks. It was considered a justified act by the Persians because the Greeks had already broken the truce when they burnt down some houses – most likely as a way of trying to stay warm (Xenophon, *Anabasis*, IV.4.14).

8. Xenophon, *Anabasis*, IV.5.7–16; Bulimia, translated as 'hunger-faintness', meant people felt unable to continue moving due to a lack of energy caused by starvation, it was associated with cold weather. Depression was evident in many of the men's refusal to move from their seated position, even when under the

threat of death – either from the snow, from their commanders, or from the enemy.

9. Xenophon, *Anabasis*, IV.7.13–14.
10. This is not just a romantic, modern notion, but is explicitly described by Xenophon (*Anabasis*, III.1.3) after the capture of the commanders.
11. The Drilae were a constant burden to the Trapezuntians so, once again, the Greeks had been manipulated into fighting the enemy of their allies.
12. The Greek word *doruphoroi*, used by Xenophon (Anabasis, V.2.4), translates as 'spear-carriers'. These were most likely lightly armed hoplites, eschewing armour and/or shields for mobility in climbing the rugged terrain and palisades, or camp followers who had armed themselves in search of loot.
13. The javelin had a loop on its handle which was used to create a greater throwing distance. Modern studies show an improved throwing distance of 58 per cent from a static position using these loops, so Xenophon's order had them fully prepared for an optimal attack. S.R. Murray, W.A. Sands, N.A. Keck, and D.A. O'Roark, 'Efficacy of the Ankle in Increasing the Distance of the Ancient Greek Javelin Throw', in *Nikephoros*, 23 (2010), pp.329–33.
14. Enyalius was a minor god of war in his own right, but he was often used as an epithet for Ares himself.
15. In siege warfare one could not claim to have control of a city without taking the central citadel that most acropolises served as.

Chapter 15: The Battle of Marathon (490 BC)

1. The exact events surrounding Darius' ascendency are controversial. We have three sources which contradict one another: Herodotus' account (III.61–65), the Bisitun monument commissioned by Darius, and economic documents from Babylon. The documents from Babylon show a simple transition from brother to brother, before Darius intervened. Whereas Darius' inscription describes Cambyses killing his brother before he died, and this new 'Bardiya' was an imposter. Herodotus mostly continues the tradition set by Darius with a few minor changes. I have chosen the traditions that comes down through the Babylonian documents as they seem more reliable. M. Waters, *Ancient Persia: a Concise History of the Achaemenid Empire, 550–330 BCE* (Cambridge, 2014), pp.58–69.
2. This period of continuous warfare was worth it for Darius as it resulted in the subjugation of nine different claimants to the throne. The entire list of (known) military action during this period is given in the Bisitun inscription, an English translation of which is freely available on http://www.livius.org/be-bm/behistun/behistun03.html (accessed 23/4/15).
3. The Scythian tactics during this campaign are often portrayed in modern accounts as 'running away', as if they were trying to bore Darius into leaving. But this does not seem easy to reconcile with the warrior ethos that underpinned

Scythian culture. C. Tuplin, 'Revisiting Dareios' Scythian Expedition', in *Achaemenid impacts in the Black Sea: Communication of powers*, edited by Jens Nieling and Ellen Rehm (Aarhus, 2010), pp. 281–312.

4. A tyrant was someone who took power of a city, outside of the realms of a constitution, and held it as an individual. Tyranny did not, automatically, hold the same negative connotations that it does today. This tyrant in question was the son of a tyrant called Pesistratus who was beloved by the Athenians.

5. Aristotle, *Athenian Constitution*, 22.1.

6. Isagoras was successfully voted in as eponymous archon for the year 508/7 BC, which made Cleisthenes turn to the public for support.

7. Cleisthenes' ancestors had been involved in the sacrilegious murder of suppliants in the Acropolis during an attempted coup in 632 BC. Cities who harboured criminals such as this would earn the anger of the gods, and that continued through the family line until the city and/or the family were cleansed of this pollution.

8. Herodotus does imply that the Athenians were furious with their envoys for the deal, but Krentz makes the strong argument that this Persian demand could not have come as a surprise, due to the various Asiatic Greek dealings with Persia, some of whom were Athenian colonies. Therefore the Athenians would have most likely agreed these terms before the envoys were sent. P. Krentz, *The Battle of Marathon* (London, 2010), pp.38–9; Waters, *Ancient Persia*, p.84.

9. It was a common practice for the Persians to support tyrants of Greek cities in their empire, so that they maintained control through the loyalty of that one man, rather than enforcing a Persian-led government over the Greek cities, which would harbour strong ill-feeling.

10. Ionia had little to complain about under Persian rule, in some ways, because they were thriving both culturally and economically; P. George, 'Persian Ionia under Darius: The Revolt Reconsidered', in *Historia*, 49:1 (2000), pp.1–39. There is a suggestion that the city of Miletus, perhaps overly epitomized by Aristagoras in Herodotus' account, was looking to replace Persian rule in the region with a Milesian hegemony, something we first see in the failed attempt to take Naxos (Herodotus, *Histories*, V.50.3).

11. He claimed that the Persians used neither shield nor spear, which is a blatant lie.

12. Excitingly the archaeology of sites like Soloi and Paphos show the extent of this resistance. Finds include siege mounds crossing defensive ditches and a tunnel dug beneath a city wall, as well as a concentration of missiles used by both sides. Krentz, *The Battle of Marathon*, p. 74.

13. Herodotus makes this a blanket statement - that all of the tyrants were deposed in place of democratic rule - but we know this was not the case on the island of Samos, for instance, where the tyrant Aeaces continued to rule. The historian seems to be trying to defend an earlier statement he made regarding Persian

attitudes to government, where one Persian is said to champion democracy whilst another oligarchy, and Darius argued for monarchy. Waters, *Ancient Persia*, p.88.

14. 'Medizing' was the act of submitting to, and supporting, the Persians, who were often called Medes, although this is an inaccurate term based upon one ethnic group within the Persian Empire.

15. 'The Lindos Chronicle', FGrH 532 (trans. A Kuhrt) in *The Persian Empire: A Corpus of Sources from the Achaemenid Period* (New York, 2010) p. 224. The dating of the events described in the monumental inscription known as the Lindos Chronicle has never been satisfactorily resolved. I have placed these events during the Marathon campaign, as opposed to the Ionian revolt, due to the role ascribed to Datis and the reference to Rhodes being the first island that the fleet met on the expedition. If this was during the Ionian revolt, the first island the fleet would have encountered would have been the rebellious island of Cyprus not Rhodes, implying that Cyprus was already under Persian control. Krentz, *The Battle of Marathon*, pp. 94–5; N. Sekunda, *Marathon 490 BC: The First Persian Invasion of Greece* (Oxford, 2002), pp.29–30. For an argument contrary to this timing see the influential work of A. Burn, *Persia and the Greeks: The Defence of the West, C. 546–478 BC* (Stanford, 1984), pp. 210–11, 218.

16. It has been suggested that the presence of Hippias shows that Athens was always a major target for the expedition, but it may not suggest that military action was inevitable. The size of the Persian force was not enough to launch a viable campaign against Athens, but perhaps Datis had hoped the threat of force might encourage the Athenians to take Hippias back. Or else he was simply there to offer his local knowledge, and get him out of Artaphernes' court.

17. The small amount of cavalry is substantiated by the difficulty of transporting them, and their lack of activity in the subsequent battle. C. Tuplin, 'Marathon: In Search of a Persian Dimension', in (eds) K. Buraselis and K. Meidani, *Marathon: Deme and Battle* (Athens, 2010), pp. 268–9; Krentz, *The Battle of Marathon*, pp.92–3.

18. Tuplin, 'Marathon: In Search of a Persian Dimension', p. 265.

19. The commander, or *polemarch*, was an official selected by lot and not one based on military merit. The *polemarch* had the honour of leading the right wing of the army and for breaking any ties in the voting of the ten generals, but he did not hold the authoritative position we associate with a general.

20. Neither army is given a fighting strength by Herodotus, while the later traditions subscribe to the astronomical figures that so often followed Persian armies (ranging from 90–600,000 men). For a thorough break down of the various academic arguments for a variety of estimated fighting strengths see D. Fink, *The Battle of Marathon in Scholarship: Research, Theories and Controversies since 1850* (Jefferson, 2014), pp. 126–134.

21. Krentz, *The Battle of Marathon*, p.107.

22. The reasoning for the Athenians deciding to fight is as contentious as almost every other aspect of the battle. I have followed the reasoning of Krentz, *The Battle of Marathon*, p.142–3, but for a large array of solutions see Fink, *The Battle of Marathon in Scholarship*, pp. 145–51.

23. The generals shared command on a daily rota. It is said by Herodotus (VI.110) that Miltiades was given the command days of the other generals who voted to fight, but that he still waited until his official day to act.

24. Billows is right in his assertion of the tactical ingenuity this battle took; from a Greek perspective this running advance and uneven line depth was unprecedented. It is certain that Miltiades must have informed his soldiers of the plan before the day of battle, and maybe even practised some basic drills to make sure everyone knew what was expected of them. R. Billows, *Marathon: How One Battle Changed Western Civilization* (New York, 2010), p.214.

25. More accurately it would have been a hearty jog rather than a run. Krentz, *The Battle of Marathon*, p.143–52, 156.

26. The historical interpretation of Persian tactics relying strongly on the horse has been, I think, successfully debunked, at least during this early period, by Tuplin. While the Greeks most likely did hold great fear for the Persian cavalry, and this influenced Miltiades battle plan, it does not necessarily equate that the Persians intended to use their cavalry in that exact way. While modern historians obsess over the role of the 'missing' cavalry, we may be missing the point that Datis had no intention of using them in any decisive and critical way. C. Tuplin, 'All the King's Horse: In Search of Achaemenid Persian Cavalry', in M.Trundle & G.Fagan (eds.), *New Perspectives on Ancient Warfare* (Leiden, 2010), pp. 158–74; C. Tuplin, 'Marathon: In Search of a Persian Dimension', pp. 269–71;

27. Aristophanes, *Wasps*, 1084.

28. Epizelus was possibly suffering with a form of 'conversion disorder' that is often associated with extreme trauma (within the modern parlance this would come under Post-traumatic Stress Disorder). Unlike PTSD, however, this injury worked in his favour as he became a hero of Athens. His blindness made him akin to the blind poets of the age, who were considered touched by the gods. H. King, 'Recovering hysteria from history: Herodotus and the first case of "shell-shock"', in P. Halligan, C. Bass and J. Marshall (eds), *Contemporary Approaches to the Science of Hysteria: Clinical and Theoretical Perspectives* (Oxford, 2001), pp. 42–2.

29. Psuedo–Plutarch, *Greek and Roman Parallel Stories*, 1.

30. This unfortunate man was called Cynegeirus, he was a brother of the famous tragedian Aeschylus who also fought in the battle.

31. Philostratus, *Life of Apollonios*, 1.24.

Chapter 16: The Battle of Plataea (479 BC)

1. Xerxes was not the eldest son, but Herodotus claims that he convinced Darius to name him as his heir because Xerxes was the first son of Darius after he

had become a king – amazingly this worked and he was named heir apparent (Herodotus, *Histories*, VII.3.1–4).

2. M. Dandamaev, *A Political History of the Achaemenid Empire* (Leiden, 1989), p.178

3. J. Boardman, N.G.L. Hammond, D.M. Lewis, M. Ostwald (eds.) *Cambridge Ancient History Volume IV (second edition): Persia, Greece and the Western Mediterranean, c.525 to 479 BC*, (Cambridge, 2002), p.72–3.

4. It is important to note that, for the Persians, stability in Egypt was vastly more important than invading Greece. Whereas our sources imply that the Egyptian rebellion was a non-event, something that got in the way of the Persians true ambition to take Greece; it is just as likely that the Egyptian rebellion was the only reason that Greece had maintained its independence in the first place.

5. Herodotus tells us that one of his advisors, Mardonius, had convinced him to continue Darius' plan to invade Greece. (*Histories*, VII.5)

6. Dandamaev, *A Political History of the Achaemenid Empire*, p.184.

7. Any new king needed to receive a crown from the hands of Marduk at the New Year festival. Xerxes had already been through this ceremony himself.

8. The size of army is hotly debated, with Herodotus estimating it at 1.8 million in Asia Minor, rising to 2.1 million by the time it reached Greece. Modern estimates range between 50,000–200,000 with most fence-sitters settling at 100–150,000 as a reasonable figure; P. De Souza, *The Greek and Persian Wars, 499–386 BC* (2003) p. 41.

9. Herodotus, *Histories*, VII.174; Dandamaev, *A Political History of the Achaemenid Empire*, p.197; P. De Souza, *The Greek and Persian Wars*, p. 49.

10. Much ink has been spilt about this famous battle between 8,000 Greek hoplites and the great Persian army attacking them, but ultimately it is disproportionate in the grand scheme of military development or even interest. Ultimately the stand lasted three days until the Persians found another path to circumnavigate the Greeks' defensive position, after which a massacre ensued. For a good retelling of the Battle of Thermopylae see P. Cartledge, *Thermopylae: the Battle that Changed the World* (Oxford, 2006).

11. The Greeks were first positioned near the town of Erythrae, then after their initial success in the skirmish they decided to move west and nearer Plataea.

12. For an interesting interpretation of the *helots'* role in this battle see P. Hunt, 'Helots at the battle of Plataea', in *Historia*, 46: 2 (1997), pp. 129–44.

13. Herodotus lists: Persian troops from the 10,000 immortals, the troops that were known simply as 'wearing breastplates' and 1,000 horsemen; Medes; Bactrians; Indians, both horsemen and infantry; Sacae; Boeotians; Locrians; Malians; Thessalians; 1,000 Phocian hoplites; Macedonians, Phrygians, Thracians, Mysians, Paeonians, Ethiopians and Egyptians. Herodotus estimates that the Greek allies of Persia numbered 50,000, the number was probably nearer 20,000. (Herodotus, *Histories*, VIII.113.2–3, IX.31–2). As always, these figures

are contentious. Just pick up a book on the Persian wars and you will read a slightly different estimate. For the sake of this book it is important to show that the numerical difference between the two armies was nowhere near as dramatic as has been often depicted.

14. There is a story that Herodotus tells that whilst the Persians began to prepare for battle that night, the Greeks were visited by Alexander I of Macedon who was on the side of the Persians. Alexander is meant to have informed the Greeks that Mardonius intended to attack the next day, giving them the chance to prepare. We are told that Pausanias panicked, because his Spartans were to face the Persian elite troops (the Immortals) and he asked to change positions with the Athenians, which they did, but then changed back after being counter-moved by the Persians. These two tales are usually dismissed by historians because the Alexander episode is all too convenient for the story to progress, and the Pausanias tale flies in the face of everything we know about the Spartans' sense of superiority and their general military arrogance.

15. It should be noted that this episode is also contended by scholars, such as P. Cartledge, *After Thermopylae: The Oath of Plataea and the End of the Greco-Persian Wars* (New York, 2013), p.114, because such insubordination is so conflicting with the image we have of Sparta. It has been suggested that this was actually a tactical decision to give a staggered, feigned, retreat, in keeping with Sparta's tactics in later battles. I have decided to leave it in because I believe it to be a highly possible event due to the cognitive strain that such an order would have had on a Spartan officer. Ultimately, it was considered wrong for a Spartan to not hold their ground after setting up for battle and this officer could not find congruence between his commander's orders and the Spartan warrior ethos.

16. A large force led by Artabazus never joined in the fighting.

17. Do not be fooled by the use of wicker, these were light but also very durable and resilient pieces of equipment. R. Konijnendijk, 'Neither the Less Valorous Nor the Weaker: Persian Military Might and the Battle of Plataea', in *Historia*, 61 (2012), p. 15 n.82; N. Sekunda, *The Persian Army 560–330* (Oxford 1992), p.16–17

18. Of the 300,000 – so that does not include Artabazus' troops – not even 3,000 survived (Herodotus, *Histories*, 9.70.5).

19. Konijnendijk, 'Neither the Less Valorous Nor the Weaker', p. 15 n.82.

Chapter 17: The Battle of Cunaxa (401 BC)

1. This actually contradicts one of our main sources, which claims that the decision was made on Darius' deathbed (Plutarch, *Life of Artaxerxes*, 2.2.3). But Pierre Briant seems correct when he observes that it would be very unlikely that Darius would wait until the end of his life to name a successor, and Arsicas' natural position of successor as the eldest son (over the age of 20 no less) does suggest that a crown prince would have needed to be named, maybe a few years

earlier. P. Briant, *From Cyrus to Alexander: A History of the Persian Empire*, trans. Peter Daniels, (Paris, 2002), p.615. Cyrus the Younger must not to be confused with his illustrious ancestor Cyrus the Great.

2. Plutarch, *Life of Artaxerxes*, 2.2.3.

3. Xenophon, *Hellenica*, II.1.8. The 'crime' committed by those who were executed was that they did not place their hands in the longer sleeves of their clothing, which was required in the presence of the Great King.

4. For the relationship, and changing circumstances, between Cyrus and Tissaphernes see S. Ruzicka, 'Cyrus and Tissaphernes, 407–401 BC', in *The Classical Journal*, 80:3 (1985), pp. 204–11.

5. The precise date for this event is not clear from our sources, but it seems more likely that this was arranged before Cyrus returned to his lands. Ruzicka, 'Cyrus and Tissaphernes', pp. 207–8.

6. If it were not for the pressing issue of a revolt in Egypt, Artaxerxes may well have tried to rid himself of Cyrus that campaign season.

7. The governments had been set up by the Spartan commander Lysander who was a close ally of Cyrus.

8. The superiority of the Greek hoplite is often overemphasized in their role as mercenaries (thanks to our sources having been written by Greeks). Whilst their experience of the Peloponnesian War made them desirably battle hardened, it is perhaps more important that there were so many of them available. That being said, Tissaphernes did feel fit to hire a mercenary hoplite expert named Phalinus, to use his expertise in dealing with Cyrus' army.

9. For the Greek cities this was not a matter of democracy versus oligarchy, at least not in all cases. It was a question of one Persian overlord versus another, so it was more pragmatic for them to wait and see who was victorious.

10. One force was amassed by the Spartan exile Clearchus, who had been given the funds to wage his own private war against the Thracians for over a year. Another was given to Aristippus of Thessaly who wanted help against his political enemies; Cyrus gave him a very large force and ordered him to maintain the conflict and to not settle it without consulting him first.

11. Diodorus (XIII.46.4). S. Ruzicka, *Trouble in the West: Egypt and the Persian Empire 525–332 BCE* (Oxford, 2012), p.36.

12. Athens had supported Egyptian revolts in the mid-fifth century as it was an efficient way of distracting the Persians, and also an effective way of undermining the cohesion of the empire. For the end of the Peloponnesian War and the parallel events in Egypt see Ruzicka, *Trouble in the West*, p.35–8.

13. Allegedly the army was 300,000 men strong, from a possible 1,200,000 available to the Persian King. This is an obvious exaggeration, but the army would still have been very strong.

14. Diodorus states that the warning came from another *satrap*, Pharnabazus (XIV.11.1–2; 22.1), which would mean that Artaxerxes would have known as

early as 404 BC of Cyrus' intent. This does not match the overall narrative we have from our sources, which depict the King's response as being reactive and unprepared. It is also hard to believe that Artaxerxes would have endorsed his brother's fighting with Tissaphernes (Xenophon, *Anabasis*, I.1.8), knowing that Cyrus was in the process of planning a rebellion.

15. Ruzicka, 'Cyrus and Tissaphernes, 407–401 BC', p. 211.

16. Xenophon, *Anabasis*, I.2.11.

17. The full story of this episode (Xenophon, *Anabasis*, I.3.1–21) is fascinating and deserves more coverage than it can receive here. The twenty-day pause also ended with Clearchus becoming the unofficial leader of the Greeks.

18. Meno had lost 200 men in the march to Tarsus, or else the figure would have been 10,600 men.

19. Abrocomas had no intention of cutting off Cyrus' army, which appears to have been Xenophon's assumption when discussing the commander's actions. When Abrocomas received the orders from Artaxerxes, he intended to join the king as he drew his forces together, which meant having to cross the Euphrates. The important point for Cyrus was that he needed to cross the river and engage his brother in battle, before Artaxerxes could be joined by such a sizeable army.

20. The lack of resistance by the Greeks certainly shows how unsurprised they were by this 'revelation'.

21. Orontas, the man who tried to take Sardis from Cyrus, sent word to Artaxerxes saying that he would join the king with as many of Cyrus' cavalry as he could commandeer. The message was intercepted and Orontas was tried and executed.

22. J. Rop, 'Reconsidering the Origin of the Scythed Chariot', in *Historia*, 62:2 (2013), pp.168–70.

23. G. Wylie., 'Cunaxa and Xenophon', in *L'Antiquité Classique*, 61 (1992), pp.122–3.

24. The Paphlagonian cavalry is a reliable figure due to its position on the right wing next to the Greeks, where Xenophon was most likely positioned.

25. Xenophon (I.7.10) states 100,000 non-Greeks; Diodorus (XIX.7) says 70,000. For the modern estimates see J.M. Bigwood, 'The Ancient Accounts of the Battle of Cunaxa', in *The American Journal of Philology*, 104:4 (1983), p.341, especially n.5.

26. Wylie, 'Cunaxa and Xenophon', p.123.

27. Bigwood, 'The Ancient Accounts of the Battle of Cunaxa', p.342, especially n.6.

28. The topic of the Immortals is highly contentious in academic circles. For the question of their presence at Cunaxa see M. Charles, 'Immortals and Apple Bearers: Towards a Better Understanding of Achaemenid Infantry Units', in *The Classical Quarterly*, 61:1 (2011), pp. 124–5.

29. Xenophon (*Anabasis*, I.9.31) specifically describes Ariaeus commanding the cavalry, but Cyrus must have had more infantry that the Greek portion of his army, and he would have had hitherto-unmentioned archers as well.

30. It is unfair to blame the commander for this, he did control over half of the entire army by himself, as opposed to the Greeks who had at least three commanders to themselves.

31. The positioning of Tissaphernes within the battle is greatly debated because Diodorus' account (XIV.23.6) places him in the centre of the army, taking command when the king leaves the field. I have followed the analysis of Bigwood in keeping Tissaphernes within his placement by Xenophon, due in no small part to the events that occurred there. I would also argue that Tissaphernes' experience in fighting with Greek mercenaries in Anatolia made him a prime candidate to command the forces that faced them. Bigwood, 'The Ancient Accounts of the Battle of Cunaxa', p.355.

32. The vagueness of this description is unfortunately a true reflection of our sources. It most likely reflects Xenophon's vision on the battlefield, he could not see beyond the Egyptians and so generalizes that the rest of the line was made up of archers and cavalry, which is highly unlikely.

33. It is not clear if Cyrus meant to attack from the position the Greeks were already in, or to relocate in the battle formation to a more central position. The close proximity of the enemy meant that neither idea was a viable one.

34. The watchword was a way to notify people of your allegiance during the chaos of battle.

35. Diodorus (XIV.23.1) describes this as a deliberate tactic by Clearchus and that the Greeks began to run when they entered missile range. Taking into account Diodorus' emphasis of the role of Clearchus throughout his narrative, this seems a little suspect. The broken run is in keeping with the portrayal of the Greeks as impetuous, and at times ill-disciplined. If we are to expect these veterans to maintain their composure in battle, would we not also expect them to remain on the field and not chase after a solitary company? Cf. Wylie, 'Cunaxa and Xenophon', p.126.

36. The ability to let the chariots through their lines implies three things – 1) the lines were back in formation after the running, 2) this was a drilled move that must have been practised, 3) the lines of the formation must have been in a loose formation rather than the traditional model of a tight, closed phalanx.

37. For the possible use of the levees by the *peltasts* see Wylie, 'Cunaxa and Xenophon', p.126.

38. Whilst I would not go as far as to describe this as a planned retreat from the Persian line, it does appear (through the anti-Persian narrative) that Tissaphernes was placed on the wing specifically to react to the Greek offensive. The fact that he did not attack the phalanx from the rear implies that it was never his intention to attack the Greeks but to allow them to leave the field, while he regrouped behind Cyrus' lines. R. Waterfield, *Xenophon's Retreat: Greece, Persia and the End of the Golden Age* (London, 2006), p.18.

39. This element of the battle is not found in Xenophon's personal account (he references Ctesias twice in quick succession) and is based upon Plutarch, *Life of Artaxerxes*, 9–11, which makes more extensive use the works of Deinon and Ctesias.

40. All of the accounts of Cyrus' death differ from each other, with the longest account by Ctesias coming under specific scrutiny for dragging it out for too long (Fr. 20=Plutarch, *Life of Artaxerxes*, 11.5). This means there is no reliable story to explain his death so I have gone for the shortest.

41. Xenophon places the king in the heart of the action at all times, but the description by Ctesias cannot be completely discounted. This final phase of the battle is based upon Ctesias' original placements of the king's entourage (Fr. 20=Plutarch, *Life of Artaxerxes*, 11.2) but still follows Xenophon's description of events wherever possible.

42. It is commonly written, in accordance with Xenophon, that the Greeks broke the 'weak' Persian lines with a charge, but this does not make much sense. The Persians were in a very strong position with the majority of their forces intact, they could easily have outflanked the Greek position and enacted the slaughter that Clearchus was so afraid of when planning his ambitious manoeuvre. It seems more likely, taking into account the late hour of the day, that Artaxerxes put on a show of force before re-evaluating the situation, maybe with guidance from his experienced commanders, and ordering an orderly retreat that was disrupted by the Greek charge.

43. According to Ctesias this was the number reported to the king (Fr. 22–3=Plutarch, *Life of Artaxerxes*, 13.3–5), but the physician thought the number to be nearer 20,000, which was still low given his own estimates of the king's original forces (400,000).

44. See Chapter 14: The Siege of the Drilae (400 BC) for the continuation of their story.

Bibliography

Ancient Works and Selected Translations
Aeschines, *Against Ctesiphon*.
Andocides, *On the Peace*.
Aristophanes, *Plutus*.
Aristotle, *Athenian Constitution*.
Athenaeus, *The Deipnosophists*.
Ctesias, *Persica*.
Demosthenes, *Speeches*.
Diodorus Siculus (Diodorus), *Library of World History*.
Ephorus, *Histories*.
Frontinus, *Strategemata*.
Herodotus, *Histories*.
Pausanias, *Description of Greece*.
Philostratus, *Life of Apollonios*.
Polyaenus, *Stratagems*.
Polybius, *World History*.
Plato, *Symposium*.
Plutarch, *Life of Agesilaus*.
—— *Life of Artaxerxes*.
—— *Life of Nicias*.
—— *Life of Pelopidas*.
—— *Life of Pericles*.
—— *Love Stories* (*Amatoriae narrations*).
—— *Sayings of the Spartans*.
Pseudo-Plutarch, *Greek and Roman Parallel Stories*.
Thucydides, *History of the Peloponnesian War*.
Xenophon, *Agesilaus*.
—— *Anabasis*.
—— *Hellenica*.
—— *Cyropaedia*.
Unknown, *Hellenica Oxyrhynchia*.
The Lindos Chronicle.
McKechnie, P R, & S J Kern, *Hellenika Oxyrhynchia* (fourth impression), (Warminster, 1993).

Sage, M, *Warfare in Ancient Greece: A Sourcebook* (1996, London).

Strassler, R, *The Landmark Thucydides: A Comprehensive Guide to the Peloponnesian War* (New York, 1996).

Strassler, R, *The Landmark Herodotus: The Histories* (London, 2008).

Strassler, R, *The Landmark Xenophon's Hellenika* (London, 2011).

For free translations on the internet there are no better resources than the Perseus Project, Lacus Curtius, and Livius. There are also numerous research projects online that are making valuable translations available to the wider public. See 'Websites' below for relevant URLs.

General works on classical Greek military history

Anderson, J K, *Military Theory and Practice in the Age of Xenophon* (Berkeley, 1970).

Borza, E, *In the Shadow of Olympus: The Emergence of Macedon* (Princeton, 1990).

Campbell, B, & L Tritle (eds.), *The Oxford Handbook of Warfare in the Classical World* (Oxford, 2013).

Echeverría, F, 'Hoplite and Phalanx in Archaic and Classical Greece: A Reassessment', in *Classical Philology*, 107: 4 (2012), pp. 291–318.

Fagan, G, and M Trundle (eds.), *New Perspectives on Ancient Warfare* (Leiden, 2010).

Goldsworthy, A, 'The *Othismos*, Myths and Heresies: The Nature of Hoplite Battle', in *War in History*, 4:1 (1997), pp.1–26.

Hanson, V D, *The Western Way of War: Infantry Battle in Classical Greece* (Berkeley, 1989).

Hanson, V D, *Warfare and Agriculture in Classical Greece* (London, 1998).

Hanson, V.D. (ed.), *Hoplites: The Classical Greek Battle Experience* (London, 1999).

Kagan, D, & G F Viggiano (eds.), *Men of Bronze Hoplite Warfare in Ancient Greece* (Princeton, 2013).

Krentz, P, 'Casualties in Hoplite Battles', in *Greek, Roman and Byzantine Studies*, 26:1 (1985), pp.13–20.

Lazenby, J F, *The Spartan Army* (Barnsley, 2012).

Lendon, J, *Soldiers & Ghosts: A History of Battle in Classical Antiquity* (New York, 2005).

Matthew, C, *A Storm of Spears: Understanding the Greek Hoplite at War (Barnsely, 2012)*.

Pritchett, W K, *The Greek State at War*, 5 vols, (Berkeley, 1971–1991).

Ray Jr, F E, *Greek and Macedonian Land Battles of the 4th Century BC: A History and analysis of 187 engagements* (Jefferson, 2012).

Sabin, P, *Lost Battles: Reconstructing the Great Clashes of the Ancient World* (London, 2009).

Tritle, L, *Melos to My Lai: War and Survival* (London, 2000).

van Wees, H, *Greek Warfare: Myths and Realities* (London, 2004).

van Wees, H (ed.), *War and Violence in Ancient Greece* (London, 2000).

Whatley, N, 'On the Possibility of Reconstructing Marathon and Other Ancient Battles', in *The Journal of Hellenic Studies*, 84 (1964), pp. 119–139.

Peloponnesian War:

Anderson, J K, 'Cleon's Orders at Amphipolis', in *The Journal of Hellenic Studies*, 85 (1965), pp. 1–4.

Boegehold, A, 'Thucydides' Representation of Brasidas before Amphipolis', in *Classical Philology*, 74: 2 (1979), pp. 148–152.

Bugh, G, *The Horsemen of Athens* (Princeton, 1988).

Cooper III, G L, 'Thuc. 5.65.3 and the Tactical Obsession of Agis II on the Day before the Battle of Mantinea', in *Transactions of the American Philological Association (1974–)*, 108 (1978), pp. 35–40.

Ellis, J R, 'Thucydides at Amphipolis', in *Antichthon*, 12, (1978), pp.28–35.

Gomme, A W, *A Historical Commentary on Thucydides*, Vol. III (Oxford, 1956).

Gomme, A W, Andrewes, A, & K Dover, *A Historical Commentary on Thucydides*, *IV* (Oxford: 1970).

Hammond, N, 'The Campaigns in Amphilochia during the Archidamian War', in *The Annual of the British School in Athens*, 37 (1936/7), pp. 128–140.

Hanson, V D, *A War Like No Other: How the Athenians and Spartans Fought the Peloponnesian War* (New York, 2005).

Hornblower, S, *A Commentary on Thucydides: Volume II: Books IV-V. 24* (Oxford, 1996).

Jones, N, 'The Topography and Strategy of the Battle of Amphipolis in 422 B.C', in *California Studies in Classical Antiquity*, 10 (1977), pp. 71–104.

Kagan, D, *The Outbreak of the Peloponnesian War* (London 1969).

Kagan, D, *The Archidamian War* (New York, 1974).

Kagan, D, *The Peace of Nicias and the Sicilian Expedition* (New York: 1981).

Kagan, D, *The Fall of the Athenian Empire* (New York, 1987).

Koukouli–Chrysanthaki, C, 'Excavating Classical Amphipolis', in M Stamatopoulou and M Yeroulanou (eds.), *Excavating Classical Culture: Recent Archaeological Discoveries in Greece*, BAR International Series 1031 (2002).

Lendon, J, *Song of Wrath: The Peloponnesian War Begins* (New York, 2010).

Nevin, S, 'Military Ethics in the Writing of History: Thucydides and Diodorus', in Bragg, E, L I Hau and E Macaulay-Lewis (eds.), *Beyond the Battlefields: New Perspectives on Warfare and Society in the Graeco-Roman World* (Cambridge, 2008).

Roisman, J, *The General Demosthenes and His Use of Military Surprise* (Stuttgart, 1993).

Toher, M, 'Diodoros on Delion and Euripides' Supplices', in *The Classical Quarterly*, 51:1 (2001), pp. 178–182.

Tritle, L, *A New History of the Peloponnesian War* (Oxford, 2010).

Westlake, H D, 'Thucydides and the Fall of Amphipolis', in *Hermes*, 90:3 (1962), pp. 276–287.

Wylie, G, 'Brasidas: Great Commander or Whiz-Kid?', in *Quaderni Urbinati di Cultura Classica*, 41:2 (1992), pp.75–95.

Spartan Hegemony

Anderson, J K, 'The Statue of Chabrias', in *American Journal of Archaeology*, 67:4 (Oct., 1963), pp. 411–413.

Anderson, J K, *Military Theory and Practice in the Age of Xenophon*, (Berkeley, 1970).

Buck, R, *Boiotia and the Boiotian League, 432–371 BC*, (Edmonton, 1994).

Buckler, J, 'Plutarch on Leuktra', in *Symbolae Osloenses: Norwegian Journal of Greek and Latin Studies*, 55:1 (1980), 75–93.

Burliga, B, 'Did they Really Return upon Their Shields? The Hubris of the Spartan Hoplites at Lechaeum, 390 BC', in N. Sekunda and B Burliga (eds.), *Iphicrates, Peltasts and Lechaeum* (Gdansk, 2014).

Cartledge, P, *Sparta and Lakonia: a Regional History 1300–362 BC* (New York, 2002).

Cawkwell, G, 'Epaminondas and Thebes', in *Classical Quarterly*, 22:2 (1972), pp. 254–78.

Craven, B, *Dionysius I: War-Lord of Sicily* (London, 1990).

Delorme, J, *Gymnasion: Étude sur les monuments consacrés à l'éducation en Grèce* (des origines à l'Empire romain) (Paris, 1960).

Deltenre, F-D, 'La datation du début de la troisième guerre sacrée. Retour sur l'interprétation des comptes de Delphes', in *Bulletin de Correspondance Hellénique*, 134 (2010), pp. 97–116.

Gaebel, R, *Cavalry Operations in the Ancient Greek World* (Norman, 2002).

Grey, V, *The Character of Xenophon's Hellenica* (London: 1989).

Griffith, G T, 'The Union of Corinth and Argos (392–386 BC)', in *Historia: Zeitschrift für Alte Geschichte*, 1:2 (1950), pp. 236–56.

Grote, G, *History of Greece*, vol.9 (London, 1854).

Hanson, V D, 'Epameinondas and the "Embolon"', in *Phoenix*, 39:2 (1985), pp. 134–43.

Hanson, V D, 'Epameinondas, the Battle of Leuktra (371 BC), and the "Revolution" in Greek Battle Tactics', in *Classical Antiquity*, 7:2 (1988), pp. 190–207.

Hanson, V D, 'Epaminondas at Leuctra, 371 B.C', in B. Campbell & L. Tritle (eds.), *The Oxford Handbook of Warfare in the Classical World* (Oxford, 2013).

Hornblower, S, 'When Was Megalopolis Founded?', in *The Annual of the British School at Athens*, 85 (1990), pp. 71–7.

Kagan, D, 'Corinthian Politics and the Revolution of 392 BC', in *Historia: Zeitschrift für Alte Geschichte*, Bd. 11, H. 4 (Oct., 1962), pp. 447–57.

Konecny, A, '"Κατέχοψεν την μόραν 'Ιφιχράτης", The Battle of Lechaeum, Early Summer, 390 BC', in N. Sekunda & B. Burliga (eds.), *Iphicrates, Peltasts and Lechaeum* (Gdansk, 2014).

Rhodes, P J, *A History of the Classical World: 478–323 BC* (Oxford, 2010).

Rothaus, R, 'Lechaion, Western Port of Corinth: a Preliminary Archaeology and History', in *Oxford Journal of Archaeology*, 14: 3 (1995), pp.293–306.

Salmon, J B, *Wealthy Corinth: A History of the City to 338 BC* (Oxford, 1997).

Sekunda, N, and B Burliga (eds.), *Iphicrates, Peltasts and Lechaeum* (Gdansk, 2014).

Shrimpton, G, 'Plutarch's Life of Epaminondas', in *Pacific Coast Philology*, 6 (1971), pp. 55–9.

Shrimpton, G, 'The Theban Supremacy in Fourth-Century Literature', in *Phoenix*, 25:4 (1971), pp. 310–18.

Spence, I G, *The Cavalry of Classical Greece: a Social and Military History* (Oxford, 1993).

Sprawski, S, 'Battle of Tegyra (375 BC). Breaking through and the opening of the ranks', in *Electrum*, 8 (2004), pp.13–26.

Tuplin, C, 'Pausanias and Plutarch's Epaminondas', in *The Classical Quarterly*, 34 (1984), pp 346–58.

Wiseman, J, 'Ancient Corinth: the Gymnasium Area', in *Archaeology*, 22:3 (June, 1969), pp. 216–25

Wiseman, J, *The Land of the Ancient Corinthians* (Studies in Mediterranean Archaeology vol. 50), (Goteborg: 1978).

Sieges

Abbott, E, 'The Siege of Plataea', in *The Classical Review*, 4:1/2 (Feb, 1890), pp. 1–3.

Aravantinos, V, A Konecny and R Marchese, 'Plataiai in Boiotia: A Preliminary Report of the 1996–2001 Campaigns', in *Hesperia: The Journal of the American School of Classical Studies at Athens*, 72:3 (2003), pp. 281–320.

Bosworth, B, 'Athens' First Intervention in Sicily: Thucydides and the Sicilian Tradition', in *The Classical Quarterly*, 42:1 (1992), pp. 4–55.

Campbell, D, *Ancient Siege Warfare: Persians, Greeks, Carthaginians and Romans 546–146 BC* (Oxford, 2005).

Campbell, D, *Besieged: Siege Warfare in the Ancient World* (Oxford, 2006).

Flower, H, 'Thucydides and the Pylos Debate (4.27–29)', in *Historia: Zeitschrift für Alte Geschichte*, 41:1 (1992), pp. 40–57

Grundy, G, *The Topography of the Battle of Plataea: The City of Plataea. The Field of Leuctra* (London, 1894).

Harrison, E L, 'The Escape from Plataea: Thucydides 3. 23', in *The Classical Quarterly*, 9:1 (May, 1959), pp. 30–33

Jordan, B, 'The Sicilian Expedition was a Potemkin Fleet', in *The Classical Quarterly*, New Series, 50:1 (2000), pp. 63–79.

Kagan, D, *The Peace of Nicias and the Sicilian Expedition* (New York, 1981).

Kern, P, 'Military Technology and Ethical Values in Ancient Greek Warfare: The Siege of Plataea', *War and Society*, 6:2 (1988), pp.1–20.

Konecny, A, V Aravantinos and R Marchese, *Plataiai. Archäologie und Geschichte einer boiotischen Polis*, (Vienna, 2013).
Liebeschuetz, W, 'Thucydides and the Sicilian Expedition', in *Historia: Zeitschrift für Alte Geschichte*, 17:3 (Jul., 1968), pp. 289–306.
McLeod, W, 'The Range of the Ancient Bow', in *Phoenix*, 19:1 (Spring, 1965), pp. 1–14.
Murray, S R, W A Sands, N A Keck and D A O'Roark, 'Efficacy of the Ankyle in Increasing the Distance of the Ancient Greek Javelin Throw', in *Nikephoros*, 23 (2010), pp. 329–33.
Rubincam, C, 'The Topography of Pylos and Sphakteria and Thucydides' Measurements of Distance', in *The Journal of Hellenic Studies*, 121 (2001), pp. 77–90.
Sears, M, 'The Topography of the Pylos Campaign and Thucydides' Literary Themes', in *Hesperia*, 80 (2011), pp.157–68.
Shepherd, W, *Pylos and Sphacteria 425 BC* (New York, 2013).
Woodhead, A G, 'Thucydides' Portrait of Cleon', in *Mnemosyne*, 13:4 (1960), pp. 289–317.
Wilson, J, and T Beardsworth, 'Pylos 425 B. C.: "The Spartan Plan to Block the Entrances"', in *The Classical Quarterly*, 20:1 (1970), pp. 42–52.
Wilson, J, and T Beardsworth, 'Bad Weather and the Blockade at Pylos', in *Phoenix*, 24:2 (1970), pp. 112–18.
Zatta, C, 'Conflict, People, and City-Space: Some Exempla from Thucydides' History', in *Classical Antiquity*, 30:2 (October 2011), pp. 318–50.

Greco-Persian Conflict
Bigwood, J M, 'The Ancient Accounts of the Battle of Cunaxa', in *The American Journal of Philology*, 104:4 (1983), pp. 340–57.
Billows, R, *Marathon: How One Battle Changed Western Civilization* (New York, 2010).
Boardman, J, N G L Hammond, D M Lewis, and M Ostwald, *Cambridge Ancient History Volume IV (second edition): Persia, Greece and the Western Mediterranean, c.525 to 479 BC* (Cambridge, 2002).
Bovet, C, 'Egyptian Warriors: The *Machimoi* of Herodotus and the Ptolemaic Army', *Classical Quarterly*, 63:1 (2013), pp.209–36.
Briant, P, *From Cyrus to Alexander: A History of the Persian Empire*, trans. Peter Daniels (Paris, 2002).
Briant, P, 'The Achaemenid Empire', in K Raaflaub and N Rosenstein (eds.), *War and Society in the Ancient and Medieval Worlds: Asia, The Mediterranean, Europe and Mesoamerica* (London, 1999), pp 105–28.
Buraselis, K, & K Meidani (eds.), *Μαραθών: η μάχη και ο αρχαίος Δήμος / Marathon: the Battle and the Ancient Deme* (Athens, 2010).

Burn, A, *Persia and the Greeks: The Defence of the West, C. 546–478 BC* (Stanford, 1984).

Carey, C, and M Edwards (eds.), *Marathon – 2,500 Years: Proceedings of the Marathon Conference 2010* (London, 2013), pp. 35–44.

Cartledge, P, *Thermopylae: the Battle that Changed the World* (Oxford, 2006).

Cartledge, P, *After Thermopylae: The Oath of Plataea and the End of the Greco-Persian Wars* (New York, 2013).

Charles, M, 'Immortals and Apple Bearers: Towards a Better Understanding of Achaemenid Infantry Units', in *The Classical Quarterly*, 61:1 (2011), pp. 114–33.

Dandamaev, M, *A Political History of the Achaemenid Empire* (Leiden, 1989).

De Souza, P, *The Greek and Persian Wars, 499–386 BC* (Oxford, 2002).

Fink, D, *The Battle of Marathon in Scholarship: Research, Theories and Controversies since 1850* (Jefferson, 2014).

George, P, 'Persian Ionia under Darius: The Revolt Reconsidered', in *Historia*, 49:1, (2000), pp.1–39.

Hewitt, J, 'The Second Phase of the Battle of Cunaxa', in *The Classical Journal*, 15: 2 (1919), pp. 83–93.

Hunt, P, 'Helots at the battle of Plataea', in *Historia*, 46: 2 (1997), pp. 129–44.

Hyland, J, 'Pharnabazos, Cyrus' Rebellion, and the Spartan War of 399', in *Arta* (2008), pp. 1–27.

King, H, 'Recovering hysteria from history: Herodotus and the first case of "shell-shock"', in P Halligan, C Bass and J Marshall (eds), *Contemporary Approaches to the Science of Hysteria: Clinical and Theoretical Perspectives* (Oxford, 2001), pp. 36–48.

Konijnendijk, R, 'Neither the Less Valorous Nor the Weaker: Persian Military Might and the Battle of Plataea', in *Historia*, 61 (2012), pp.1–17.

Krentz, P, *The Battle of Marathon* (London, 2010).

Krentz, P, 'Marathon and the development of the exclusive hoplite phalanx', in C Carey and M Edwards (eds), *Marathon – 2,500 Years: Proceedings of the Marathon Conference 2010* (London, 2013), pp. 35–44.

Kuhrt, A, *The Persian Empire: A Corpus of Sources from the Achaemenid Period* (New York, 2010).

Nefedkin, A, 'The Tactical Development of Achaemenid Cavalry', in *Gladius*, 26 (2006), pp. 5–18.

Nefiodkin, A, 'On the Origin of the Scythed Chariots', in *Historia*, 53:3 (2004), pp. 369–78.

Rahe, P, 'The Military Situation in Western Asia on the Eve of Cunaxa', in *The American Journal of Philology*, 101: 1 (1980), pp. 79–96.

Rop, J, 'Reconsidering the Origin of the Scythed Chariot', in *Historia*, 62:2 (2013), pp.167–81.

Ruzicka, S, 'Cyrus and Tissaphernes, 407–401 BC', in *The Classical Journal*, 80:3 (1985), pp. 204–11.

Ruzicka, S, *Trouble in the West: Egypt and the Persian Empire 525–332 BCE*, (Oxford, 2012).

Sekunda, N, *The Persian Army 560–330*, (Oxford, 1992).

Sekunda, N, *Marathon 490 BC: The First Persian Invasion of Greece* (Oxford, 2002).

Shepherd, W, *Herodotus: The Persian War* (Trowbridge, 1987)..

Shepherd, W, *Plataea 479: The Most Glorious Victory Ever Seen* (Oxford, 2012).

Steinhauer, G, *Marathon and the Archaeological Museum* (Athens, 2009).

Summerer, L, 'From Tatarlı to Munich: The Recovery of a Painted Wooden Tomb Chamber in Phrygia', in İ Delemen (ed), *The Achaemenid Impact on Local Populations and Cultures in Anatolia (Sixth-Fourth Centuries BC): Papers presented at the International Workshop Istanbul 20–21 May 2005* (Istanbul, 2007).

Tuplin, C, 'Revisiting Dareios' Scythian Expedition', in Jens Nieling and Ellen Rehm (eds), *Achaemenid impacts in the Black Sea: Communication of powers* (Aarhus, 2010), pp. 281–312.

Tuplin, C, 'All the King's Horse: In Search of Achaemenid Persian Cavalry', in M.Trundle & G.Fagan (eds), *New Perspectives on Ancient Warfare* (Leiden, 2010), pp. 101–182.

Tuplin, C, 'Marathon: In Search of a Persian Dimension', in Kostas Buraselis and Katerina Meidani (eds), *Μαραθών: η μάχη και ο αρχαίος Δήμος / Marathon: the Battle and the Ancient Deme* (Athens, 2010), pp. 251–74.

Waterfield, R, *Xenophon's Retreat: Greece, Persia and the End of the Golden Age* (London, 2006).

Waters, M, *Ancient Persia: a Concise History of the Achaemenid Empire, 550–330 BCE* (Cambridge, 2014).

Westlake, H D, 'Diodorus and the Expedition of Cyrus', *Phoenix*, 41: 3 (1987), pp. 241–54.

Wu, X., '"O Young Man … Make Known of What Kind You Are": Warfare, History, and Elite Ideology of the Achaemenid Persian Empire', in *Iranica Antiqua*, 49 (2014), pp. 209–99.

Wylie, G, 'Cunaxa and Xenophon', in *L'Antiquité Classique*, 61 (1992), pp.119–34.

Websites (all URLs are accurate at time of print):

http://www.achemenet.com/

http://www.ashmolean.museum/ash/faqs/q004

http://corinth.sas.upenn.edu/corinth.html

http://www.livius.org/be-bm/behistun/behistun03.html

http://penelope.uchicago.edu/Thayer/E/Roman/home.html

http://www.perseus.tufts.edu/hopper/collection?collection=Perseus:collection: Greco-Roman

Index